Poets Historical

Poets Historical

Dynastic Epic in the Renaissance

Andrew Fichter

YALE UNIVERSITY PRESS
NEW HAVEN AND LONDON

*Published with the assistance of the Elizabethan Club of Yale
University from the foundation established in memory of
Oliver Baty Cunningham of the Class of 1917, Yale College.*

*Designed by James J. Johnson
and set in Palatino Roman type.
Printed in the United States of America by
Edwards Brothers Inc., Ann Arbor, Mich.*

Library of Congress Cataloging in Publication Data

*Fichter, Andrew, 1945–
  Poets historical.*

  Includes bibliographical references and index.
  1. Epic poetry—History and criticism.
2. Virgil—Influence. 3. European poetry—Renaissance, 1450–1600—History
and criticism. 4. Literature, Comparative—Classical and modern. 5. Literature, Comparative—Modern and classical. I. Title.
PN1303.F5   809.1'3   81–19795
ISBN 0–300–02721–4   AACR2

10   9   8   7   6   5   4   3   2   1

To Margaret and Jonathan

Contents

Preface

Among those who helped bring this book into being, Thomas P. Roche, Jr., deserves first mention. To him I am deeply grateful for advice, inspiration, moral support, and friendship. I could wish for no better introduction to Renaissance epic literature than I was given by my teachers, Thomas Greene and A. Bartlett Giamatti. The guidance they provided for the doctoral thesis from which this book evolved was invaluable. My debt to the scholarship of all three of the above goes far beyond the capacity of footnote documentation to reveal. I would also like to thank those who read part or all of the manuscript at various stages of completion and offered useful suggestions: Lawrence Danson, John Fleming, William Kennedy, Earl Miner, David Quint, D. W. Robertson, Jr., Thomas P. Roche, Jr., and Daniel Seltzer. I am indebted as well to Ellen Graham, a gracious and resourceful editor, to the American Council of Learned Societies and the Princeton University Committee on Research in the Humanities and Social Sciences for financial support, and to Marilyn Walden for skillful assistance in preparing the manuscript.

Let me also make explicit part of what is implied in the dedication of *Poets Historical* by expressing my gratitude to my wife, Margaret, for the unbounded sympathy and patience with which she shared the travails of this project.

Poets Historical is intended for the use of professional scholars and students alike. Accordingly, most verse citations are provided both in their original forms and in English translations, which I have selected in part for their availability in print. Those

instances where I have felt it necessary to supply my own translations are indicated in the text. Since a study of this scope cannot
expect to find a wide readership with an even familiarity with the
subjects of all its chapters, I have quoted generously. Other
scholars, notably C. M. Bowra, Thomas Greene, Robert M. Durling, and A. Bartlett Giamatti, have preceded me in tracing epic
poetry's line of descent from Virgil through the Renaissance; I
have tried to avoid treading on ground they have already covered.

Introduction

The poems discussed in this book come together under the heading of dynastic epic.[1] Their common theme is the rise of *imperium*, the noble house, race, or nation to which the poet professes allegiance. To this subject the dynastic poet imports the narrative strategy established by Virgil in the *Aeneid* (*Aen.*): action is set in the period of the historical or quasi-historical past during which the struggle for the formation of *imperium*, the laying of geographical, genealogical, cultural, and moral foundations, takes place. The dynastic poet's concerns, then, overlap those of the historian, but their methods, as Spenser observes, are different:

> For the Methode of a Poet historical is not such, as of an Historiographer. For an Historiographer discourseth of affayres orderly as they were donne, accounting as well the times as the actions, but a Poet thrusteth into the middest, euen where it most concerneth him, and there recoursing to the thinges forepaste, and diuining of thinges to come, maketh a pleasing Analysis of all.   [Letter to Ralegh][2]

The "Poet historical" speaks of the past as if it were a future—a future to which he and his heroes are granted access only in extraordinary moments of prophetic vision during which the scroll of fate is unrolled and the divine plan is for an instant revealed. In such moments the narrative future (the historical present) is seen as the Golden Age in which the struggles dramatized in the poem are completed; "impious Rage" is restrained within the temple gates (*Aen.* 1.291–96) and the task of forging a civilization is finished.

The dynastic theme brings into focus what must be consid-

1

ered one of the most basic elements of epic from Virgil onward, its consciousness of history. The narrative strategy of the dynastic poem reflects the assumption of a historically oriented mind that the present may be regarded as the culmination of a course of events set in motion in the remote past. The dynastic prophet is an analyst of historical experience. He bestows on himself as historian the same privilege Horace grants him as narrative poet, the privilege of shaping his material so that "beginning, middle, and end all strike the same note."[3] The Golden Age is an imaginative construct constituting a determinative end, the knowledge of which enables the poet to interpret history as a coherent process, reducible into certain basic paradigms. Or, to take the poet at his word, the Golden Age is a future to which he has access by virtue of his insight into the divine plan that governs the movement of temporal events. The strategy of the dynastic poet, then, is born of the desire, if not to order historical experience, to reveal whatever principle of order is thought to inform it.

The obvious problem confronting the Virgilian prophet is that to which Auden has called attention:

> How was your shield-making god to explain
> Why his masterpiece, his grand panorama
> Of scenes from the coming historical drama
> Of an unborn nation, war after war,
> All the birthdays needed to pre-ordain
> The Octavius the world was waiting for,
> Should so abruptly, mysteriously stop,
> What cause could he show why he didn't foresee
> The future beyond 31 B.C.,
> Why a curtain of darkness should finally drop
> On Carians, Morini, Gelonians with quivers,
> Converging Romeward in abject file,
> Euphrates, Araxes and similar rivers
> Learning to flow in a latinate style,
> And Caesar be left where prophecy ends,
> Inspecting troops and gifts for ever?
> Wouldn't Aeneas have asked:—"What next?
> After this triumph, what portends?"
>
> ["Secondary Epic"][4]

If Aeneas does not ask the question, Virgil's readers, living as they do in the world the poem prophetically anticipates, might well have. The aura of finality created by the poet's prophetic utterances conspicuously jars against the reader's experience of time as open and ongoing. But this openness does not go unacknowledged by Virgil. The *Aeneid*, for all its characterization of the Augustan moment as climactic, carries an implication of inconclusiveness in its form. If the epic poet "hastes into the midst of things" at the outset, it is there too, in one sense, that the poem ends. If we consider what Northrop Frye has called epic's "total action" (the story, say, of the Trojan wars), any given epic poem recounts only a fragment of that action—the anger of Achilles or the homecoming of Odysseus.[5] The *Aeneid* closes with Aeneas triumphant over Turnus but still hopelessly distant in time from the Rome toward which he has bent all his heroic efforts. Indeed even the Rome of Augustus has a distance to go before it can be unambiguously identified with the Golden Age prophetically projected in Virgil's poem.

It is here that the Renaissance emulators of Virgil depart from their model. To be sure, they are no less aware than we may suppose Virgil was that history does not draw to a close with the advent of contemporary rulers; yet the Renaissance poet believes himself capable of transcending the limitations of the Virgilian prophet. The Renaissance poet could speak with more certainty of last things. The whole course of human history from first things to last, after all, had been charted in Scripture. He could solve the problem of Virgilian prophecy because Christian revelation had lifted the veil obscuring the future and had disclosed not an unending pattern of recurrences but an absolute end, the Apocalypse. He could see the whole of what Virgil knew only in part. If it did not stand at the end of time, his contemporary dynasty could be portrayed in the clear light of that end, as an image of the Apocalypse. His knowledge of history, the Renaissance poet believes, permits him to rewrite the *Aeneid*—in effect to complete it. And in the course of doing so he transforms the original, for his knowledge gives him a new perception of man's relationship to history and thus a new conception of the epic hero. But before we turn to this crucial difference between the *Aeneid* and the Renaissance dynastic poem—a difference that will constitute the principal focus of this study—let us establish the common ground.

Epic is built to evoke man's struggle to orient himself in time. With its episodic structure, its variety of incident, its considerable cast of characters, and its sheer length, which is still not enough to encompass the "total action," epic reflects the human experience of time as a vast and an ongoing process. But epic also celebrates those moments when individuals and communities locate themselves in relation to parents and children, ancestors and posterity, beginnings and ends. The dynastic poet carefully selects the historical setting of his poem with the aim of checking the impression of temporal indeterminateness his narrative otherwise generates. Spenser's claim that the archaic setting of *The Faerie Queene* is security against "the daunger of enuy, and suspition of present time" (Letter to Ralegh) goes only part of the way toward explaining his motives. Tasso goes a step further when he argues in his *Discourses on the Heroic Poem* that the epic poet should choose a historical subject "so nearly buried in antiquity" as to permit him to arrange events as he pleases with little fear of contradicting his reader's memory of the facts, thereby preserving his "freedom to invent and imitate."[6] But beyond the arguments for protective distancing lies a more positive principle. The dynastic poem locates its action at what is in several senses a conspicuously crucial moment. In historical terms it marks the close of one era and the dawning of another; in cultural terms, a transition between two orders of civilization; in geographical terms, a westward relocation of the City; in mythical terms, a *renovatio*; and in literary terms, the "overgoing" of previous epics by a new poet.[7]

The narrative present, moreover, stands in significant relation to the poet's real present, both chronologically and analogically. Aeneas is both the ancestor and the prototype of Augustus. The genealogical thread connecting the past and the present is important; but perhaps more important, because it is the premise on which the interpretation of history as a pattern rather than an indefinitely extended sequence of events rests, is the association of the past and the present by way of analogy. Ariosto looks back to the Carolingian past to find an instance of imperial renovatio that can serve as a prefiguration, if not of his contemporary world, of the ideal toward which he urges his world. He sees in Carolingian empire *Romanitas* and *Christianitas* reconciled, Europe uniting politically and morally against the pagan Orient. The narrative setting of *Orlando Furioso (OF)* is charged with implications for the real present, and it is the purpose of the prophetic voice of the poem to bring these to light. Tasso makes explicit the relevance of the First Crusade to the Europe of his day as he exhorts his contemporary audience at the outset of *La Gerusalemme Liberata:*

> È ben ragion, s'egli avverrà ch'in pace
> il buon popol di Cristo unqua si veda,
> e con navi e cavalli al fero trace
> cerchi ritôr la grande ingiusta preda,
> ch'a te lo scettro in terra, o, se ti piace,
> l'alto imperio de' mari a te conceda.
> Emulo di Goffredo, i nostri carmi
> in tanto ascolta, e t'apparecchia a l'armi.   [1.5][8]

> [For if the Christian princes ever strive
>   To win fair Greece out of the tyrant's hands,
> And those usurping Ismaelites deprive
>   Of woful Thrace, which now captived stands,
> You must from realms and seas the Turks forth drive,
>   As Godfrey chased them from Judah's lands,
> And in this legend, all that glorious deed
> Read, whilst you arm you: arm you, whilst you read.][9]

The Arthurian setting of *The Faerie Queene* also evokes a contemporary imperial ideal: a realm wholly united, a Golden Age of chivalry centered upon the royal court, an era in which the purity of religion and the security of the nation alike are assured by a heroic monarch. To the extent that Spenser explores an analogy between Arthurian and Tudor times he follows a tradition propagated by the Tudor monarchs themselves, who claimed descent from Arthur and sought thereby to assert their right to his empire. We need not impute the same belief to Spenser, but we should observe that for him, as for Tasso, Ariosto, and Virgil, the business of forging links between the present and the past is more than incidental to the poem. Such connections argue against the view of time as a random, discontinuous, and irrational succession of events.

In some respects the setting of the dynastic poem constitutes what a historian might label a turning point. We should note, however, that for the dynastic poet something more is at issue: the narrative present dramatizes not only a historical transition but also a transition in the way history is perceived. From the standpoint of the epic hero the view into the past and the view into the future represent two distinct modes of vision. To look backward is to see the ashes of Troy, to evoke the image of the ancestral city's great disaster, whereas to look ahead is to see that city's reincarnation in a new place:

> And *Troy* againe out of her dust was reard,
> To sit in second seat of soueraigne king,
> Of all the world vnder her gouerning.   [3.9.44]

Memory, that is, attests to the futility of human achievements, the most glorious of which was Troy; prophecy, on the other hand, gives assurance of the continuity of the City, however transformed, and so seeks to counter tragic consciousness. In his role as prophet, then, the poet reinterprets tragic history as destiny, making Troy's fall part of the larger plan that mandates that city's resurrection in a new form. The poet's pretense to a knowledge of the future is in effect a way of gaining a new and more tolerable perspective on loss.

The decisive moment in the life of the dynastic hero is that in which he ceases to dwell solely on the tragedy of the past. Such a moment occurs in the elaborate rite of passage in book 6 of the *Aeneid*, where Anchises orchestrates and Aeneas witnesses the pageant of the Roman future. Up to this point, as readers have noted, Aeneas seems destined only to accumulate losses and to reenact in various settings his painful exile from Troy. The cities he builds or visits on his way from Ilium to Cumae are effigies of Troy, and as such they are inevitably touched by the tragedy emanating from the thing they recall. The surrogate Troys, Aeneados and Pergamea, the futile replica of Troy Aeneas finds at Buthrotum, the false Troy he makes of Carthage, and the substitute Troy he builds at Acesta for those too feeble and fainthearted to continue the journey are all monuments to the pathos of attempting to arrest time. Only as he shifts his orientation from the past to the future does the landscape of the poem begin to suggest fertility and promise. This is not to say, however, that the dynastic poet seeks simply to displace a tragic memory with a vision of a future sufficiently glorious to console the hero. Prophetic revelation involves historical consciousness of a more inclusive nature. The descent of Aeneas into Avernus in book 6 embraces the whole dialectic of loss and gain. And Rome itself, for that matter, is in a sense a new Troy; the voyage to Italy, seen in a larger historical framework, is a return to a place of origin. Italy, after all, is the land of Dardanus, father of the Trojan race (3.167–68); and Latium will have its copy of Troy's river Xanthus, its Achilles, and its Doric camp (6.88–90). But Rome will be no sterile replica of Troy. If the yearning of Aeneas for a return to his personal past is inherently tragic, that yearning is redeemed as it serves the Roman destiny. *Recursus* becomes a vital historical principle rather than a moribund and illusory obsession. The past is not to be obliterated but is given new meaning in the light of knowledge of things to come.

What we witness in the dynastic hero, in other words, is not so much a simple shifting of perspective from the past to the future as it is a change from seeing things in part to seeing the larger design. The corresponding moment in the career of the hero of Renaissance epic-romance is that in which he ceases to experience movement as aimless wandering through an uncharted labyrinth and comes to understand that the journey has been directed all along, that the mage, unbeknownst to the hero, has been expecting his arrival. It is a transition from seeing time as the antagonist of human aspirations to seeing history as a plan in which the hero is to play a crucial role.

From this observation it is a short step to seeing that heroism and historical consciousness are closely interrelated matters in the dynastic epic. Only as the hero comes fully to understand his place in history and to appreciate the significance of accepting such a place are his heroic energies released. The dynastic epic reinterprets the prideful, recalcitrant inaction of Achilles as avoidance of or ignorance of historical destiny, the effect of which is self-defeating. Thus the armies of Charlemagne and Goffredo steadily disintegrate until their heroes experience their moments of historical *anagnorisis,* and Spenser's Red Cross Knight exhausts himself canto by canto until he learns his historical (and spiritual) identity from the prophet Contemplation. To such a moment the dynastic poem brings its interpretation of Achilles' legendary choice of a short and glorious rather than a long and inglorious life. The revelation of the dynastic future contains a prophecy of the hero's death; emergence into history involves an awareness of the individual's mortality. But participation in history is also the condition of the hero's greatness. Historical awareness is for the hero of dynastic epic self-awareness in the fullest sense. He attains his full stature only as he aligns himself with the process of change. He is *homo historicus,* the creature of history who, when he comes to know himself as such, is also a creator and a builder. But only as he engages history and sees himself defined by it can he also determine its course.

Such a hero is essentially unlike his Homeric prototypes. Homer celebrates men's capacities to assert themselves, to impose their wills on a hostile or an indifferent universe. The Homeric hero leaves his mark but it is not a signpost pointing the direction history will take after him. His life and death and the rise and fall of his cities affirm the existence of no grand design. Virgil's hero, by contrast, must subordinate his will to something larger than himself. It is not his own personal destiny he advances, except as that destiny becomes indistinguishable from Rome's. But here the fundamental difference between the *Aeneid* and Christian epic surfaces once again. The hero of Renaissance epic, too, must subordinate his will to that of his God, but as he does so the central paradox of the Christian notion of Providence comes into play. The hero discovers that the two imperatives of personal fulfillment and duty to a higher authority are not really antithetical, that history is in fact organized for the sole purpose of accomplishing man's salvation. Fulfillment comes as the hero rededicates himself to his epic destiny. Indeed, in light of this revelation, he discovers that it was his former recalcitrance to destiny that was truly burdensome.

II

If we look far enough into the past and the future, Virgil tells us, or go deep enough into the mystery at the center of things, where we hear Anchises speaking of the *anima mundi* (6.724–51), we encounter a universal principle of renewal. Troy dies to be reborn as Rome; death gives way to life. Such a principle is in some sense inherent in nearly all historical interpretation, whether history is construed as movement according to cyclical or linear patterns, as progress and decline, fall and redemption, renascence, revolution, conversion, or reformation. [10] That Virgil's epic should feed the imaginations of the poets of the Renaissance, that other historically oriented era of renewal, should not, then, be surprising. The *Aeneid* holds much fascination for Renaissance humanists, in part because it provides them with a literary vehicle for historical thought. But we should note that Virgil's appeal to the Renaissance is also in part an outgrowth of a tradition considerably older than the Renaissance. Christian readers since Augustine have dealt in one way or another with the apparent relationship between Virgilian ideas of renewal and the fundamental principle of Christian thought, the belief that all things are made new in Christ.

There are important differences, however, between Virgilian and Christian historiography, and between the *Aeneid* and the epic romances of Ariosto, Tasso, and Spenser. Virgil's idea of Roman destiny, despite its characterization as a divine mandate, does not naturally translate into the Christian idea of Providence. Virgil does not moralize the process of Rome's growth as Christianity moralizes man's movement in time or God's interaction with history. The fall of Troy is no Fall, and the ascent of Rome is not authorized by an absolute deity to demonstrate his grace or to affirm Rome's goodness. [11] There is no moral justification for the deaths of Dido and Turnus. Rome is the issue of a compromise ending the struggle between Juno, the divine patroness of the Greeks, Carthage, and Turnus, and Venus, the mother of Aeneas (*Aen*. 12.834–40). Such a struggle may tell us something about the nature of cosmic and historical processes but does not affirm the triumph of good over evil. Aeneas is asked to surrender to his fate, to shoulder the weight of a destiny of which he will always be partly ignorant. He is not, like the hero of Christian epic, paradoxically liberated for having done so. History, that is, is not that movement of grace in time to which one has only to accede (or to be raised up to see) in order to be fulfilled.

It would at first glance seem to have been a simple matter for the post-Augustinian poet to rewrite Virgil's tale of two cities, Carthage and Rome, in Christian terms: one would need only to substitute Augustine's city of man for Carthage, the false *imperium* of cupidinous passions (as Virgil's allegorizers had identified it), and the City of God for Rome. In fact, the Renaissance epic poet does make such a substitution, and its importance cannot be underestimated, but the result is a poem moved to a metaphysical plane wholly apart from that on which the *Aeneid* exists. For the relationships between Carthage and Rome and the two cities of man and God are not the same. The difference lies not so much, as one might suppose, in the otherworldliness of Augustine's City of God, since service to God, at least for the Renaissance epic poet, is not mutually exclusive with worldly, civic concerns. On this point Ariosto, Tasso, and Spenser are insistent; their poems are no less oriented toward Ferrara, London, or Cleopolis because they are also directed toward the New Jerusalem. (By the same token, we need not suppose that the emergence in the Renaissance of dynastic epic, with its emphasis on the earthly city, is symptomatic of a departure from orthodox Christian idealism.) The real difference between the *Aeneid* with its Carthage and Rome and the Christian epic with its cities of man and God is precisely that in the latter case there need be no substantive opposition. The Christian poet writes within the framework of a system that abhors and finally denies dualism. Virgil had written of the conflict of personal love and duty to empire, the antithetical urges between which Aeneas is forced to choose; for Augustine, love is the very foundation of *imperium*. The relevant passage in *The City of God* has often been quoted, but in view of its centrality to this study I shall quote it once again:

> Accordingly, two cities have been formed by two loves: the earthly by the love of self, even to the contempt of God; the heavenly by the love of God, even to the contempt of self. The former, in a word, glories in itself, the latter in the Lord. For the one seeks glory from men; but the greatest glory of the other is God, the witness of conscience. The one lifts up its head in its own glory; the other says to its God, "Thou art my glory, and the lifter up of mine head." In the one, the princes

and the nations it subdues are ruled by the love of ruling; in the other, the princes and the subjects serve one another in love, the latter obeying, while the former take thought for all. The one delights in its own strength, represented in the persons of its rulers; the other says to its God, "I will love Thee, O Lord, my strength." And therefore the wise men of the one city, living according to man, have sought for profit to their own bodies or souls, or both, and those who have known God "glorified Him not as God, neither were thankful, but became vain in their imaginations, and their foolish heart was darkened; professing themselves to be wise"—that is, glorying in their own wisdom, and being possessed by pride—"they became fools, and changed the glory of the incorruptible God into an image made like to corruptible man, and to birds, and four-footed beasts, and creeping things." For they were either leaders or followers of the people in adoring images, "and worshipped and served the creature more than the Creator, who is blessed for ever." But in the other city there is no human wisdom, but only godliness, which offers due worship to the true God, and looks for its reward in the society of the saints, of holy angels as well as holy men, "that God may be all in all."[12]

There are in the realm of human experience two cities, one based on the form of love that is the soul's movement toward self-enjoyment, self-aggrandizement, the illusion of self-sufficiency—*cupiditas*—and the other on the soul's movement toward God—*caritas*.[13] These are the two cities that oppose each other in Renaissance epic. These are the respective provinces of Agramante and Charlemagne, Solimano or Armida and Goffredo. Yet in the long run the two cities and the two kinds of love on which they are grounded are really one, for there is finally but one order of being in Augustinian metaphysics.[14] The city of man is a false objective, not only in the sense that it is the locus of moral error but also as it is the negation of that upon which being depends. To follow one's cupidinous desires, the promptings of one's own pride or passion, is to move not toward an alternative city, a Carthage rather than a Rome, but toward nonbeing.

Conflict conceived in such terms can have but one resolution, the discovery that there was never any contest to begin with, except in the mind of the imperfectly enlightened beholder. An epic poem built on such a premise would then be radically unlike the *Aeneid*, for what room would be left for epic *agon*, for the dramatization of a decisive struggle between opposing forces, where in the last resort only one of those forces is to be granted real existence? The reader for whom the clash of equal or nearly equal contraries is the sine qua non of epic may ultimately wish to exclude the poems of Ariosto, Tasso, and Spenser from the genre. But for their part, as we shall see, the Renaissance poets accept Christian doctrine's requirement of a drastic reassessment of the norms of classical epic and continue nevertheless to proclaim themselves Virgil's literary heirs.

As it is seen from the vantage point of orthodox Christian thought, the *Aeneid* is metaphysically as well as narratively incomplete. It is the record of universal discord that precedes (in human history, in the individual's experience) the perception of cosmic unity that Christian revelation grants. In this light the narrative inconclusiveness of the *Aeneid* takes on added meaning for the Christian reader. To the Renaissance poet the non-ending of Virgil's poem signals the pagan poet's crucial limitation, his inability to see the conclusion toward which history had been aimed by Providence. Thus, given what he takes to be the fuller knowledge of history imparted to him by revelation, the Renaissance poet undertakes to finish what Virgil began. The fifteenth-century poet Maphaeus Vegius does so literally by writing a conclusion to the *Aeneid* in the form of an additional book. "The Thirteenth Book of the *Aeneid*" enjoyed a wide readership during the Renaissance and was commonly appended to editions of Virgil's poem from the sixteenth to the mid-seventeenth century. As poetry Vegius's "Thirteenth Book" no longer attracts many readers, but as an expression of the humanist impulse to place classical literature in a Christian perspective it deserves our attention.

In one sense Vegius does no more than tie up all the loose narrative threads in the *Aeneid*. After killing Turnus, Aeneas accepts the surrender of the Rutulians; the Trojans bury their dead and the Latins mourn Turnus; Aeneas returns the body of Turnus to his father Daunus, who grieves the loss of his only son; the

Rutulian city Ardea is burned and its spirit rises in the form of a heron (*ardea*) from its ashes; Latinus offers his daughter Lavinia to Aeneas in marriage and the event is celebrated in nine days of feasting; Aeneas marks out with a plough the boundaries of a new city, Lavinium, in which Trojan and Latin blood will mingle equally; a flame portending future prosperity appears playing about the head of Lavinia; Aeneas eventually succeeds Latinus to the throne, rules for three years, and at his death is by the decree of Jupiter stellified. What is so striking about Vegius's "Thirteenth Book" is that very little is added to the plot already projected by Virgil himself. Even the stellification of Aeneas is simply the fulfillment of the prophecy of Jove in book 1 (258–60). It is evidently not so much a notion that material additions to the plot are required as a feeling that there is a need to bring into balance a narrative that would otherwise end on a note of violence that motivates Vegius. He seeks a resolution of human passions through ceremony: death must be mourned and marriage publicly celebrated. Vegius has a good eye for symmetries and parallels, which he employs to bring the narrative to a state of equilibrium. The burning of Ardea concludes the action begun with the burning of Troy; the funeral of Turnus recalls that of Pallas in book 11 and thus confirms that retributive justice has run its course. Daunus loses a son but Latinus gains one, and Aeneas finds a new Troy in Lavinium, a new Creusa in Lavinia, a new Anchises in Latinus:

> "I now am come at last, and thee with ioy whatever chance
> For father heere mine I take, and once againe for to advance
> Anchises image old in thee I shall begin, and heere
> Most fervently in sunlike love to hold, with dutie deere."[15]

It is more than an instinct for tidiness, however, that motivates Vegius to compose his "Thirteenth Book." Vegius is finishing a story he finds morally as well as narratively incomplete. He writes within a tradition that interprets the *Aeneid* as an allegory of the pilgrimage of the soul through material existence, a journey that cannot be concluded until the soul attains the kingdom of heaven. Vegius provides his own allegorical gloss for the "Thirteenth Book" in *On Perseverance in Religion* (1.5), in which he suggests that for Latium we read "heaven," for Troy, "life," for Turnus, "the devil," for the Latins, "worldliness," for Lavinia, "the soul," and for Aeneas, "goodness watching and striving for the benefit of others," or the Christian virtue of perseverance.[16] The "Thirteenth Book" supplies the action that makes these interpretations possible. The extent to which Vegius manages to educe such meanings without substantially altering the plot provided by the *Aeneid* itself is the measure of his skill and testimony to his conviction that Virgil's poem is adaptable to a Christian universe. "The Thirteenth Book of the *Aeneid*" is an extension of the medieval characterization of Virgil as an unknowing prophet of Christian truth and an expression of the general belief that classical thought, although limited, is not finally incompatible with Christian doctrine. The *Aeneid* need not be wholly rewritten; the truth is there and has only to be discovered by the Christian reader, equipped with the superior knowledge Revelation has imparted to him. Later critics of the "Thirteenth Book," particularly those of the late seventeenth century and after, would object to Vegius's contribution as a piece of supererogation, an unnecessary appendage to a poem already narratively complete;[17] but this is to miss the point that it is not Virgil's poetic abilities but what are perceived as his spiritual limitations to which Vegius responds.

In one notable instance in which he does supplement Virgil's narrative with material external to the *Aeneid*, Vegius still confines himself to the corpus of pagan literature. The account of Aeneas's translation to the stars is in part derived from Ovid's *Metamorphoses* (14.581–608). This conflation of the narratives of two classical poets only serves to make Vegius's intentions more obvious, since the Ovidian episode would have been for the Renaissance reader an even more conspicuous signal of the potential of classical legend to find completion in Christian myth. In Ovid, Venus petitions Jove to fulfill his promise that Aeneas be deified and the Olympian gods, including Juno, consent. The mortal parts of Aeneas are washed away in the river Numicius and Aeneas is transported into the heavens. Medieval and Renaissance moralizations of Ovid construe the apotheosis of Aeneas as a foreshadowing of Christ's ascension: Christ, seeing his mission on earth completed, petitions God to release him from his body (Aeneas); God and the Holy Spirit give their consent. Ovid's Venus, Juno, and Jove thus adumbrate the Christian Trinity.[18] Vegius shows himself an adherent to this tradition, if not to this particular interpretation of Ovid, when he permits his Jove to allude forward to future stellifications:

> Yea, others that with vertue fraught herafter shall arise,
> And eke themselves adorne with praise eterne not to decay,
> Fulfilling eke the world with noble deedes of glory gay,
> Those likewise will I to the skies advance. [617–19]

The "others that with vertue fraught herafter shall arise" may be Julius and Augustus but they are also, for Vegius, Christ and the Christian heroes of perseverance.

If Vegius has in mind something more than rounding off the edges of Virgil's narrative, he is also something more than an allegorical commentator. His moral interpretations do not intrude into the text of the "Thirteenth Book." He seems equally divided between a desire to produce a plausibly Virgilian narrative, full of verbal echoes and imitations of the original, and a wish to point that narrative in the direction of Christian truths. In his awareness that the act of imitation can also be an act of interpretation he has something in common with the epic poets of the Renaissance. Ariosto, Tasso, and Spenser do not attempt to "complete" the narrative of the *Aeneid* in so direct a manner as Vergius—partly because they understand that epic must remain inconclusive, open to history, in order to remain epic; yet it is apparent that in certain respects they have allowed their minds to move in the direction of a thirteenth book. To choose as a point of reference a theme that will necessarily occupy a significant place in this study, we may note that, like Vegius, Ariosto, Tasso, and Spenser appreciate that the *Aeneid* is, after all, potentially a marriage poem. Thus marriage becomes a focal issue for the Renaissance epic. Through marriage the dynastic poet forges the genealogical chain that links the world of his poem with his contemporary world. As it involves simultaneously a recognition of the mortality of the individual and a promise of the continuity of the bloodline, marriage serves the poet in his search for a symbol of permanence in a mutable, time-bound world. The Renaissance poet conceives of marriage as a way of putting death into perspective as an aspect of the greater, fundamentally vital, providential scheme of things. As such the dynastic marriage in Renaissance epic is a comment on Virgil to the effect that the pagan poet, as he does not give us the marriage of Aeneas and Lavinia, shows himself incapable of sufficiently transcending the tragic fact of human mortality. With his celebration of marriage, moreover, the Renaissance poet proclaims his belief that true *imperium*, empire as an image of Augustine's City of God, is established by love rather than arms. Above all, marriage is for the Renaissance poet the means of attaining the narrative and thematic closure the *Aeneid* lacks. With the dynastic marriage the Renaissance poet sees the history of his nation recapitulating the universal history of mankind as it begins with the union of Adam and Eve and ends with the apocalyptic wedding of the Lamb in Revelation.

In the chapters that follow I shall pursue the careers of the dynastic heroes of Renaissance epic: Ruggiero and Bradamante in Ariosto's *Orlando Furioso*, Rinaldo and Armida in Tasso's *Gerusalemme Liberata*, Artegall and Britomart in Spenser's *Faerie Queene*. It is within the context of these narrative threads that the Renaissance poet's effort to assimilate the *Aeneid* reveals itself most clearly. The dynastic narrative typically includes, for one thing, imitations of Virgilian prophecy, selected instances of which I shall examine for what they tell us of the difference between Virgil's and the Renaissance poet's conceptions of historical processes. But the implicit subject of this study is broader than such a focus can always accommodate. I am generally concerned with the "overgoing" of Virgil, the redefinition of classical epic from a Renaissance and Christian perspective, and this subject will require some consideration of the Renaissance epic as imitation. It will be my contention that we should not invoke the criterion of resemblance too strictly as we assess Virgilian echoes in Renaissance narrative poetry. If we assume the Renaissance poet's objective to be no more than the replication of the *Aeneid* in a new setting, without taking into account all that that change of setting implies, we are bound to conclude that he failed to achieve his purpose. He seems strangely deaf to the tone of Virgil's poem; he seems incapable of reproducing the pathos of the original.[19] But such a judgment misses the point: the Renaissance poet does not restrict himself to imitation in the narrowest sense of the word. His allusions to the *Aeneid* are deliberately designed to reflect the difference between Virgil's world and the world under the dispensation of grace.

The subject of Virgilian imitation in turn invites a discussion of poetic form as the matter was debated in the sixteenth century. Up to a point we may distinguish between romance and epic as two divergent narrative categories, each with its own separate potential for reflecting the image of Virgil. In general the presence of a fully developed dynastic plot in the Renaissance poem is an indication of the author's intention of assuming the mantle of the epic rather than the romance poet. But in the long run, as Tasso argues in the *Discourses on the Heroic Poem*, romance and epic are best viewed as two aspects of a single undertaking, unified and consistent with respect to its critical assessment of the *Aeneid*. The apparent distinction between romance and epic parts within the Renaissance narrative poem begins to fade once it is understood that both parts are components of what has been conceived as a new entity, the Christian epic.

Were it my purpose in this study to pursue all the avenues connecting Virgil to the Renaissance, I might have taken into account the medieval tradition of allegorical commentary on the *Aeneid*. I have preferred not to do so, however, in part because the ground has been covered elsewhere,[20] but also because the commentaries are finally a genre apart from the works I wish to examine. The commentaries are not, that is, imitative overgoings of the *Aeneid*; there is little in the nature of Fulgentius's *Exposition of the Content of Virgil* or Bernardus Silvestris's *Commentary on the First Six Books of Virgil's Aeneid* to suggest the impulse to construct epic narrative that flourishes in the Renaissance. It has seemed to me more useful to treat the matter of the continuity of Christian responses to Virgil from the Middle Ages to the Renaissance in theoretical rather than historical terms. It is to this end that I have focused my attention on Augustine, whose *Confessions (Conf.)*, I suggest (chap. 2), lay the metaphysical foundations for the narrative assimilations of Virgilian epic undertaken by Renaissance poets.

Some of the salient features of medieval allegorical commentary on the *Aeneid*, however, deserve mention here. The three interpretive commentaries,[21] those by Fulgentius (sixth century),

Bernardus Silvestris (twelfth century), and Cristoforo Landino (fifteenth century), all attest to the importance of book 6 of the *Aeneid*—the book on which I shall concentrate in chapter 1—in Christian readings of the poem. Indeed, the remaining six books of the *Aeneid* are ignored by Bernardus and are given only cursory treatment by Fulgentius and Landino. The reason for the emphasis on the first half of the poem is implicit in the interpretive scheme the commentators follow. The *Aeneid* is read as the allegory of the journey of an Everyman through six ages of life, each represented by one of the first six books.[22] Thus, according to Fulgentius, book 1 is an allegory of birth (the storm and shipwreck, "the pangs of the mother in giving birth and the hazards of the child in its need to be born"[23]; 2, infancy (Aeneas sees but does not recognize his mother, Venus); 3, childhood (Aeneas is diverted by fabulous adventure tales); 4, adolescence (Aeneas, "on holiday from paternal control, goes off hunting, is inflamed by passion"); 5, young manhood (the games; learning discipline); 6, mature manhood (the attainment of wisdom through the instructions of Apollo and Anchises). Bernardus observes a distinction between the narrative and chronological ordering of events in the *Aeneid* but generally follows Fulgentius's plan, whereas Landino rearranges the sequence of the books (2, 3, 1, 4, 5, 6) to reflect true chronology in his interpretation.

A second assumption held in common by the commentators is that the *Aeneid* reflects Platonic or Neoplatonic doctrine.[24] Thus the itinerary of Aeneas represents the progress of the soul from its initial, violent entrance into the body (as Bernardus would have it, the etymology of Aeneas's name identifies him as the soul inhabiting or imprisoned in the flesh) to its attainment of knowledge of the "secret mysteries of nature" (Fulgentius, 22) by means of the descent into the underworld. The soul is conceived, in accordance with Neoplatonic thought, as pure, and the body, or matter, as the source of all corruption—hence the violence of the birth scene. The first six books of the *Aeneid* dramatize the inevitable antagonism between the flesh and the spirit as it struggles to return to its true home. (This, according to Fulgentius, has been achieved by Anchises, whose name he understands to mean "living in one's own land.") The soul, moreover, is regarded as immortal whereas corporeal existence is only temporary. Thus

Anchises teaches "how men's spirits are brought back again and again from [or to] life and makes clear the future (22)."[25]

In many ways the preoccupations of the commentators are not congenial to the production of epic literature. For all the commentators, the *Aeneid* is a poem written *sub integumentum*. It is the commentator's purpose, then, to expose wherever he can Virgil's concealed meanings, the "natural secrets" that lie beneath the poem's narrative surface. In doing so the commentator seems willing to leave behind him much of what is essential to an epic, its literal and historical dimensions, its attachment to a particular time, place, and culture (an attachment the dynastic poems of the Renaissance seek to restore), and the fundamental individuality of its heroes. Indeed it is the explicit purpose of Neoplatonic allegory to discredit the sensible world in the eyes of the reader and thereby to turn his mind toward the realm of invisible things where reality and goodness reside. Another important reason for distinguishing between Augustine and the Renaissance epic poets on the one hand and the allegorists on the other is that the latter, in their enthusiasm to distill from the *Aeneid* a body of universal truths and moral *sententiae*, tend not to emphasize the differences between pagan and Christian thought. In a more fully articulated Christian orthodoxy, such as we shall encounter in Augustine, the Platonic notions of the immortality of the soul, the soul's purity and matter's inherent corruption, and the theory of metempsychosis espoused by Anchises are not received without strong objections. In the commentaries, however, the stress falls not so much on Virgil's deficiencies in the area of theology as on his excellence as a philosopher, as the guardian of the secrets of nature. Bernardus, for one, carefully restricts his discourse to what Virgil tells his reader "about the nature of human life."[26] Landino's *Camaldulensian Dialogues*, as Michael Murrin observes, have a similarly delimited scope.[27] Landino generally confines himself to the exploration of lessons that the *Aeneid* and Platonism are capable of teaching. Such lessons, or at least the methods by which they are taught, are essentially negative. In the course of the *Dialogues* the reader is called upon to question the validity of the alternatives with which the visible, external cosmos presents the hero: pleasure, civic glory, the virtues of the active life. "Thus the *Camaldulensian Dialogues*, by shattering our false conceptions of human ends, prepares us to see clearly and shelters us from the ills of life."[28] The *Aeneid*, that is, illustrates the *via negativa* of Neoplatonism, which, if it does not directly express the nature of the supreme being, the final object of philosophical contemplation, does at least clear away the obstacles to such knowledge.[29]

The commentators, in other words, set out to discover in the *Aeneid* the path toward Christian truths. Virgil's pagan philosophy, as Fulgentius observes, contains wisdom of which Christians can readily approve. Thus the demise of Misenus ("vain praise") illustrates "the wholesome and God-given precept of us Christians [that] charges that 'a broken and a contrite heart, O God, thou wilt not despise'" (19). As Bernardus reads the *Aeneid*, it teaches us to turn "from the nature of the flesh toward the spirit," to avoid the temptations of Carthage ("the new city of the world," the Virgilian analogue of the scriptural Babylon), to shun Dido ("passion"), Circe ("earthly wealth"), Iris ("the senses"), and so forth. In general the commentators pursue a line of interpretation that underscores the continuity of pagan and Christian thought. In their respect for Virgil as a philosopher they do not, as Augustine does, dwell on that aspect of the poem which might to a Christian reader attest to the need for the New Dispensation.

I do not wish to draw the line between Augustine and the Virgilian commentators too firmly, however. What separates them is in the last analysis a matter of emphasis. The commentators may allow their reverence for Virgil to weigh more heavily in the balance than their sense of his limitations, but such a sense does exist. Fulgentius, for instance, takes his own Christianity and Virgil's paganism into account in *The Exposition*, in which the ghost of Virgil is imagined to have returned from the grave to explain the mysteries of his poem to the commentator. Fulgentius characterizes himself as Virgil's intellectual inferior, a schoolboy being instructed by a condescending *magister*, but Fulgentius simultaneously recognizes the advantage his knowledge of Christian revelation has given him over the pagan sage. On the one hand Virgil chides Fulgentius for his obtuseness, his "fatheadedness," and his age's "distrust of . . . dangerous doctrine" (6). On the other hand, Virgil acknowledges his limits:

"You may see what the true Majesty has taught you, while I can only set forth what I see" (8). The commentators celebrate Aeneas's *descensus ad inferos* in book 6 as the climax of the quest for such knowledge and virtue as can be attained through Platonic contemplation, but they remain tacitly aware that the journey toward enlightenment can be completed only with the Pauline *ascensus ad coelis*. In this life, Bernardus tells us, one may, like Aeneas, contemplate the Creator through his creatures; "and then in the other life one attains vision—that is, he sees face to face."[30] This assessment of Virgil is apparent throughout the Middle Ages. The *Aeneid* is seen as the repository of all knowledge accessible to human reason but Virgil remains deprived of the higher truth Christian revelation affords. Virgil becomes, as Dante's Statius describes him, a figure "that goes by night and carries the light behind him and does not help himself but makes wise those that follow."[31]

If Augustine pays more attention to the differences between Virgil's (supposed) Platonism and Christian doctrine, Augustine is not blind to the greatness of the *Aeneid* or to its usefulness to Christian readers. Augustine, like the commentators and like the epic poets of the Renaissance, seeks finally to reserve a place of honor for the *Aeneid* in world literature. And if the Renaissance epic poets produce something quite unlike allegorical commentary, it is not because they have rejected the principles on which allegorical interpretation is based. They would have understood that the allegorist's pursuit of meaning beyond the letter of Virgil's text proceeded not from utter disregard for the importance of the poem's literal dimension but from a desire, ultimately, to confirm and preserve it.[32] What divides the tradition of allegorical commentary from the works I shall examine in the following pages is, as I have said, not so much a difference in basic assessments of Virgil as a difference in emphasis. But the emphases are crucial since it is above all a consciousness of Virgil's "limitations" that motivates the Renaissance attempts to rewrite—to overgo—the *Aeneid*.

In the end the epic sense of history reveals itself most clearly in the history of epic itself, and of this the epic poet is always acutely aware. Each successive poet in the tradition measures himself against his forerunners: Ariosto makes himself the successor of both Virgil, the first great author of the dynastic poem, and Boiardo, whose unfinished romance, *Orlando Innamorato*, Ariosto sets out to complete. Tasso seeks to reformulate the relationship between classical epic and Ariostan romance so that both may be brought into the service of an explicitly Christian theme in *La Gerusalemme Liberata*, and Spenser puts himself at the end of the long line of "Poets historical." Each new poet adopts an attitude of deference toward his predecessors, but he is also quick to assert himself and to announce his intention of producing something new, of saying something "never said before in prose or rime" (*OF* 1.2), of overgoing the authors of the past. This formulaic boldness on the part of the epic poet is in part a declaration made on behalf of his dynasty, the particular form of *imperium* in which all others, he maintains, culminate. The westering of Troy begins as Aeneas comes to Italy but does not end until Troy has become Spenser's Troynovant, "that with the waues / Of wealthy *Thamis* washed is along. . . ." (*FQ* 3.9.45)

The epic poet's alternating postures of deference and self-assertiveness signal the complexity of the issue of epic continuity. On the one hand the very fact of the Renaissance dynastic poem is a tribute to Virgil. The *Aeneid* is for the modern poet a model that he might hope to imitate but not, in many respects, to equal. On the other hand the Renaissance poet claims it his privilege and responsibility to overgo Virgil. To overgo, however, is not to overthrow; Virgil is to be assimilated, not vanquished. What sustains the dynastic poets of the Renaissance in their somewhat paradoxical endeavors to produce works at once classical and modern, Virgilian and Christian, is their conviction that through their art they are reflecting the coherence and continuity that obtains to human history in general by virtue of the existence of a providential plan, the universal scheme in which the classical past and the Christian present are equally included.

CHAPTER ONE

VIRGIL:
Aeneas and the Augustan Future

In book 6 of the *Aeneid* the hero descends into the underworld to see the shade of his father, who has in turn long yearned for his son's arrival in order to be able to present him with a prophecy of the future of his race. Father Anchises foretells the advent of Augustus, the greatest of Aeneas's descendants, destined to establish a universal empire and to restore the Golden Age of Saturn (792–94). We have heard the dynastic prophecy before, when in book 1 Jove unrolled the scroll of fate for Venus to reveal a future age of peace, a Trojan Caesar, and a Roman *imperium sine fine*, dominion without end (1.257–96); and we will hear of the future again in book 8, when Aeneas receives from Venus the shield on which Vulcan has engraved the story of Rome from Romulus to Actium. What distinguishes Anchises' prophecy from those of Jove and Vulcan is that it unfolds in the context of a dialogue with the dynastic hero. The voice of Roman destiny in book 6 is therefore subjected to interrogation by the hero who is to be the instrument of that destiny. It is, to be sure, an unequal dialogue; Aeneas is for the most part a silent spectator of the pageant over which Anchises eagerly presides. But what little Aeneas does say confirms that he is weary of his wanderings, weary even of life. His presence thus determines the dramatic function that the dynastic prophecy must perform. The image of future Roman greatness must serve to resolve what amounts to the hero's doubt concerning the meaning of his existence. It becomes the objective of the prophet to provide Aeneas with a reason and an incentive for going on, and it is in this spirit that Anchises undertakes his task. He becomes the advocate of the

Roman future, presenting it as a goal sufficiently glorious to justify whatever hardships its pursuit might entail.

Later Christian readers of the *Aeneid* would credit Anchises
with only qualified success in achieving his purpose. Aeneas
reenters the world of the living and proceeds to shoulder the
burden of his destiny, but St. Augustine, for one, would maintain
that the need Aeneas expresses in book 6 for a motive for doing so
is at best imperfectly met by the vision of destiny with which
Anchises provides him.[1] When the dynastic poets of the Renaissance reduplicate Anchises' prophecy, substituting their own
contemporary forms of *imperium* for Virgil's Rome, they preserve
Anchises' enthusiasm for the future, but they do so in the conviction that they also satisfy more fully than Anchises could the
personal needs of the hero. The Christian poet bases his claim to
have overgone Virgil on the belief that the destiny to which the
Christian hero accedes is not burdensome but fulfilling. Thus to
see the *Aeneid* as the Renaissance epic poet sees it, as a poem
whose vision of destiny begs to be reinterpreted in the light of
Christian belief, we must first alert ourselves to the tragic sense
that pervades the Virgilian discourse on man and history.[2]

Anchises, as Aeneas first sees him in Avernus, is engaged in
recounting the tale of the Trojan people and surveying "the imprisoned souls that were to pass to the light above" (679–81).
Aeneas sees a crowd thronging to the banks of Lethe and asks for
an explanation, which Anchises provides:

> "Animae, quibus altera fato
> corpora debentur, Lethaei ad fluminis undam
> securos latices et longa oblivia potant.
> has equidem memorare tibi atque ostendere coram,
> iampridem hanc prolem cupio enumerare meorum,
> quo magis Italia mecum laetere reperta."   [713–18]

> ["Spirits they are, to whom second bodies are owed by
> Fate, and at the water of Lethe's stream they drink the sooth-
> ing draught and long forgetfulness. These in truth I have long
> yearned to tell and show thee to thy face, yea, to count this,
> my children's seed, that so thou mayest rejoice with me the
> more at finding Italy."][3]

Then Aeneas asks what one modern reader has called "perhaps the saddest question of the *Aeneid*":[4]

"O pater, anne aliquas ad caelum hinc ire putandum est
sublimis animas iterumque ad tarda reverti
corpora? quae lucis miseris tam dira cupido?"   [719-21]

["But, father, must we think that any souls pass aloft from here to yon sky, and return a second time to sluggish bodies? What means, alas! this their mad longing for the light?"]

The question betrays Aeneas's despair. It is indirectly a request on his part for a justification for his own resumption of the *iter durum* (688), the "toilsome way" that has taken him from Troy to Italy. But the question is also a demand for a reason for reentering the realm of the living, and as such it is for Augustine, as we shall see, a question to which Virgil can supply no answer.[5]

Anchises' response to the question suggests that he is aware of Aeneas's mood but unwilling to indulge it. The father exhorts the son to overcome his hesitations, prodding him with an insinuation that his question implies faintheartedness:

"Et dubitamus adhuc virtutem extendere factis,
aut metus Ausonia prohibet consistere terra?"   [806-08]

["And do we still hesitate to enlarge our prowess by deeds, or does fear forbid our settling on Ausonian land?"]

If the tone of Anchises' response is somewhat disconcerting, so too is its substance. Anchises' answer is in effect an elaborate evasion of Aeneas's question. The full reply is twofold. First Anchises explains, in terms that lead Giordano Bruno to label Virgil "the Pythagorean poet,"[6] the cycle of reincarnation by which souls reenter bodies after a period of purgation in the underworld. Then, moving from philosophical to historical matter, Anchises presents to Aeneas a pageant of the heroes of the Roman future up to Augustus. Either part of Anchises' response might have served adequately had Aeneas asked how time is structured or what the future entails, but Aeneas has asked something else. He has asked, as Otis observes, for a reason for being, and in this respect the answer he receives is disappointing.[7]

In fairness to Anchises, however, it must be said that his response is justified within the terms of Virgil's poem; nor will Christian poets deny the validity of his justification, given what they will take to be the limits of pagan thought. Anchises' reply can be regarded as a deliberate, tactical evasion of the spirit of a question which if pursued might have led in the direction of self-pity. Anchises' vision of cosmic cycles of purgation and reincarnation and of the Roman future offer an antidote to tragic self-absorption. Aeneas is urged to expand his self-awareness, to see himself as part of the greater continuum that includes a Rome as well as a Troy. He is being instructed in the nature of *pietas*, the civic virtue of the Roman hero, and in the process his personal yearnings must be converted into a sense of duty to both family and *patria*, father and fatherland. If his quest to see his father in some ways comes short of the conclusion we may suppose he originally envisioned (106–23), his longing for a reunion with his father is fulfilled in another sense as he learns to see himself in that role, the primogenitor of a new race. Thus Anchises' avoidance of complicity in his son's evident despair is perhaps the best possible method for transforming Aeneas into the kind of hero the poem requires. The father's reply to the son's question is wholly consistent in both statement and strategy with Virgilian epic's premise that men must accommodate to history, not history to men.

But the frustration underlying this encounter between father and son cannot be ignored. It can be felt as Aeneas vainly attempts to embrace the shade of Anchises, only to see it flee from his hands (699–702). The gesture evokes the pathos of earlier scenes of loss and disappointment, that in which Aeneas tries to clasp the fleeing shadow of his wife, Creusa, in Troy (2.792–94) and that in which he realizes he has been speaking to his immortal parent, Venus, only as she transforms herself and evades his grasp (1.407–09). Virgil's theme is the disequilibrium between men and gods, or between the living and those mortals who in their deaths have become voices of Roman destiny. However ennobling Anchises' implicit argument for acceptance of destiny may be, his remains a vision in which personal desires are not fulfilled but subordinated to and redirected by an impersonal ideal.

To Aeneas, Anchises' promise that he will earn for himself a place in history must seem something of a consolation, and one whose shortcomings he has already witnessed earlier in book 6.[8] Misenus, the hero whose death occasions the funeral that frames Aeneas's descent into the underworld, has, for instance, similarly been granted eternal fame with the promise that his name would be given to the mountain on which he perished, challenging the gods to a musical contest (234–35). What is memorialized, however, is not only a name but an event by which we are reminded of the tragic inequality of men and gods and, in some measure, the cruelty of the latter. Palinurus, the pilot who drowned before the Trojan ships reached the Italian shores, has likewise suffered death at the hands of a god (5.838) and is likewise compensated with *aeternum nomen:* "aeternumque locus Palinuri nomen habebit" ("and for ever the place shall bear the name of Palinurus") (6.381). Once again, however, the consolation is equally a reminder of the hostility of the Virgilian universe to mortals. "Guiltless" Palinurus (5.841) has deserved his death far less than Misenus. Aeneas, moreover, has been rather cruelly deceived in the case of Palinurus by a divine prophecy that is fulfilled in letter but not in spirit:

> "quis te, Palinure, deorum
> eripuit nobis medioque sub aequore mersit?
> dic age. namque mihi, fallax haud ante repertus,
> hoc und responso animum delusit Apollo,
> qui fore te ponto incolumem finisque canebat
> venturum Ausonios. en haec promissa fides est?"
>
> (6.341–46)

["What god, Palinurus, tore thee from us and plunged beneath the open ocean? O tell me! for Apollo, never before found false, with this one answer tricked my soul, for he foretold that thou wouldst escape the sea and reach Ausonian shores. Lo! is it thus his promise holds?"]

Palinurus does arrive on Ausonian shores but only to be killed by barbarous natives as he climbs out of the sea. Palinurus's plight, his desperate request for the burial that will permit his soul to find a quiet resting place (370–71), can be assumed to touch Aeneas deeply since it mirrors his own search for permanence and an end of the iter durum.[9] To the extent that the promise of aeternum nomen is another point of parallelism with Aeneas it is significant that we are told the assurance satisfies the ghost of Palinurus only for a little while (382–83).[10] The adequacy of the same consolation when Anchises offers it to Aeneas has thus already been thrown into doubt.

As Adam Parry observes, "We hear two distinct voices in the *Aeneid*, a public voice of triumph, and a private voice of regret."[11] Anchises speaks with the public voice of a mission that justifies whatever personal sacrifice might be required, and he does so with an eagerness that is disturbingly discordant with the mood of his son. Aeneas, however, has listened to the voices of human suffering as well. The cases of Misenus and Palinurus make us painfully aware of the obliquity of the discourse wherever both voices are heard in dialogue.

This obliquity is carried to its extreme in the interchange (or lack of it) between Aeneas and Dido in Avernus. It is one of the most poignant moments in the *Aeneid* and its impact will be felt by the poem's Christian readers from Augustine through the Renaissance. Aeneas discovers Dido wandering ("errabat," 451) in a landscape to which the epic-romance poet will return. Her wandering is in a sense a recapitulation of that of Odyssean Aeneas, relocated in the narrower space of the forest in the part of Avernus where

> quos durus amor crudeli tabe peredit,
> secreti celant calles et myrtea circum
> silva tegit   [442–44]

[those whom stern Love has consumed with cruel wasting are hidden in walks withdrawn, embowred in a myrtle grove.]

Aeneas speaks to her through tears:

> "Infelix Dido, verus mihi nuntius ergo
> venerat exstinctam, ferroque extrema secutam?
> funeris heu! tibi causa fui? per sidera iuro,
> per superos, et si qua fides tellure sub ima est,
> invitus, regina, tuo de litore cessi.
> sed me iussa deum, quae nunc has ire per umbras,

per loca senta situ cogunt noctemque profundam,
imperiis egere suis; nec credere quivi
hunc tantum tibi me discessu ferre dolorem.
siste gradum teque aspectu ne subtrahe nostro.
quem fugis? extremum fato, quod te adloquor, hoc
    est."   [456–66]

["Unhappy Dido! then was the tale brought me true, that thou
wert no more, and hadst sought thy doom with the sword?
Was I, alas! the cause of death to thee? By the stars I swear, by
the world above, and whatever is sacred in the grave below,
unwillingly, O queen, I parted from thy shores. But the gods'
decrees, which now constrain me to pass through these
shades, through lands squalid and forsaken, and through
abysmal night, drove me with their behests; nor could I deem
by going thence would bring on thee distress so deep. Stay
thy step and withdraw not from our view. Whom fleest thou?
The last word Fate suffers me to say to thee is this!"]

But Dido merely turns away in bitter silence. As an attempt to
soothe his lover's anger or to justify himself in her eyes Aeneas's
speech is a failure. He can only plead the inflexibility of the demands of his destiny.

The encounter between Aeneas and Dido in Avernus is an
extension of their final discourse in book 4, in which Dido
passionately charges Aeneas with cruelty and faithlessness for
leaving her (4.305–30) and receives from him an answer that reveals the gulf between them. The theme of Aeneas's speech is his
inability to resist fate:

"Me si fata meis paterentur ducere vitam
auspiciis et sponte mea componere curas,
urbem Troianam primum dulcisque meorum
reliquias colerem."   [340–43]

["Did the Fates suffer me to shape my life after my own pleasure and order my sorrows at my own will, my first care
should be the city of Troy and the sweet relics of my kin."]

He has been commanded to move forward to Italy by the mes-
senger of Jove himself (356–59): "Italiam non sponte sequor" (361)

("Not of free will do I follow Italy!"). To this he can add a list of excuses made dubious not only by the inappropriately legalistic spirit in which they are offered but also by their sheer number: he did not intend to depart from Dido in stealth; he never entered into a contract of marriage; he has a right to his own city; Anchises' ghost has urged him forward; Ascanius is being deprived of his "predestined lands" (331–61). He can excuse himself but he has nothing to confess.[12] His destiny puts him unalterably at odds with Dido and seems to obstruct even his wish "to soothe and assuage her grief" (393–94). Aeneas inhabits a world in which there can be no resolution when the requirements of love and those of empire conflict.

II

That Aeneas asks why the souls in the underworld should desire to return to the light is perhaps not surprising, even if we put aside the fact that he has witnessed the inadequacy of consolations for personal suffering before he reaches Anchises. After death, as Anchises explains it, the soul must undergo a process of purgation, including punishment for sins, and then have its memory of its former existence erased before it can conceive a desire to return again to the body. The basic precept of Anchises' disquisition, and of the Neoplatonic doctrine from which it is derived, is that the human soul is contaminated when it assumes bodily form. Within the dualism of body and soul it is the body that corrupts and burdens the soul:

> "Igneus est ollis vigor et caelestis origo
> seminibus, quantum non noxia corpora tardant
> terrenique hebetant artus moribundaque membra."
>
> [6.730–32]

["Fiery is the vigour and divine the source of those life-seeds, so far as harmful bodies clog them not, nor earthly limbs and mortal frames dull them."]

Anchises does not, however, speak of an ultimate reunion of the purified soul with the divine mind, as he might have, had he chosen to follow Platonic or Neoplatonic doctrine to a further stage. His discourse on the anima mundi, the fiery spirit that sustains the cosmos and is the source of all life, does not provide a teleological justification for the soul's repeated acceptance of the dull, corrupting mortal frame. [13] Even if he had pursued Pythagorean or Platonic doctrine more fully, however, Anchises would not have satisfied Augustine, who can be heard in *The City of God* giving his own answer to the question Aeneas now poses:

> For it is indeed foolish to believe that souls should desire to return from that life, which cannot be very blessed unless by the assurance of its permanence, and to come back into this life, and to the pollution of corruptible bodies, as if the result of perfect purification were only to make defilement desirable. For if perfect purification effects the oblivion of all evils, and the oblivion of evils creates a desire for a body in which the soul may again be entangled with evils, then the supreme felicity will be the cause of infelicity, and the perfection of wisdom the cause of foolishness, and the purest cleansing the cause of defilement.   [10.30][14]

The question Aeneas asks of Anchises is for Augustine the crucial one since the inability of Anchises, or even the hypothetical Platonic thinker, to answer it identifies clearly the need to which Christianity responds.

That Anchises does not speak of a possible end to the cycles of reincarnation, however, serves him well enough, given his purpose. His intention is to shift Aeneas's eyes toward Rome as the chief goal of his aspirations. As Anchises narrows the scope of his discourse in moving from philosophical to historical matters, he raises to a higher degree of visibility the objective of the epic quest. History will provide the *telos* that Anchises' philosophy does not. (From an Augustinian point of view it might be said that the problem with Anchises' prophecy in general is that philosophical and historical matters do not perfectly coincide, that history cannot be presented as the manifestation of truth and truth as the form of history.) Anchises' true concerns, then, are revealed in the second, historical part of his answer to Aeneas's question.

If Anchises' intention is to stir Aeneas with a vision of a glorious Roman future, however, it is somewhat surprising that the prophet does not orchestrate the pageant of the future to culminate with Augustus in his role as "son of a god" (792) and restorer of the Golden Age. Given Virgil's earlier suggestion that Anchises reveals things "in order" (723), it is worth investigating the structure of the historical prophecy. At least one of the implications of that structure must be, I think, that history is not easily made tractable to the prophet's apparent desire to construe it as an incentive or as a consolation for personal suffering.

Anchises' prophecy does not adhere strictly to the chronological order of the events of Roman history. Chronology is violated at crucial moments in order to allow a threefold thematic structure to emerge. The three themes are identified by Anchises in three separate exhortations.[15] The first thematic section begins with Aeneas's first unborn descendant, Silvius, but interrupts chronological order after an allusion to Romulus in order to identify Augustus:

> "Hic vir, hic est, tibi quem promitti saepius audis,
> Augustus Caesar, Divi genus, aurea condet
> saecula qui rursus Latio regnata per arva
> Saturno quondam."   [791–94]

["This, this is he, whom thou so oft hearest promised to thee, Augustus Caesar, son of a god, who shall again set up the Golden Age amid the fields where Saturn once reigned."]

The theme is the preservation through history of Trojan seed and Trojan *nomen* (756–58; 766; 768; 778; 789–90). The leap from Romulus to Augustus is justified on the grounds that each is, like Hercules (801), a *conditor*, a founder-hero, who acts to rid the city of a threat to its existence and to establish for it new and wider boundaries. Anchises' exhortation is correspondingly positive: "And do we still hesitate to enlarge our prowess by deeds, or does fear forbid our settling on Ausonian land?"

The second section resumes chronological order with Numa, second king of Rome and successor to Romulus, but then interrupts the sequence again shortly after mention of Brutus, founder of the Republic, who executed his sons for plotting to restore the Tarquin kings. The incident calls for an allusion forward in time to the civil and familial strife between Caesar and Pompey, *gener* and *socer*, father- and son-in-law. The theme is the evolution of

Roman government from the institution of laws by Numa to the period of Tarquin kingship to the establishment and finally the collapse of the Republic. But the theme is also civil war, illustrated in terms of conflicts between fathers and sons. History now conveys a grim lesson, which Anchises in his role as father articulates in his second exhortation:

> "Ne, pueri, ne tanta animis adsuescite bella,
> neu patriae validas in viscera vertite viris;
> tuque prior, tu parce, genus qui ducis Olympo;
> proice tela manu, sanguis meus!"   [832-35]

["O my sons, make not a home within your hearts for such warfare, nor upon your country's very vitals turn her vigour and valour! And do thou first forbear, thou who drawest thy race from heaven; cast from thy hand the sword, thou blood of mine!"]

At this point we must ask whether the effect of Anchises' ordering of themes is not to qualify the initial impression that history provides a consolation for undertaking the "toilsome way." History now seems unable to support the earlier exhortation to "enlarge our prowess by deeds."[16] So Augustine, at least, seems to feel as he comments in *The City of God* on this passage of Anchises' prophecy. Augustine argues that Virgil is at best unconvincing when he seems to wish to console Brutus for what must have been the torment of killing his sons:

> It is this deed that Virgil shudders to record, even while he seems to praise it; for when he says,
>> "And call his own rebellious seed
>> For menaced liberty to bleed,"
> he immediately exclaims,
>> "Unhappy father! howsoe'er
>> The deed be judged by after days";
> that is to say, let posterity judge the deed as they please, let them praise and extol the father who slew his sons, he is unhappy.   [3.16][17]

The theme of the third part of Anchises' prophecy is the expansion of empire through the actions of a series of hero-avengers. Conflict is international rather than internal to Rome.

Chronology is disturbed again in order that we may see first Troy taking a belated revenge on Agamemnon (in the form of the victories of Mummius, 146 B.C., and L. Aemilius Paulus, 168 B.C., in Greece) and then Rome's gradual ascendancy over Carthage in the Punic Wars. Anchises' exhortation is once again positive, but the statement of Roman destiny is also strangely qualified— qualified, as Adam Parry remarks, by the exclusion of the very things Virgil as a man prized most:

> "Excudent alii spirantia mollius aera,
> (credo equidem), vivos ducent de marmore voltus;
> orabunt causas melius, caelique meatus
> describent radio et surgentia sidera dicent:
> tu regere imperio populos, Romane, memento
> (hae tibi erunt artes) pacique imponere morem,
> parcere subiectis et debellare superbos."   [847-53][18]

["Others, I doubt not, shall beat out the breathing bronze with softer lines; shall from marble draw forth the features of life; shall plead their causes better; with the rod shall trace the paths of heaven and tell the rising of the stars: remember thou, O Roman, to rule the nations with thy sway—these shall be thine arts—to crown Peace with Law, to spare the humbled, and to tame in war the proud!"]

For Augustine the last line of this prophecy, despite or perhaps because of its parallelism with scriptural pronouncements on divine prerogative, reveals the moral chasm between the visionary who looks to Rome and the one who looks beyond to the City of God. *The City of God* opens juxtaposing the two:

> For the King and Founder of this city of which we speak, has in Scripture uttered to His people a dictum of the divine law in these words: "God resisteth the proud, but giveth grace unto the humble." But this, which is God's prerogative, the inflated ambition of a proud spirit also affects, and dearly loves that this be numbered among its attributes, to
> > "Show pity to the humbled soul,
> > And crush the sons of pride."
> And therefore, as the plan of this work we have undertaken requires, and as occasion offers, we must speak also of the

earthly city, which, though it be mistress of the nations, is
itself ruled by its lust of rule.   [1.1]

We need not invoke Augustine's heavenly city, however, to
grasp the limitations of the prophet of Rome. Had he arranged
things chronologically, Anchises might have shown Roman history building toward an apocalyptic climax with the advent of
Augustus and the restoration of the Saturnian Golden Age. Why,
then, has Anchises not done so? One answer, to infer his motive
from what he has accomplished, is that he wishes to avoid men-
tioning Augustus in the context of Rome's recent civil wars or in
proximity to Julius Caesar and Pompey. [19] Anchises, that is, finds
himself faced with what according to Kenneth Quinn is the
Aeneid's central moral problem, how to write a poem ostensibly
celebrating Augustus as the great bringer of peace when he had
been for many years one of the principals in the wars that had
ravaged the empire. [20] Anchises' prophecy represents a solution
to that problem in the form of a subtle evasion of it. By arranging
things thematically rather than chronologically, Anchises can introduce Augustus in the context of a speech arbitrarily limited to
the subjects of nomen and bloodline. The issue of civil strife is
relegated to another section of the prophecy. Anchises' solution
to the problem is admittedly an imperfect one, and perhaps deliberately so. The very dexterity with which the dilemma is han-
dled, it may be argued, serves to draw attention to it. We see the
prophet, and behind him the poet, maneuvering with almost
conspicuous delicacy to avoid embarrassing the emperor. In any
case, Anchises' prophecy is from an Augustan point of view
somewhat anticlimactic. The tribute to Augustus is followed by
allusions to human actions that are far from godlike, the effect of
which is to diminish the impact of the Augustan panegyric of
lines 777–807. Anchises' prophecy concludes on a strangely sober
note with a peroration apparently concerned with establishing
the limits of the role Rome is destined to play in history.

Anchises' prophecy, then, contains a tacit admission that history cannot be made to conform to the needs of either the hero or
the prophet. To the former history offers an imperfect consolation
for the sacrifice it requires; to the latter it presents obstacles to
envisioning a continuous movement toward a glorious apoc-

alypse. Virgil does not have available to him the principle that allows the Renaissance epic poet to rewrite history to conform to an ideal vision of it without compromising his belief in the veracity of what he records. The Virgilian prophet is constrained by the intransigence of historical fact to the meaning he seems to wish it to illustrate. Virgilian prophecy, to the extent that it wishes to remain truthful, is bound to the literal truth of history. The Christian poet-prophet, on the other hand, seeks to go beyond the letter of recorded fact, even where the immediate past is concerned. He is capable of attributing a more substantial reality to events as they conform to a providential plan than as they arrange themselves in human experience.

The appearance of the last figure in Anchises' pageant of future heroes underscores the point. Aeneas catches sight of the sad shade of Marcellus, Augustus's nephew, adopted son, and designated successor, who is destined to die before attaining his full glory. In Marcellus, Anchises is confronted with a figure who confirms the tragic nature of history that the prophet has so far seemed to struggle to deny. For the reader the touching eulogy Anchises now delivers for Marcellus may come as a relief since it breaks the tension created by the discrepancy that has existed up to this point between the moods of the son and the father. Anchises' eagerness for the future is finally subdued by the prospect of a tragedy for which he can only offer *inani munere*, "empty service" (885–86). There is irony, however, in the realization that whatever sense of relief we may feel is the result of an acknowledgment of the futility of human yearnings for fulfillment in history.

III

The Marcellus passage brings into focus what may be considered, from the later, Christian point of view, the limitations of the Virgilian vision of history. That Anchises can only lament the death of Marcellus is a reminder, after all, of the inability of the Virgilian prophet finally to dissuade his audience from conceiving of the human condition as tragic. History can provide only a partial and an impersonal compensation for death. Death remains a tragedy to which the only response is an "unavailing" commemoration:

> "Manibus date lilia plenis,
> purpureos spargam flores animamque nepotis
> his saltem accumulem donis et fungar inani
> munere."   [883–86]

["Give me lilies with full hand; let me scatter purple flowers; let me heap o'er my offspring's shade at least these gifts and fulfill an unavailing service."]

The Virgilian vision of the future, to be complete in its own terms, must contain the sight of a figure unable to "break the harsh bonds of fate" (882). Philosophically, the distance is great between this view of fate as harsh, inflexible, and intractable to any moral interpretation and the Christian conception of a benevolent providence.[21]

The Marcellus passage makes apparent a further limitation of Virgilian prophecy when we consider that it brings us, after all, only to the poet's immediate present. At some point it becomes necessary to address ourselves to Auden's question, "What next? / After this triumph, what portends?" ("Secondary Epic"). Are we to believe that the drama of history is somehow brought to a conclusion with Augustus? If not, do the prophecies of the return of the Golden Age not deteriorate into a device for Augustan propaganda? Virgilian prophecy, Augustine insists, is finally no more than a contrivance to view the past in the future tense (*City of God* 5.12). The Christian poet-prophet, on the other hand, will claim for himself knowledge of a greater sweep of time. He will see history unfolding from first things to last, according to the divine plan documented in Scripture: the beginning is the universal beginning of mankind and the end is absolute. He has available to him as a model not only Anchises, the prophet of dynasty, but also the prophet of Revelation.

What the Christian poet-prophet thereby asserts for himself, however, is not just a knowledge of greater amplitude but a different relation to historical knowledge altogether. The difference is visible in his hero. Aeneas, despite the fact that the Augustan future is fully known to Virgil, will always be in the process of discovering what lies ahead. Even when he is informed in detail of the future in prophetic revelations he remains in a sense ignorant of it, as Virgil intimates when Aeneas receives Vulcan's shield in book 8:

> Talia per clipeum Volcani, dona parentis,
> miratur rerumque ignarus imagine gaudet. [729-30][22]

[Such sights he admires on the shield of Vulcan, his mother's gift, and, though he knows not the deeds, he rejoices in their portraiture.]

His grasp of the future is imperfect in part because he is, like Virgil himself, limited to knowledge of what he has experienced, and in part because realization of the ultimate goal of which Virgil speaks, the restoration of the Golden Age, will always be a remote and an unattainable prospect, for the poet no less than for the hero. For the hero of Christian epic, on the other hand, the issue of historical knowledge acquires an added dimension. If he himself is constrained by time, he has access to the mind of a God who is not. To the extent that the Christian hero is cut off (or cuts himself off) from divine omniscience he exists in darkness, but when revelation does come he can undertake his pilgrimage with a degree of certainty Aeneas cannot possess.

I emphasis the tragic sense rather than the triumph of the *Aeneid* in order to establish the differences between Virgil's and the Christian view of history. Aeneas inhabits a universe whose hostility the Christian reader could believe his God had mollified. He could see in the austerity of the Virgilian hero's condition the limitations of a vision of destiny embodied in the earthly, historical city of Rome. But it is important to recognize that the difference between these two conceptions of history is at the same time the source of the great attraction the *Aeneid* holds for its Christian reader. The constraints that Roman destiny imposes on its hero are precisely those which Christianity sees itself in a position to break. In retrospect the *Aeneid* could be seen as a compelling document of the condition from which humanity was reprieved with the advent of Christ. Such an approach to Virgil's poem need not imply contempt. It is testimony to the complexity of the Christian response to Virgil that Augustine can use the language of Jove's prophecy of Augustan Rome, *imperium sine fine*, dominion without end (1.278–79), in an exhortation to his reader to renounce paganism:

> Lay hold now on the celestial country, which is easily won, and in which you will reign truly and for ever. For there shalt thou find no vestal fire, no Capitoline stone, but the one true God
>> "No date, no goal will here ordain:
>> But grant an endless, boundless reign."
>>> [*City of God* 2.29]

Augustine, as we shall see in the next chapter, would redefine dynastic epic in light of his understanding that its true objective is the City of God rather than the city of man. But by the same token he would grant the *Aeneid* a crucial place in his thought. In the *Confessions* he casts himself in the role of Aeneas in his conviction that he and Virgil's hero are fundamentally alike. They differ not so much in the nature of their yearning as in their respective capacities to attain its fulfillment.

CHAPTER TWO

AUGUSTINE:
The *Confessions* and the *Aeneid*

Augustine's *Confessions* have yet to be allotted the place they deserve among the documents basic to our understanding of Christian epic. Recognition of the significance of the *Confessions* in this regard awaits in turn fuller recognition of the importance of the *Aeneid* to our understanding of the *Confessions*. Readers who recall Augustine's account of the tears he shed for Dido in his youth and his subsequent condemnation of that sentiment from the perspective of his later moral enlightenment (1.13) are apt to take the apparent disapprobation registered there as a definitive statement of his attitude toward Virgil. But Augustine is not so hostile to the *Aeneid* as this passage might seem to suggest, and Virgil's epic is not so summarily dismissed from Augustine's thought as would appear to be the case, given the absence of explicit mention of it in later books of the *Confessions*. We continue to be conscious of Aeneas's epic itinerary as Augustine recounts his own journey from Carthage to Rome and his gradual discovery of his spiritual destiny. That Augustine's travels partly parallel those of Aeneas is, to be sure, a historical accident but one whose implications Augustine deliberately exploits. The *Confessions* are in a sense a recapitulation of Virgilian epic in a Christian universe. The elements of dynastic epic appear as they have been transformed in the light of Christian revelation. Augustine addresses himself not to an imperial patron but to God; he charts the evolution not of an earthly city or a ruling family united in blood but of a community of the faithful united spiritually in Christ. He celebrates a marriage not to a human dynastic copartner but, paradoxically, to Continence (8.11). The crisis of his life concerns his submission to a divine destiny, but the destiny to which he accedes is that of his personal salvation rather than that of a nation. The *Confessions* are a record of a quest into which that of Aeneas has been subsumed and by which it has been redefined, and as such the *Confessions* constitute an act of literary assimilation that goes far toward illuminating the undertakings of the epic poets of the Renaissance.[1]

Augustine never explicitly acknowledges the *Aeneid* as a subtext, but his first reference to Virgil is a subtle invitation to explore such a connection to the extent that it reveals his fascination with the analogies that can be drawn between himself and Virgil's heroes:

> I was obliged to memorize the wanderings of a hero named Aeneas, while in the meantime I failed to remember my own erratic ways. I learned to lament the death of Dido, who killed herself for love, while all the time, in the midst of these things, I was dying, separated from you, my God and my Life, and I shed no tears for my own plight.
>
> What can be more pitiful than an unhappy wretch unaware of his own sorry state, bewailing the fate of Dido, who died for love of Aeneas, yet shedding no tears for himself as he dies for want of loving you? O God, you are the Light of my heart, the Bread of my inmost soul, and the Power that weds my mind and the thoughts of my heart. But I did not love you. I broke my troth with you and embraced another while applause echoed about me. For to love this world is to break troth with you, yet men applaud and are ashamed to be otherwise. I did not weep over this, but instead I wept for Dido, who surrendered her life to the sword, while I forsook you and surrendered myself to the lowest of your created things. [1.13][2]

This passage occurs in the context of a criticism of the methods of education to which Augustine had been subjected in his youth. Later in the same chapter Augustine makes his distaste for such methods clear: "It is true that curtains are hung over the entrances to the schools where literature is taught, but they are not so much symbols in honour of mystery as veils concealing error."[3] It is easy to come away from this first mention of Virgil with the impression that Augustine means to classify his boyish enthusiasm for pagan literature among the errors he eventually learns to eschew, but on closer scrutiny we note that it is not so much classical literature itself as a way of reading it that Augustine means to censure. The youthful Augustine engages the *Aeneid* mindlessly, ironically unaware of its relevance to his own condition. The "wanderings" of Aeneas find their parallel in the erratic ways of the reader (both as reader and as an unregenerate youth), as do Dido's self-destructive passions. Dido's love of Aeneas has its counterpart in Augustine's cupidinous love of this world (a love in which the profane passion for literature being dramatized is reflected), and Aeneas's infidelity to Dido, which is implied in the same sentences, is echoed in Augustine's betrayal of his God: "I did not love you. I broke my troth with you and embraced another while applause echoed about me."

Such parallels, it might be argued, are meant to lead us to the conclusion that Virgilian epic should be censured on the grounds that it incites false passions, propelling its reader into complicity with its heroes in their moral depravity. But Augustine pointedly places the blame for his error on himself and his schoolmasters rather than Virgil. The inference we are to draw from the passage is not that Virgil should not be read but that he should not be read falsely. Classical literature may in fact serve Christian ends, as Augustine tells us in *On Christian Doctrine:*

> We should not think that we ought not to learn literature because Mercury is said to be its inventor, nor that because the pagans dedicated temples to Justice and Virtue and adored in stones what should be performed in the heart, we should therefore avoid justice and virtue. Rather, every good and true Christian should understand that wherever he may find truth, it is his Lord's. [2.18.28][4]

Thus, for instance, had the youthful Augustine been fully aware of the parallels between his own and Aeneas's "wanderings," or his and Dido's passions, the *Aeneid* might have served as an exemplum to move him in the direction of moral insight. He is impeded only by his inability in his youth to distance himself from the narrative, by his lack of a moral vantage point beyond the literal text. Or, to put it another way, he is impeded by his inability to distinguish between "wanderings" ("errores") in the literal and moral senses of the word.

Augustine makes no further open references to the *Aeneid* in the *Confessions* after book 1, but it would be a mistake to conclude from this that he has dismissed Virgil from his thoughts. We know from the *De ordine* (1.26), for one thing, that Augustine continued to read Virgil after his conversion.[5] But there is also evidence of an interest in the *Aeneid* internal to the *Confessions* that deserves our consideration. Virgilian echoes continue to reverberate in crucial moments later in Augustine's narrative. Augustine's pursuit of higher education takes him from his home in Thagaste to Carthage, which from the perspective of his later moral consciousness he views as a snare set in the path of his progress toward spiritual enlightenment, a "hissing cauldron of lust" (3.1). There he enters into a sexual relationship with a woman in whom we may see a Dido (if again we are willing to make the changes Augustine's morality imposes on Virgil): "In those days I lived with a woman, not my lawful wedded wife but a mistress whom I had chosen for no special reason but that my restless passions had alighted on her" (4.2). Augustine's mother, Monica, has already expressed her objections to marriage under such circumstances in terms that may recall Venus's opposition to a marriage between her son and Dido: "She was afraid that the bonds of marriage might be a hindrance to my hopes for the future" (2.3; cf. *Aen.* 1.664–75). Eventually Augustine, like Aeneas, responds to divine promptings to make the voyage from Carthage to Rome. The scene of Augustine's nocturnal, secret flight from Carthage and from Monica has distinct Virgilian overtones, this time with Monica cast in the role of Dido:

> She wept betterly to see me go and followed me to the water's edge, clinging to me with all her strength in the hope that I would either come home or take her with me. I deceived her with the excuse that I had a friend whom I did not want to leave until the wind rose and his ship could sail. . . . During the night, secretly, I sailed away, leaving her alone to her tears and her prayers. . . . The wind blew and filled our sails, and

the shore disappeared from sight. The next morning she was wild with grief, pouring her sighs and sorrows in your ear, because she thought you had not listened to her prayer. [5.8]

We glimpse the imprint of the *Aeneid* again when Augustine disentangles himself from his mistress, despite his passionate love for her, in order to clear the way for a career marriage of which Monica approves (6.13, 15).

It is finally not only where the narrative of the *Confessions* parallels the *Aeneid* but also where the two diverge that the nature of their relationship is defined. For if Augustine means for us to see that the Christian quest recapitulates the pagan one, he also takes care to show that the former eventually overgoes the latter. Thus Augustine's destiny lies not with his "Lavinia," the woman Monica for a time hopes he will marry, but with Continence, not in Rome but in Milan, the monastic communities at Thagaste and Hippo, and ultimately in the heavenly city of which the earthly Rome is false shadow. The boundaries of the world of Aeneas seem to have been extended in the *Confessions*, both geographically and spiritually, and in the larger space of the Christian universe the crises of the pagan one seem to dissolve. Thus, for instance, Monica wins a reprieve from the tragic fate that awaits her counterpart, Dido, in the scene of Augustine's departure for Rome: Monica later rejoins him in Italy. If we permit ourselves to think of the *Confessions*, mutatis mutandis, as an *Aeneid*, they are an *Aeneid* that has been expanded (in purely formal terms, from twelve books to thirteen) and brought to closure. In a sense the closing books of the *Confessions*, with their extended meditation on time and their allegorical interpretation of Genesis, represent the ultimate comment on the epic sense of history from a Christian perspective. The *Aeneid* ends looking ahead to the vision of a historical future, a Golden Age—but one from which by Augustine's time the glitter had fallen; the *Confessions*, by virtue of the perception that all moments in time, past, present, and future, are circumscribed by God (book 11), look beyond history. The *Aeneid*, like all epic, ends with what is in terms of its "total action" a beginning, the beginning of the historical process of building the Roman Empire. The *Confessions* overgo the *Aeneid* with respect to their conception of a total action as well; they conclude with a return to absolute beginnings, the Creation, and glimpse there a foreshadowing of the absolute end:

> But the seventh day is without evening and the sun shall not set upon it, for you have sanctified it and willed that it shall last for ever. Although your eternal repose was unbroken by the act of creation, nevertheless, after all your works were done and you had seen that they were very good, you rested on the seventh day. And in your Book we read this as a presage that when our work in this life is done, we too shall rest in you in the Sabbath of eternal life.   [13.36]

The line of speculation I am pursuing inevitably raises the question of the historicity of Augustine's narrative. Does seeing a sustained and deliberate relationship between the *Confessions* and the *Aeneid* mean we are not to regard the accounts of certain events in Augustine's life as factual? Or, if they are factual, would that not militate against speaking of them as somehow indebted to the *Aeneid* as a literary antecedent? Both questions, I believe, must be answered negatively. It is a matter of record, for instance, that Augustine studied in Carthage and subsequently went to Rome, and we have no compelling reason to doubt that the circumstances of his departure were as he describes them. But we have not seen the whole truth if we stop there. Truth, for Augustine, does not reside at the level of historical accident. The events of human experience become more significant in the degree to which they reveal the pattern of divine truth lying beyond them, the "invisible things" of God; the journey is fully understood only in terms of its goals. Such is the principle that informs the allegorical interpretation of Genesis expounded in the last books of the *Confessions*. Augustine elaborates in *On Christian Doctrine* in terms that hold implications for the *Confessions*:

> Suppose we were wanderers who could not live in blessedness except at home, miserable in our wandering and desiring to end it and to return to our native country. We would need vehicles for land and sea which could be used to help us to reach our homeland, which is to be enjoyed. But if the amenities of the journey and the motion of the vehicles itself

delighted us, and we were led to enjoy those things which we should use, we should not wish to end our journey quickly, and, entangled in a perverse sweetness, we should be alienated from our country, whose sweetness would make us blessed. Thus in this mortal life, wandering from God, if we wish to return to our native country where we can be blessed we should use this world and not enjoy it, so that the "invisible things" of God "being understood by the things that are made" [Rom. 1. 20] may be seen, that is, so that by means of corporal and temporal things we may comprehend the eternal and spiritual.   [*On Christian Doctrine* 1.4.4]

At the very least it must be acknowledged, as O'Meara points out, that Augustine uses the idea of memory as it is established in book 10 of the *Confessions* (8) to justify arranging the events of his life selectively, as he wishes to call them up, so that the providential pattern can be revealed.[6] To this end he has altered the chronological order of certain incidents as that order is documented in other treatises. He has antedated, for instance, the moment of his conversion, apparently with a view to clarifying the internal structure of the *Confessions*.[7] We do the *Confessions* an injustice to think of them as simply a record of the author's life;[8] they are at once something more and something less than that. They are neither complete as autobiography nor completely autobiographical. Their purpose is to bear witness to the fact of and the nature of divine intervention in human life in the form of spiritual revelation, and as such they narrate a story that is essentially typical rather than specific, potentially universal in its relevance.[9] Moreover, Augustine applies the principle by which he has designed the *Confessions* to his interpretation of the *Aeneid*. There too he sees a pattern, an account of a quest in which not just Aeneas but pre-Christian man could be thought to be engaged. And it is important for Augustine to take the pattern of that quest into account, not only because it could serve, in juxtaposition with that of the Christian pilgrim, to show the difference Christian revelation had made but also because the Virgilian quest, as Augustine sees it, is part of the Christian one. The *Aeneid* represents a stage in the continual unfolding of the providential scheme through which humanity had passed collectively and through which each individual must pass in his own life.[10]

While it is important to recognize that the *Confessions* aim at conveying more than the immediate, circumstantial facts of the author's life, it is equally important—for our understanding of both the *Confessions* and later Renaissance epic—to see that Augustine does not thereby mean to deny the historicity of such facts. History and the providential plan by which God works the individual's salvation are by no means mutually exclusive matters. Indeed, it is a fundamental tenet of Augustine's belief that history everywhere attests to Providence. By the same token we are not meant to construe the *Confessions,* for all their distortions of chronology and their elaborations upon pure fact, as fiction. Our eyes are continually shifted from the realm of historical accident to that of providential truth so that we may see the former confirmed by the latter, "the sole Truth by which all else is true" (10.23), and not because Augustine senses any alienation of the one from the other. It is upon such a notion of the continuity of history and divine truth that the efforts of Renaissance poets to construct Christian epics from historical *matière* will be based.

II

Among other things the *Confessions* are a quest for what is in the broadest sense of the term a concept of integrity. The *Confessions* depict a mind initially divided against itself, torn in different directions by conflicting impulses. Such is the natural condition, we are told, of a temporal being: "You, my Father, are eternal. But I am divided between time gone by and time to come" (11.29). The narrative strategy of the *Confessions* reinforces the impression of divisiveness. Augustine writes from two temporal perspectives simultaneously, from that of a consciousness moving in stages through time and that of one who has already completed the journey. Thus the enlightened, spiritually mature Augustine stands ready at any moment to utter his judgment on the experiences of Augustine the child, the adolescent, or the catechumen as these unfold. As Augustine comes to grasp the fundamental

unity of time through his meditation on memory in books 10 and
11, he also learns to look ahead to the moment of his own eventual
integration:

> My thoughts... are torn this way and that in the havoc of
> change. And so it will be until I am purified and melted by the
> fire of your love and fused into one with you. Then I shall be
> cast and set firm in the mould of your truth.   [11.29–30]

It is in the context of this quest, I believe, that Augustine's
allusions to the *Aeneid* should be read. That is, in the sequence of
references, overt and covert, that Augustine makes to Virgil in
the course of the *Confessions* we see a recapitulation of the larger
quest for a unification of the self. Thus the first mention of the
Aeneid, the passage in which Augustine implies an association
between himself in his truancy to God and Aeneas in his "wanderings" (1.13), establishes at least in part the existence of conflicts in the young Augustine's mind. So much becomes apparent
when we notice that it is not only Aeneas with whom Augustine
identifies himself. He sees in himself, rather surprisingly, parallels with both Aeneas and Dido, sometimes with each in turn and
sometimes with both simultaneously. He sees his reflection with
equal clarity in the betrayer and the betrayed.

It is worth returning to the passage to pursue its intricacies.
Augustine associates himself first with Aeneas in his moral way-
wardness, then with Dido as a spiritual suicide:

> I learned to lament the death of Dido, who killed herself for
> love, while all the time, in the midst of these things, I was
> dying, separated from you, my God.

He then reiterates the parallelism between himself and Dido,
"who died for love of Aeneas," but bases the parallel on contrast:
his own spiritual death is caused by not loving God. At this point,
having admitted that he most nearly resembles Dido in her tragic
fidelity to Aeneas through his own infidelity to God, he compli-
cates matters further by reasserting the parallel with Aeneas—for
it is Aeneas as well as Augustine whom we recognize as the
breaker of troth whom the world applauds: "But I did not love
you. I broke my troth with you and embraced another while
applause echoed about me." He is Dido in the fact of his spiritual

death and Aeneas in the act of betraying his love. He is both Aeneas and Dido, moreover, in the moment the gulf between the two Virgilian heroes is widest.

That Augustine may in this early stage of his life be construed as both an Aeneas and a Dido no doubt signals a certain lack of self-awareness on his part, but there is more to be inferred from such ambivalence than the uncertainty of a youth concerning his identity. We are witnessing deliberate manipulations of perspective on the Virgilian text, the implications of which will become fully clear only in the light of the notion of integrity that emerges as the goal of Augustine's personal pilgrimage. The conflation of apparently antithetical Virgilian personae within a single Augustinian one points us toward the principle on which the attempt to assimilate and overgo the *Aeneid* is grounded: Augustine's conviction that as a Christian he can achieve a resolution of the antagonisms that divide the soul of fallen man, including those dramatized in Virgilian epic. Thus had he fully grasped the nature of Christian paradox in his youth, he might have seen in himself the capacity to span the great rift opened in the *Aeneid* by the conflicting imperatives of love and empire. He might have understood the Christian promise of an empire founded on love, and he might have seen in this, and in himself as a Christian man, an end in which both the passion of Dido and the pietas of Aeneas could find expression.

This first mention of the *Aeneid* is significantly a description of an act of reading. It introduces not only Augustine's quest for salvation but also the quest for a principle of exegesis that is so obviously central to Augustine's concerns in the *Confessions*. The two pursuits are coextensive and analogous: the *Aeneid* no less than Augustine himself is to undergo a process of redemption. The strategy of the epic's redemption has been announced in 1.13 and will manifest itself again wherever allusions to the *Aeneid* seem to elicit a similar ambiguity. Thus Monica, as I have suggested, bears a resemblance to the Venus of the *Aeneid* in her capacity as principal guardian of her son's welfare and advocate of what she believes to be his destiny. But in the scene of Augustine's departure from Carthage to Rome Monica is decidedly cast in the role of Dido. Her frenzied grief, her prayers that Augustine's voyage might be prevented can be interpreted only as expressions of a will opposed to divine purpose in the light of Augustine's retrospective realization that his journey was a pilgrimage for his soul's salvation (5.8). If the scene of Augustine's departure to Rome deliberately echoes the *Aeneid*, the conflation of the roles of Venus and Dido in the person of Monica can be construed as a comment from the perspective of Christian enlightenment on the ironic meaninglessness of epic choice. Venus and Dido, the advocate and the opponent of Roman destiny, are from Augustine's point of view indistinguishable since both urge the hero in the direction of the city of man rather than the City of God. The antithesis between Carthage and Rome which Virgil keeps so clearly in view from the outset of his epic collapses in the presence of the greater alternative Augustine envisions between the earthly and the heavenly cities.

Monica, to be sure, has her son's spiritual welfare foremost in mind and so identification with neither Venus nor Dido is appropriate in the long run. But at this point an irony involving a discrepancy between motive and outcome comes into play. For the moment, at least, Monica's maternal devotion works against the higher goal she has in view: "For as mothers do, and far more than most, she loved to have me with her, and she did not know what joys you had in store for her because of my departure." The same discrepancy applies where Augustine is concerned: his journey will prove to be a further stage in his movement toward God, but it will be so in spite of his intentions. Augustine sees in Rome the promise of a better educational environment, where he will be permitted to conduct his lectures without the disruptions customary in the schools of Carthage. In retrospect Augustine expresses shame for his motives: he had fled a real misery in Carthage but pursued a false felicity in Rome. To the extent that he is moved by self-interest and Monica by maternal possessiveness, neither can fully comprehend the significance of the present event. The providential plan unfolds nonetheless, despite their ignorance of its direction: "You knew, O God, why it was that I left one city and went to the other. But you did not make the reason clear either to me or to my mother."

The difference between the forces governing the Virgilian and the Augustinian worlds seems to be that Augustine's God does not require conscious human compliance. In the scene of Augustine's departure from Monica there is no equivalent of Mercury, descending from heaven to jolt the hero out of his truancy to his destiny. The nature of the irony involved in the *Confessions* is not fully grasped, however, until it is seen that Augustine's God can use even human intransigence:

> In secret you were using my own perversity and theirs to set my feet upon the right course. For those who upset my leisure were blind in their shameless violence, and those who tempted me to go elsewhere knew only the taste of worldly things.

The providential plan, in other words, is so comprehensive as to include apparent deviation as part of the itinerary of salvation. Movement away from God may in the long run be movement toward him. With this principle Augustine gives new meaning to the circuity that characterizes the movement of the epic hero: "circumflectere cursus," the injunction under which the epic hero moves, translates into the Christian precept that to be saved one must first be lost.

One further step in Augustine's logic reveals the distance he has come from Virgilian epic in his reinterpretation of it. Monica's grief and the pain Augustine feels in leaving her are perhaps Virgilian in their intensity, but in Augustine's presentation of it the experience of tragic passion is circumscribed by an awareness that such passion is ultimately groundless. Monica has no more cause to lament her son's departure than he has to move in stealth or to torment himself with guilt for deceiving her, if events could be seen in the light of their eventual outcome. For one thing, the separation of Monica and Augustine is not final; she subsequently joins him in Italy (6.1). But it is the tragic sensibility itself against which Augustine really argues, and in doing so he implicitly revises the assumptions on which book 4 of the *Aeneid* is based. Dido's *furor* and the regret Aeneas feels for her loss go unresolved, as their meeting in Avernus (6.440–76) reveals. But Christian Providence works differently from Roman destiny. God does not exact a sacrifice in terms of human suffering for the advancement of his purposes; he may allow human passions to run their course but only to fulfill what is finally a benevolent justice. God does not answer Monica's prayers that Augustine be restrained from leaving for Rome but he refuses only in order to grant her unspoken prayers for her son's eventual salvation, "the wish that was closest to her heart." He does so in part to chastise her for what amounts to her momentary cupidity, her "too jealous love for her son" and her lack of faith in Providence. Her grief is "proof that she had inherited the legacy of Eve, seeking in sorrow what with sorrow she had brought into the world." This conception of a divine plan conspiring for what is best for the individual, often despite his immediate wishes, dissipates the urgency of Virgilian epic choice and subverts the sense of finality attached to it. Augustine's notion of Providence leaves little room for the melancholy that lies at the core of Virgil's epic, given its assumption that human gains are always accompanied with losses, that fate and the individual can never be perfectly reconciled.

Augustine's implicit reassessment of Virgil clearly entails a radical philosophical change. Augustine sees himself in a position to resolve the conflicts of Virgilian epic by virtue of his access to the paradoxical logic of Christian revelation. Thus the distinction between Virgil's Dido and Venus collapses when viewed from Augustine's perspective. Similarly, Augustine's "Lavinia," the woman whom Monica at first hopes he will marry (6.13), becomes his "Dido" in the light of his subsequent paradoxical betrothal to Continence and his decision not to place his hope "in this world." His visionary "marriage" to Continence at once parodies Aeneas's destined marriage to Lavinia and overgoes the *Aeneid* by celebrating the event that Virgil relegates to his poem's future:

> I could see the chaste beauty of Continence in all her serene, unsullied joy, as she modestly beckoned me to cross over and to hesitate no more. She stretched out loving hands to welcome and embrace me, holding up a host of good examples to my sight. With her were countless boys and girls, great numbers of the young and people of all ages, staid widows and women still virgins in old age. And in their midst was Continence herself, not barren but a fruitful mother of children, of joys born of you, O Lord, her Spouse.   [8.11]

Augustine's vision of chastity and fecundity paradoxically united in a principle of spiritual engendrure constitutes a climactic transformation of the Virgilian dynastic theme, a translation of it from the realm of flesh to that of spirit. The epic poets of the Renaissance, as we shall see, will look back on Virgil from the vantage point of a similar idealism. The dynasties they trace are the products of unions in which we see not only the crossing of different genealogical lines but also the *discordia concors* of chastity reconciled to love.

The possibility that Augustine's discovery of Providence implies a comment on the *Aeneid* seems to be confirmed in the moment of his conversion, the famous *tolle lege* passage of book 8 (12). The moment represents the culminating episode in a series of incidents beginning with what may be construed as a reference to Virgil (or rather to the act of reading him). The sequence begins in book 4, where Augustine describes the practice of the *sortes Virgilianae* as it is explained by a *vir sagax*, Vindicianus, as a means of interpreting one's destiny:

> He said that people sometimes opened a book of poetry at random, and although the poet had been thinking, as he wrote, of some quite different matter, it often happened that the reader placed his finger on a verse which had a remarkable bearing on his problem. It was not surprising, then, that the mind of man, quite unconsciously, through some instinct not within its own control, should hit upon some thing that answered to the circumstances and the facts of a particular question.   [4.3]

Vindicianus disabuses Augustine of his notion that fate can be read by this method, with its dubious mixture of chance and design. But Augustine returns to the practice later in the *Confessions*, this time having exchanged the "book of poetry" (Virgil would have been usual) for Paul's Epistles, that is, for a text in which the providential plan is fully revealed.

He recounts first the incident in which his friend Ponticianus finds a copy of the Epistles on a gaming table in Augustine's house (8.6). In the detail of the gaming table we notice a recurrence of the theme of chance on which the sortes Virgilianae is based, but in this case chance will give way to providential design. Ponticianus is stirred by his discovery, for reasons that will become clear, to speak of St. Anthony and then of the story of the conversions of two of his acquaintances and their fiancées. The two acquaintances, both employed in the service of the state and having wandered one day into a garden near the city walls of Trêves (while the emperor was watching the games in the circus), had chanced upon "a house which was the home of some servants of yours, men poor in spirit, to whom the kingdom of heaven belongs," where they found a book containing the life of St. Anthony.[11] In the process of reading it they are converted to a life of Christian asceticism. The incident is suggestive in all its details of the transformation of epic into spiritual pilgrimage we have seen taking place throughout the *Confessions*. In the course of their wanderings the two are converted from the service of the state, the earthly city (where the emperor sits watching the games in the circus), to the service of the kingdom of God. The story Ponticianus tells is digressive but Augustine is fully conscious of its relevance to himself: "But while he was speaking, O Lord, you were turning me around to look at myself. For I had placed myself behind my own back, refusing to see myself" (8.7).

Not long after this incident, in the crucial moment of his own conversion, Augustine returns again to a reenactment of the sortes. In his desperate struggle to come to a decision in the matter of Continence, he hears, or thinks he hears, a child's voice repeating, "Tolle lege, tolle lege" ("Take it and read").[12] Once again we are invited to contemplate the subtle interplay between accident and design, game and reality:

At this I looked up, thinking hard whether there was any kind of game in which children used to chant words like these, but I could not remember ever hearing them before. I stemmed my flood of tears and stood up, telling myself that this could only be a divine command to open my book of Scripture and read the first passage on which my eyes should fall. . . . I seized it and opened it, and in silence I read the first passage on which my eyes fell: "Not in revelling and drunkenness, not in lust and wantonness, not in quarrels and rivalries. Rather, arm yourselves with the Lord Jesus Christ; spend no more thought on nature and nature's appetites." I had no wish to read more and no need to do so. For in an instant, as I came to the end of the sentence, it was as though the light of confidence flooded into my heart and all the darkness of doubt was dispelled. [8.12]

Everything about the passage suggests accident being coopted by Providence. Augustine, in despair over the difficulty of taking a vow of continence, falls somehow under a fig tree, where he laments his state in the language of Psalms: "And thou, O Lord, how long, how long, Lord, wilt thou be angry, for ever? Remember not our former iniquities" (see Ps. 6.3; 79.5, 8).[13] His Old Testament longing is answered in the sortes by the New Testament, Pauline injunction to forgo reveling and drunkenness and rather put on Christ (Rom. 13.13, 14). Augustine now recalls the story of the conversion of Saint Anthony on having entered a church while the words "Go home and sell all that belongs to you . . . then come back and follow me" were being read from Scripture. (The relevance of Ponticianus's allusion to Anthony in 8.6 now becomes clear.) Our awareness of the hand of Providence is deepened as Augustine's friend Alypius looks at the passage Augustine has just read and finds in its sequel an injunction conspicuously apposite to himself: "Find room among you for a man of over-delicate conscience" (Rom. 14.1), which leads him, too, to conversion.[14]

The tolle lege passage marks the moment in which Augustine determines to accept Continence, which is in turn the climactic moment of his spiritual autobiography. His discovery of Providence constitutes the culmination of his quest for a unified self, a mind liberated from nagging moral and philosophical doubts and a will free of concupiscent urges. He discovers that the integration of his own being lies in the prospect of integration with God and that submission to God's will is paradoxically a fulfillment rather than a suppression of his own. He realizes that indeed it is a false notion of liberty, an illusion of man in his fallen state, that maintains the viability of any choice apart from acceptance of God:

> When I was trying to reach a decision about serving the Lord my God, as I had long intended to do, it was I who willed to take this course and again it was I who willed not to take

it. . . . So I was at odds with myself. . . . All this happened to me although I did not want it, but it did not prove that there was some second mind in me besides my own. It only meant that my mind was being punished. My action did not come from me, but from the sinful principle that dwells in me. It was part of the punishment of a sin freely committed by Adam, my first father.   [8.10]

With Augustine's discovery that self-fulfillment lies in the submission of his will to God's we encounter what is perhaps the most fundamental transformation of the world view of the *Aeneid*, a resolution of the antagonism between men and gods that lies at its core. Aeneas, in the moment Dido demands of him something like a confession of guilt, can only point to that conflict: "Italiam non sponte sequor" ("Not of free will do I follow Italy!") (4.361). Aeneas, to speak of him from an Augustinian point of view, has no free will and thus nothing to confess. One need look no further than the title of Augustine's spiritual autobiography to see the difference between the two on this score.

III

The moment in which the Augustinian quest culminates, as we have just seen, is one in which what once seemed an insoluble problem is suddenly and with a rather surprising lack of apparent difficulty solved. Before he accedes to the divine will Augustine exists in a state of torment but the act of submission itself, he realizes, is easy: "And to reach this goal I needed no chariot or ship. I need not even walk as far as I had come from the house to the place where we sat, for to make the journey, and to arrive safely, no more was required than an act of will" (8.8). (Note the discarding of the paraphernalia of the epic journey, the chariot and the ship.) The reader is apt to look back on the crises of the Augustinian quest not with the sense that they have tested and confirmed any extraordinary strength of mind and will in the quester but with a feeling that he need not have taxed himself at all to have succeeded. The Virgilian hero's capacity for endurance becomes an irrelevant, even a dubious virtue. In order to understand more fully the dynamics of such crises we must look into

Augustine's account of his struggle with Manichaean heresy, the chief obstacle in the way of his intellectual progress toward acceptance of Christian doctrine. The strangely anticlimactic nature of the Augustinian quest, we shall see, implies a rejection of Manichaean doctrine, with its materialism and its conception of a universe divided by the opposing powers of good and evil. An understanding of Augustine's thinking on this subject will in turn be vital to our grasp of the quests of the heroes of Renaissance epic.

Manichaean thought, as Augustine analyzes it, is from the outset limited by its materialistic premise:

> When I tried to think of my God, I could think of him only as a bodily substance, because I could not conceive of the existence of anything else. This was the principal and almost the only cause of the error from which I could not escape.   [5.10]

From this limitation follows the basic fallacy of Manichaeanism, the belief that evil, too, must be some kind of substance, separate from and independent of God. Since God is good, he could not have created evil; there must therefore be two "antagonistic masses," according to Manichaean thought, "both . . . infinite, yet the evil in a lesser and the good in a greater degree" (5.10).

The process of overcoming the heresy of Manichaeanism involves at almost every stage a perception that an apparent conflict is in fact not one. During an early phase of his conversion to Christian thought Augustine is troubled by the seemingly irreconcilable contradictions contained in Scripture. The words "God made man in his own image," for instance, seem to confirm that God is corporeal, which would conflict with the orthodox Christian belief that he is infinite. It is Ambrose who helps Augustine over this hurdle by showing him how figurative exegesis corrects the apparent absurdities of the literal text (5.14, 6.3–4). But the problem recurs in another form when Augustine struggles for a response to the Manichaeans with regard to the question of the nature of evil. The assumption that evil exists as a power opposed to but slightly inferior to God is at first attractive because it removes the ultimate responsibility for sin from the individual to that secondary power, that "other nature that sins within us" (5.10). The same assumption, however, carries the

disadvantage of making the fact of Christ's incarnation repugnant on the grounds that his association with bodily substance
and thus with evil would have meant his corruption.

As he comes to abandon the fallacious consolation of seeing
himself as a creature acted upon rather than acting in a cosmic
struggle between the two forces of good and evil, Augustine
affirms his possession of a free will and accepts the consequences
of that assertion. But at this point comes a rush of new questions:

> But then I would ask myself once more: "Who made me?
> Surely it was my God, who is not only good but Goodness
> itself. How, then, do I come to possess a will that can choose to
> do wrong and refuse to do good, thereby providing a just
> reason why I should be punished? Who put this will into me?
> Who sowed this seed of bitterness in me, when all that I am
> was made by my God, who is Sweetness itself? If it was the
> devil who put it there, who made the devil?"   [7.3]

The way out of this morass involves a reversal of the direction of
logical inquiry. Rather than pursue a course of thought that ends
asking how God can be corrupted, Augustine begins with the
assumption that God cannot be corruptible—since otherwise he
would not be God—and proceeds from there to assess the nature
of evil (7.4). Rather than begin assuming the existence of evil and
end asking how an all-powerful and good deity could permit it,
he begins with the assumption of God's omnipotence and benevolence and then turns to consider the status of evil:

> I said to myself, "Here is God, and here is what he has
> created. God is good, utterly and entirely better than the
> things which he has made. But, since he is good, the things
> that he has made are also good. This is how he contains them
> all in himself and fills them all with his presence.
>
> "Where then is evil? What is its origin? How did it steal
> into the world? What is the root or seed from which it grew?
> Can it be that there simply is no evil?"   [7.5]

Eventually Augustine answers his question affirmatively:
"Evil is nothing but the removal of good until finally no good
remains" (3.7). Evil, that is, lacks positive existence; it is simply a

privation of good. Everything that God creates, including corruptible matter, is necessarily good. Indeed, decay, since it is a sign of a thing's existence, is a sign of goodness as well (7.1). Absolute evil, then, is a complete lack of being: "Therefore, whatever is, is good; and evil, the origin of which I was trying to find, is not a substance, because if it were a substance, it would be good" (7.12).

This philosophical stance puts the prospect of a moral epic in a new light since its central agon, the struggle between good and evil, would be a conflict with nothingness, with an illusion. As painful and real as Augustine's effort to achieve this insight may be, the solution itself is sublimely anticlimactic. It entails simply a different way of seeing things, the acquisition of a vantage from which it is not Christian paradox but the Manichaean vision of a cosmic warfare between the opposed forces of good and evil that appears absurd. The Augustinian quest may be circuitous, prolonged, and gradual, but its conclusion, instantaneous and complete, has the effect of making the journey seem almost unnecessary to the attainment of the end.

Given the understanding that evil lacks substance, that engagement with evil is ultimately engagement with illusion, we are in a position to come to terms with the notion that Providence makes use of even human perversity, as Augustine notes in his retrospective appraisal of the scene of his departure from Monica. Augustine moves in a monolithic universe in which all that is emanates from God. Since evil has no place in Creation, no independent ontological status, it exists only as parody. As nonentity, its shape is determined by that which it is not. Augustine traces the implications of this line of thought where the movement of human will is concerned in his analysis of his motive (or what appears to be his lack of one) for stealing forbidden fruit in his boyhood. All human vice, he realizes, is propelled by the desire to emulate God. Pride, for instance, is a pretense of the superiority that is properly God's; ambition is a yearning to be, like God, the object of praise and honor. "The lustful use caresses to win the love they crave for, yet no caress is sweeter than [God's] charity" (2.6). Cupidity, if it were fully understood, is an urge that is finally completed only as it transforms itself into caritas, the movement of the soul toward God. All movement of the will, in other words, even that which seems hopelessly misdirected, confirms the existence of only one true objective:

> All who desert you and set themselves up against you merely copy you in a perverse way; but by this very act of imitation they only show that you are the Creator of all nature and, consequently, that there is no place whatever where man may hide away from you.   [2.6]

The consequences of this notion are evident throughout the history of Christian epic. We are in the presence of the irony by which the antagonistic energies of Milton's Satan, for instance, are continually frustrated in *Paradise Lost* (*PL*):

> But what if he our Conqueror (whom I now
> Of force believe Almighty, since no less
> Than such could have o'erpow'rd such force as ours)
> Have left us this our spirit and strength entire
> Strongly to suffer and support our pains,
> That we may so suffice his vengeful ire,
> Or do him mightier service as his thralls?
>   [Beelzebub speaking (1.143-49)]

Augustine's solution to the problem of Manichaeanism, his substitution of a monolithic, Christian conception of the universe for a dualistic one, has its implications for the Christian epic poet attempting to assimilate Virgil. There is an obvious potential in Manichaeanism for a literature of antagonism and conflict, for Virgilian epic translated into the realm of moral struggle. Renaissance epics reveal their debt to Augustinian thought to the extent that they do not realize that potential. Their common objective, as we shall see, is instead the Augustinian one of dispelling the illusion of divisiveness and discord, which in all its manifestations constitutes an obstacle to the perception of truth and thus to genuine engagement with history. The struggle we witness in Christian epic is the effort to transform a literature of discord into one of concord.

Augustinian thought, in other words, precludes the tragic principle that Adam Parry finds in the *Aeneid*:

Aeneas' tragedy is that he cannot be a hero, being in the service of an impersonal power. What saves him as a man is that all the glory of the solid achievement which he is serving, all the satisfaction of "having arrived" in Italy means less to him than his own sense of personal loss. The *Aeneid* enforces the fine paradox that all the wonders of the most powerful institution the world has ever known are not necessarily of greater importance than the emptiness of human suffering.[15]

It is precisely this dilemma that Augustine strives to resolve as he seeks—if it can be granted that in part the *Confessions* constitute such a project—to overgo and complete the *Aeneid*. For Augustine, Virgil's fatalism derives from his ignorance of the nature of Providence, which in the light of Christian revelation is destiny whose principal concern is not Rome but man. The *Confessions* replace the paradox of which Parry speaks with another, the belief that submission to Christian Providence leads to personal fulfillment rather than loss.

IV

Much of what is essential to Augustine's sense of history can be inferred from his attitude to Virgil. That Augustine does not call for the rejection of classical epic but instead urges its completion in the light of Christian revelation attests to his belief in the inclusiveness and the continuity of the Providential plan. Such a conviction permits him to tolerate, even to respect the philosophical and moral precepts of pre-Christian cultures. Perhaps the most sustained discourse on this subject in the *Confessions* focuses on Platonism.[16] Augustine declines to revere Plato in *The City of God* (2.14) but he intimates in the *Confessions* that Platonic philosophy comes as close as is possible without the benefit of the Incarnation to seeing the truth. Platonism, to begin with, teaches one to look for truth as something incorporeal, and Christianity confirms that God is infinite, invisible except through his creatures (7.20). Reading not "word for word" (7.9) but interpretively, he finds in the writings of the Platonists implicit acknowledgment of God's eternity, the identity of God with *logos*, and the coeternity of God and the Son, if no record that "the Word was made flesh and came to dwell among us." He reads that truth is infinite and incorporeal but sees nothing of its paradoxical descent into corporeality and nothing of the sacrifice upon which the Christian notion of caritas is grounded—nothing of Christ (7.20). Pagan wisdom, to be sure, falls short of the truths of Christian revelation, which comes from beyond the realm of the human intellect and which only divine grace, not human insight, makes possible. Human reason is by definition precluded from seeing truths that transcend or subvert it in their paradoxicality. Thus a gulf lies between Platonist and Christian doctrine,

> between those who see the goal that they must reach, but cannot see the road by which they are to reach it, and those who see the road to that blessed country which is meant to be no mere vision but our home.   [7.20]

But there is also in Augustine's review of Platonism an appreciation of the fact that Revelation is a historical event of which pagan philosophers could have no knowledge.

In a similar vein Augustine delineates the differences between Virgilian and Christian thought on the subject of the immortality of the soul, and in the course of doing so the differences between Virgil's and Augustine's views of history emerge. Augustine suggests (*City of God* 22.26) that the Virgilian notion of metempsychosis as expounded by Anchises in the sixth book of the *Aeneid* derives from Platonic doctrine, which is in turn limited by its lack of access to the Christian belief in the miracle of the resurrected body. Virgil, following Plato, acknowledges the "dire craving" of the soul, once separated from the body in death, to return again to the body (*Aen.* 6.751); but since Plato and Virgil "have no acquaintance with any flesh but that which is mortal" no knowledge of that which can suffer and not die (*City of God* 21.3),[17] neither can offer a perfect gratification of the soul's "craving." Plato gives us the prospect of souls transmigrating to the bodies of beasts; Porphyry improves on this by arguing for the return of souls to human forms, but not the ones they left (10.30); Virgil envisions souls returning to bodies in an eternal round. But because Virgil, like Plato, posits that the body is the *cause* of sin (14.3), he can account for the "strange longing" of the soul to return to flesh only with the assertion that the soul becomes oblivious to the past by drinking the waters of Lethe (*Aen.* 6.750–51). If the explanation does not fully appease Aeneas, Augustine finds it even less satisfactory. Augustinian doctrine removes the problem, however, by maintaining that the soul, not the flesh, is the cause of sin (*City of God* 14.3), that death is the punishment for Adam's sin, without which the body would have been immortal (13.19), and thus that redemption from sin makes possible the soul's return to the original regenerated body. Christ's sacrifice promises the perfect fulfillment of the soul's "mad longing for the light" (*Aen.* 6.721) and an end to the eternal cycle of the soul's transmigration in and out of bodies.

In the *Aeneid* Virgil is perhaps not finally interested in applying the doctrine of metempsychosis to history generally, but this together with the notion of a resurrection of fallen Troy in Rome and that of a return of the Golden Age under Augustus does present the prospect of history conforming tc a cyclical pattern. Augustine finds such a prospect repugnant. He regards the events of Christian myth as having happened once and only once and has having made a definitive, irreversible difference:

> For once Christ died for our sins; and, rising from the dead, He dieth no more. "Death hath no more dominion over Him;" and we ourselves after the resurrection shall be "ever with the Lord," to whom we now say, as the sacred Psalmist dictates, "Thou shalt keep us, O Lord, Thou shalt preserve us from this generation." And that too which follows, is, I think, appropriate enough: "The wicked walk in a circle;" not because their life is to recur by means of these circles, which these philosophers imagine, but because the path in which their false doctrine now runs is circuitous.   [*City of God* 12.13]

The great virtue of Christian myth, according to Augustine, lies in its capacity to release the human mind from the potentially nightmarish vision of a futile, unending pattern of recurrence and thus to make engagement with history more meaningful than it could have been for Plato and Virgil. The narratives of Renaissance romance epic will turn on the same insight. The revelation that allows the chivalric hero to enter the stream of history in a meaningful way simultaneously reprieves him from his circuitous wanderings in an illusory labyrinth and from a pattern of obsessively repetitive action.

At the heart of Augustine's disagreement with Virgil and pagan historiography is the Augustinian conception of universal history as an essentially linear movement from Creation to Apocalypse, a teleological process directed toward the single goal of individual salvation. [18] Human history is a single temporal *excursus* rounded by eternity, a sequence of events defined by a distinct beginning and a distinct end. Emphasis should be placed, moreover, on the notion that it is the fate of the individual soul, not that of cities or nations, with which Christian historiography is principally concerned. In Augustine's conception of history the business of the world, the relative prosperity or decline of nations in any materialistic sense, the issue of cultural progress that so clearly occupies Virgil's thought, are essentially unimportant. [19] It is to lift Christianity out of the debate over where responsibility for the fall of the Roman Empire properly lies, after all, that Augustine set out to write *The City of God*. [20]

With this we come to the focal point of the quarrel between Virgil and Augustine: their respective attitudes to Rome itself. The greatness of Rome, the seat of world power, dominion without end (*Aen.* 1.279), and its citizens, *caelicolas*, denizens of heaven, *rerum domini*, lords of the world (*Aen.* 6.781–89) are Virgil's subjects. But this celebration of earthly glory, however closely the language approximates that of Christian vision, is to Augustine blasphemous. Rome is the earthly city, a copy of the city Cain built, similarly founded through fratricide, the killing of Remus by Romulus (*City of God* 15.5). It is a second Babylon (18.22), the Devil's city, divided against itself, neither eternal nor truly a city (15.4). The Pax Augusta is a parody of true peace:

> For [the earthly city] desires earthly peace for the sake of enjoying earthly goods, and it makes war in order to attain to this peace; since, if it has conquered, and there remains no one to resist it, it enjoys a peace which it had not while there were opposing parties who contested for the enjoyment of those things which were too small to satisfy both. This peace is purchased by toilsome wars; it is obtained by what they style a glorious victory.   [15.4]

Of the heavenly city there is only a shadow on earth, "a symbol and foreshadowing image . . . which served the purpose of reminding men that such a city was to be, rather than of making it present" (15.2).

The issue has significant implications for epic literature. The *Aeneid* deprived of Rome in its concrete, historical manifestation ceases to be the same poem. The struggle to found a specific race is the subject of the *Aeneid* (1.33): Virgil's Aeneas is the eponymous hero, not an everyman. Virgilian epic action is necessarily anchored in geographical and historical reality, not enclosed in the interior regions of the psyche or projected onto the map of a universalized, spiritualized landscape. Augustine's attitude toward Rome, to the extent that it is representative of orthodox Christian thinking, may therefore have something to do with the long disappearance of anything closely resembling Virgilian dynastic epic. Yet Augustinian thought does not preclude such an epic. In the first place let us note that Augustine preserves an analogy between Virgilian quest and Christian pilgrimage even in the act of distinguishing between them. The Christian goal remains a city, although not an earthly one, and Virgilian prophecy can be appropriated to describe it. Virgil's Rome serves as a metaphor, a *figura* of the goal toward which Augustine turns his gaze: "Of this city which served as an image, and of that free city it typified, Paul writes to the Galatians in these terms: 'Tell me, ye that desire to be under the law, do you not hear the law?' " (*City of God* 15.2). And in the second place, the typological relationship between the earthly and the heavenly cities of which Augustine speaks, as we have seen in another context, does not deny the historical reality of the former. Rome does not lose its historical status as it typifies the holy city; indeed, that status is if anything confirmed as Rome comes to be seen as something that will be fulfilled through God's providence. Augustine, in other words, ultimately accepts Rome, when Rome can be regarded with eyes that do not stop at its physical reality.[21] The objective is to contemplate Rome to see God indirectly rather than to see only Rome, or only a monument to human pride. Renaissance epic poets will return with enthusiasm to the Virgilian dynastic theme and will place a new emphasis on their earthly cities; but in doing so they will not have to abandon the fundamental precepts of

Augustinian thought. The dynastic epics of the Renaissance can be regarded rather as a continuation of a kind of thinking that permits the assimilation of pagan literature to a Christian universe.

V

One further instance of Augustine's tolerance for pre-Christian culture can be found early in the *Confessions* (3.7) as he speaks of the "equitable law" ("lege rectissima dei") by which Providence ordains different customs for different ages ("although the law itself is always and everywhere the same and does not differ from place to place or from age to age"). The notion of equitable law takes into account cultural and historical relativity and yet maintains that God's law is constant and unchanging throughout time. Given the understanding that Providence unfolds in time, judgment of one age by the standards of a later one becomes an act of presumption. One must understand that "each part of the whole has a different function suited to it" (3.7). There is room in Augustine's thought for appreciation of historical change—not accidental and random change but change directed by Providence and thus change to which it is possible to ascribe meaning and coherence.

Augustine's discussion of the equitable law that governs history is a manifestation of the double perspective that operates throughout the *Confessions* as the two realms of time and eternity are continually juxtaposed. Rules of conduct may differ from one age to the next but divine justice remains unchanged and eternal. History presents us with a succession of parts whose meanings can be fully grasped only with knowledge of the whole. This way of seeing things implies certain cognitive limitations for humanity. Only God, of course, understands the meaning of history fully because only the mind of God comprehends temporal events, past, present, and future, in its eternal present. And for the same reason, as Augustine comes to conclude in the eleventh book of the *Confessions,* it is only in the mind of God that time has substantive reality (11.27). We may speak of a division of time into the past, the present, and the future, but for time-bound mortals only the present exists (and that lacks duration); the past is that which is no longer and the future is that which is not yet (11.17,

18). To the extent that we have access to the past and the future in present perceptions of them, we may speak of "a present of past things, a present of present things, and a present of future things," or memory, attention, and expectation (11.20); but this is to experience time subjectively. Temporal existence precludes direct perception of reality or full comprehension of history's ultimate meaning. Such are the conditions imposed upon humanity with the Fall; for Augustine, the subjects of time and knowledge are in the last analysis moral issues.

Augustine represents the nature of temporal existence most concisely and compellingly in an analogy to the reading of a psalm:

> Suppose that I am going to recite a psalm that I know. Before I begin, my faculty of expectation is engaged by the whole of it. But once I have begun, as much of the psalm as I have removed from the province of expectation and relegated to the past now engages my memory, and the scope of the action which I am performing is divided between the two faculties of memory and expectation, the one looking back to the part which I have already recited, the other looking forward to the part which I have still to recite. But my faculty of attention is present all the while, and through it passes what was the future in the process of becoming the past. As the process continues, the province of memory is extended in proportion as that of expectation is reduced, until the whole of my expectation is absorbed. This happens when I have finished my recitation and it has all passed into the province of memory.
>
> What is true of the whole psalm is also true of all its parts and of each syllable. It is true of any longer action in which I may be engaged and of which the recitation of the psalm may only be a small part. It is true of a man's whole life, of which all his actions are parts. It is true of the whole history of mankind, of which each man's life is a part.   [11.28]

The human experience of time differs from God's because the divine mind is never divided between anticipating and remembering. Still, Augustine's conception of history is for him finally an argument for serenity, as the choice of a psalm as a metaphor for history suggests. The speaker knows that the psalm stands formally complete before he begins to recite it. There is a profound difference between the sense of expectation with which he faces time, transferring future to past syllable by syllable, knowing each moment will fill out the harmonious design of the whole, and the sense of awe with which Virgil's hero confronts his destiny even after it has been prophetically disclosed to him. The specific psalms to which Augustine refers in this context (63, 18, 27, 31) are hymns of confidence in divine protection. The psalmist expresses his conviction that God will deliver him from his enemies:

> The Lord is my rocke, and my fortresse, and he that deliuereth me, my God and my strength: in him wil I trust, my shield, the horne also of my saluacion, and my refuge.
> I will call vpon the Lord, which is worthie to be praised: so shal I be safe from mine enemies.   [Ps. 18.2-3, Geneva Bible]

Dynastic prophecy in the *Aeneid*, by contrast, is a pageant of glory unavoidably tempered with pain, human pride balanced against human vulnerability, an exhortation to enter the stream of history at whatever personal cost that may entail. The hero's response to his future contains an element of uncertainty that no view of history from a human perspective can ever fully dispell.

There is a difference, too, between the serenity that Augustine's view of history permits him and the pleasure that Aeneas manages to contemplate in a moment of aesthetic detachment from his present turmoil in the storm of book 1:

> "Forsan et haec olim meminisse iuvabit."
> ["Some day perhaps remembering this too will be a pleasure."]   [*Aen.* 1.203]

Augustine looks for consolation of a higher order, as when, for instance, he attempts to come to terms with the death of his friend early in the *Confessions* (4.4-11). He does not simply project himself into a future in which the present may acquire whatever attractiveness memory can bestow; rather he enlarges his scope in the belief that whatever events Providence ordains have their place in the benevolent scheme of things. He urges himself not to fix his thought on the transiency of particular things but on the pattern that emerges through their passing:

> Not all the parts exist at once, but some must come as others go, and in this way together they make up the whole of which they are the parts. Our speech follows the same rule, using sounds to signify a meaning. For a sentence is not complete unless each word, once its syllables have been pronounced, gives way to make room for the next.   [4.10]

Historical action, in other words, involves substantive reality, even if that reality is not fully comprehensible to anyone existing within time. History is the process of divine creation and destruction; its events are real and significant, and this understanding makes possible for Augustine a fuller reconciliation to momentary losses than Aeneas, who is everywhere plagued by an awareness that what meets his eye is pointless and empty, *inani*, can attain. Augustine may never acquire full knowledge of the whole but he can trust that his experience at every moment amounts to participation in that whole.

‖

CHAPTER THREE

ARIOSTO:
The Dynastic Pair, Bradamante and Ruggiero

We tend to think of Tasso as the great synthesizer of what critics of his time took to be two rival narrative forms, Ariostan romance and neoclassical epic.[1] It is true that he was that, and it is true that Tasso was aided in his project by developments in the world of Italian letters that postdated Ariosto's last edition of *Orlando Furioso* (1532), the translation of Aristotle's *Poetics* in 1536, and the subsequent emergence of a body of critical theory on the subject of classical epic. But what these truths obscure is the fact that Ariosto's *Orlando Furioso* is in its own right a poem with both romance and epic aspects. The *Furioso* is no less than Tasso's *Gerusalemme Liberata* a dialogue of two poetic forms within one frame. It is, as the second stanza of the poem informs us, a continuation of Boiardo's unfinished romance narrative, *Orlando Innamorato*, the story of Orlando's frenzied, frustrated passion for Angelica; but it is also, as the first, third, and fourth stanzas of canto 1 suggest, a poem modeled on Virgilian dynastic epic, the story of Ruggiero and Bradamante, cofounders of the house of Ariosto's patrons, the Estensi:

> Voi sentirete fra i piú degni eroi,
> che nominar con laude m'apparecchio,
> ricordar quel Ruggier, che fu di voi
> e de' vostri avi illustri il ceppo vecchio.   [1.4][2]

[Among the worthiest heroes whom I make ready to name with praise, you will hear mentioned that Ruggiero who was the ancient stock of yourself and your illustrious ancestors.][3]

In the Ruggiero–Bradamante plot Ariosto recasts the great subject of the *Aeneid,* the founding of a city and a race. Through Ruggiero and Bradamante, then, the *Furioso* finds its links with both its classical literary past, the *Aeneid,* and its historical future, the court of the Estensi.

The Orlando story too defines itself against the backdrop of the *Aeneid,* but in this respect, as in most others, the Orlando–Angelica and Ruggiero–Bradamante plots stand in inverse relation to each other. Ruggiero and Bradamante learn to act in accordance with the imperatives of dynastic epic, whereas Orlando is delinquent to these. We first meet Orlando in a context that recalls the Aeneas of book 8, embarking on his mission to establish a Trojan–Roman *imperium* in Italy, but Orlando here (canto 8) substitutes an amorous for an imperial objective, Angelica for Paris and Charlemagne, and so becomes Aeneas regressed to the truancy of book 4 and Dido. One of the earliest appearances of Ruggiero, on the other hand, recalls the Aeneas of book 4 (canto 7), but from this point onward Ruggiero proves responsive to a series of calls to reform and to fulfill his dynastic obligations. The Bradamante–Ruggiero plot is linear and progressive; the Orlando one, as readers have often observed, seems to lack unity and direction. In the Orlando story, moreover, Ariosto's fusion of the traditional Carolingian matter of war and the Arthurian matter of love produces the disastrous results familiar throughout Renaissance romance. As the hero is diverted from his proper civic and chivalric purpose by answering the call of his passions, his martial prowess is turned first against his own cause and finally against himself (for delinquency to such a cause is ultimately an act of self-betrayal). In the Ruggiero–Bradamante story, by contrast, the two matters of love and arms are gradually untangled until the love between the heroic pair becomes the principle upon which a dynasty is founded. On the one hand we witness the discord that results from a choice of love over empire, and on the other hand we see love operating in the service of empire.

But if a comparison of the two main plots of the *Furioso* suggests a division of the poem into the categories of romance and dynastic epic, a comparison of its dynastic plot to the *Aeneid* invites yet another distinction. Epic action completed in marriage argues the poet's intention of reinterpreting the *Aeneid*, as Augustine and Vegius had done, from a Christian perspective. So too does the fact that Ruggiero's "education" culminates in canto 41 in Pauline or Augustinian conversion. Indeed his spiritual regeneration, as we shall see, is the condition on which his institution as an epic hero hangs. We are once again in the realm of Augustinian thought, moreover, as we find ourselves speaking of two plots dramatizing the effects of two divergent kinds of love, one that proves self-destructive and one upon which an empire can be built.[4] The dualism of Augustine's charitable and cupidinous loves constitutes the poem's central crisis, and the Augustinian precept that both kinds of love are finally expressions of the same urge will permit the resolution of that crisis.

In this light it becomes evident that the Orlando and Ruggiero plots, the poem's romance and epic facets, are not so disparate as they may seem to be when subjected to a purely formal analysis. They proceed from the same metaphysical premise. Ultimately they are but two manifestations of a single interpretive response to the *Aeneid*. Both reflect a conception of the *Aeneid* as an inherently tragic poem, unable in the end fully to resolve the apparent conflict of love and duty. The Orlando plot differs from the Ruggiero plot only in its way of revealing its interpretation of Virgil. The Orlando plot exposes the consequences (as they are seen from a Christian vantage point) of giving oneself up to the *furor*, the self-destructive passion released into Virgil's poem by Dido, Allecto, Amata, and Turnus. Romance, as the term will apply in the following discussions of Ariosto and Tasso, is in a sense the universe of the *Aeneid* as yet unsalvaged by the Christian poet. The dynastic plot, on the other hand, shows how the *Aeneid* can be relieved of its tragic implications when rewritten to express the cosmic optimism of Christianity. In this context the poet affirms the possibility not of restraining furor and eros but of redeeming those passions so that they can be integrated into the social and historical world. Tasso in his *Discorsi del Poema Eroico* will speak more explicitly of the thematic unity of romance and epic, but what Tasso asserts in theoretical terms has already found practical application in the *Furioso*.

In the following pages I explore the implications of the *Furioso's* dynastic plot.[5] To do so, as the preceding paragraphs suggest, is to present Ariosto's poem in a light in which it has not universally been seen by its readers. Contemporary criticism of Ariosto has perhaps shifted from the position Croce took in the earlier part of this century when he offered a portrait of the poet as "untormented with doubts, not concerned with human destiny, incurious as to the meaning and value of this world";[6] but the tendency to infer Ariosto's intentions from the single perspective of the Orlando story persists. The result is often to see a poet, if not incurious as to meaning and value, then convinced of their absence from the universe he knew. But there are in fact two authorial personae in the *Furioso*, corresponding to the two main threads of the story, and the presence of the second checks whatever impressions we may take from the first. The first associates himself with Orlando to the point that he claims to share his hero's fate: he is himself the victim of an amorous passion that drives him toward madness and threatens to frustrate his efforts to complete his poem:

> Dirò d'Orlando in un medesmo tratto
> cosa non detta in prosa mai né in rima:
> che per amor venne in furore e matto,
> d'uom che sí saggio era stimato prima;
> se da colei che tal quasi m'ha fatto,
> che 'l poco ingegno ad or ad or mi lima,
> me ne sarà però tanto concesso,
> che mi basti a finir quanto ho promesso. [1.2]

[At the very same time I shall say of Orlando something never said before in prose or rime: that through love he became frenzied and insane and not that man who earlier was judged so wise,—if by her who has almost made me the same, who all the time files away my small ability, so much of it is still granted me as may suffice to finish what I have promised.]

The narrative that this poet-persona produces is an extension of his inner chaos; the disorder, the frustrating inconclusiveness, and the absurdity of narrative action reflect back on the mind of its creator. To this poet figure it is appropriate to attribute a vision of the futility of the human condition and a sense of irony that leaves nothing, however sacrosanct, unshaken. But the second poet-persona, the one who narrates the story of Bradamante and Ruggiero, acts as the spokesman for civic and moral values we need not assume Ariosto intended to ridicule. The narrative he relates takes us by stages from the "selva oscura," the landscape of romance confusion, to Paris, the locus of chivalric value, while the poet traces the process of his hero's spiritual regeneration.

This is not to say that in one aspect of his poem Ariosto puts manacles on his famous sense of irony. We need not assume, for instance, that when he presents his highly encomiastic prophecy of the birth of Ippolito d'Este in canto 46 the poet has suppressed his keen awareness of the shortcomings of his patron in real life; but neither should we doubt Ariosto's dedication to the moral standard he knew his patron ought to uphold. Readers who feel that moral consciousness cannot coexist with an ironic tempera- ment of the kind Ariosto possesses do not sufficiently appreciate the scope of that morality. Much of Ariosto's wit will be missed, moreover, if we fail to see the moral principle against which ac- tion in his poem is continually measured. We may attribute to Ariosto the qualities of urbanity, tolerance, and humor, as Giamatti has said, without concluding that he must be a cynic.[7]

I

We shall be in a position to see more clearly what is at issue in the Ruggiero–Bradamante plot if we approach it by way of its com- plementary opposite, the story of Orlando. For in Orlando Ariosto dramatizes the effects of deviation from the values Rug- giero is to acquire and uphold. Orlando establishes himself as a subverter of epic imperatives from the moment of his entrance into the poem in canto 8. The scene is Paris, where Charlemagne and the Christian forces are besieged by Agramante. The city nearly falls to the pagans but at the last moment the battle is broken off by a providential storm called down by Charlemagne's prayers. Orlando, however, has other thoughts on his mind:

> La notte Orlando alle noiose piume
> del veloce pensier fa parte assai.
> Or quinci or quindi il volta, or lo rassume
> tutto in un loco, e non l'afferma mai:

qual d'acqua chiara il tremolante lume,
dal sol percossa o da' notturni rai,
per gli ampli tetti va con lungo salto
a destra et a sinistra, e basso et alto.
   La donna sua, che gli ritorna a mente,
anzi che mai non era indi partita,
gli raccende nel core e fa piú ardente
la fiamma che nel dí parea sopita.   [8.71–72]

[In the night Orlando shares with the plaguing feathers
much of his swift thought. Now to this side now to that he
turns it, now brings it all together in one spot, and never keeps
it still, just as the trembling light from clear water struck by the
sun or the rays of the moon goes over the wide ceilings, with
long leaps to right and left and low and high.

His lady, who returns to his mind, or more truly, who
never has left it, rekindles in his heart and makes hotter the
flame that in the day seemed quenched.]

Thus Orlando's private and nocturnal frustrations on having lost
his lady are juxtaposed with Charlemagne's daytime experience
of God's grace. Whereas Charlemagne turns in prayer to God,
who quenches a fire with a rainfall, Orlando turns to his romance
deity, Angelica, who kindles a fire in his heart.

The simile describing Orlando's fretful thoughts as beams of
light reflected from water onto the ceiling of his chamber is a clear
allusion to the *Aeneid* (8.18–25), but the allusion comes in a context that only heightens our awareness of the ironic discrepancy
between the romance and epic heroes. Orlando's thinking generates a fantasy that will divert him from his epic duty, the defense
of Paris. The ruminations of Aeneas, by contrast, are immediately
followed by the appearance of the Roman river god Tiberinus,
who gives the hero assurances of his eventual success in rebuild-
ing a Troy in Italy and directs him toward Pallanteum, the site of
the future Rome (36–65). Ariosto's allusion to this passage in
Virgil is resumed in stanza 79, in which we see Orlando tossing
restlessly while the rest of the world sleeps:

Già in ogni parte gli animanti lassi
davan riposo ai travagliati spirti,

> chi su le piume, e chi sui duri sassi,
> e chi su l'erbe, e chi su faggi o mirti:
> tu le palpèbre, Orlando, a pena abbassi,
> punto da' tuoi pensieri acuti et irti;
> né quel sí breve e fuggitivo sonno
> godere in pace anco lasciar ti ponno.

[Already everywhere tired living beings were giving rest to their weary spirits, some on feathers, some on hard rocks, some on the grass, some on beeches or myrtles. You, Orlando, scarcely lower your eyelids, pricked by your sharp and pointed thoughts; nor can they even allow you to enjoy in peace that sleep so brief and fugitive.]

But once again we are meant to sense the perversity of the romance text as it seeks to recapitulate the epic one. Ariosto's words allude again to the scene in the *Aeneid* immediately preceding the appearance of Tiberinus (8.26-35), but because we see Orlando in the throes of an amorous passion we are meant to follow the allusion back to book 4 of the *Aeneid* and Dido:

> It was night, and over the earth weary creatures were tasting peaceful slumber; the woods and wild seas had sunk to rest—the hour when stars roll midway in their gliding course, when all the land is still, and beasts and gay birds, both they that far and near haunt the limpid lakes, and they that dwell in fields of tangled brakes, are couched in sleep beneath the silent night. But not so the soul-racked Phoenician queen; she never sinks to sleep, nor draws the night into eyes or heart. Her pangs redouble, and her love, swelling up, surges afresh, as she heaves with a mighty tide of passion.   [4.522-32][8]

In the *Aeneid* the recurrence of the "Nox erat" passage in book 8 illustrates the triumph of Roman pietas over Carthaginian furor, but in the *Furioso* we witness the reverse. Orlando in his passion for Angelica is Aeneas reverting to the condition of a Dido. The Virgilian landscape from which Tiberinus appears with a prophecy of success for Aeneas's mission, the pleasant stream shaded by popular leaves, is transformed in Orlando's reverie into a *locus amoenus* of cupidinous love:

Parea ad Orlando, s'una verde riva
d'odoriferi fior tutta dipinta,
mirare il bello avorio, e la nativa
purpura ch'avea Amor di sua man tinta,
e le due chiare stelle onde nutriva
ne le reti d'Amor l'anima avinta:
io parlo de' begli occhi e del bel volto,
che gli hanno il cor di mezzo il petto tolto.   [8.80]

[It seemed to Orlando that on a green stream-bank all colored with sweet-smelling flowers he was beholding the beautiful ivory and the native crimson that Love had painted with his own hand, and the two bright stars with which he fed his soul tangled in the nets of Love. I am speaking of the beautiful eyes and the beautiful face that have taken his heart from the midst of his breast.]

Thus Orlando's appearance in the poem precipitates a sudden descent from the world of epic action into the interior regions of amorous meditation. Orlando's thought is a downward spiral of recriminations and jealousy, and as such is a parody of the logic of chivalric obligation and a subversion of the tenets of Christian faith. Orlando dedicates himself not to city and emperor but to Angelica; he substitutes trust in God with the vain hope that Angelica may return his love for her. He charges himself with cowardice for having permitted Charlemagne to place Angelica in the protection of Namo; he speculates that Charlemagne might have done so out of a lack of regard for Orlando's capability and then he perversely reassures himself of that capability by musing that he could resist Charlemagne's whole army. He stirs his agony further by imagining Angelica in scenes of carnal ravagement (a lamb beset by wolves or a flower despoiled) and finally vows a desperate suicide if they should prove real. In this thought he betrays the fundamentally self-destructive nature of the course on which he has embarked in turning away from Charlemagne and God.

Orlando's meditations culminate in a dream in which he converts the providential storm that has just saved Paris from the violence of the pagans into a metaphor of sexual assault:

Sentia il maggior piacer, la maggior festa
che sentir possa alcun felice amante;
ma ecco intanto uscire una tempesta
che struggea i fiori, et abbattea le piante. [81]

[He was feeling the greatest pleasure, the greatest joy that
any happy lover can feel. But just then there rose a tempest
that tore up the flowers and struck down the trees.]

In his dream Orlando now finds himself wandering in a desert
landscape, vainly searching for shelter. What had been for Charlemagne a sign of God's grace is thus transformed by Orlando
into an image of spiritual desolation. His dream vision may be
taken as a projection of his fear of losing Angelica, but whether
we are finally to assume the ravaging storm to be Orlando himself
or someone else is appropriately ambiguous: the destructiveness
of his vision is a comment on the nature of his love. The dream
concludes with Orlando pathetically lamenting Angelica's imagined demise, grieving that he will never see her "sweet eyes"
again. Then he hears another voice calling from another direction, "Non sperar piú gioirne in terra mai" ("Do not hope to enjoy
them ever more on earth"). The direction from which the voice
comes is in fact Petrarch's *Canzoniere* (poem 250).[9] The allusion
confirms Orlando's estrangement from epic tradition and proclaims his association instead with the poetry of amorous desire
and frustration. The voice Orlando hears is that of Petrarch's
Laura telling her poet-lover of her imminent departure from
earth: "Non sperar di vedermi in terra mai." Ariosto, we note,
has changed Laura's "vedermi" ("to see me") to "gioirne" ("to
enjoy them") to underscore the spiritual poverty, the sensual
nature of Orlando's love. If the intricate pattern of Ariostan inver-
sions of the Virgilian text can be extended to include one more,
we may see in the Laura–Angelica figure of this passage an
Aeneas announcing his departure to Petrarch–Orlando, again
ironically cast in the role of Dido.[10]

Our initial encounter with Orlando, in short, amounts to a
dramatization of the psychology of the cupidinous lover. He begins by devoting himself to an ideal that the reader has ample
cause to question, since Ariosto has already shown Angelica con-
temptuously manipulating Sacripante in a situation paralleling

that which Orlando concocts in his delirium (1.40–55). Having surrendered his mind to the power of desire, he is caught in a stream of delusions that threatens to sweep him toward nonbeing. He has directed himself toward an end that is purely sensual and thus, according to the Augustinian logic that implicitly governs Orlando's whole experience of love, mutable and ultimately unreal. Throughout the episode Orlando is defined in terms of his deviation from both epic and Christian norms. Thus the dichotomy upon which Ariosto's poem is structured has been established. On one side stands Virgilian epic, seeking endorsement of its values and imperatives in an alliance with Christian doctrine; on the other side stands romance, the perfect inverse of a Christian epic.

Orlando, the reader later discovers, has in his dream in canto 8 written the scenario for his own undoing. In canto 23, the poem's midpoint, Orlando comes upon evidence that his jealous fears have been realized: Angelica has been faithless to him with the groom Medoro. Orlando arrives at a sylvan scene reminiscent of his earlier fantasy (23.100; cf. 8.80–81) and finds there proof of the love between Angelica and Medoro in the form of amorous inscriptions on all the trees and rocks. As in the dream in canto 8, the locus amoenus of canto 23 will be devastated by a violent storm; Orlando's dream proves to have been prophetic—like its parallel in the eighth book of the *Aeneid*. But Orlando's is a self-fulfilling prophecy, and self-destructive in its fulfillment. It will be Orlando himself who plays the part of the storm that uproots trees and flowers (23.130–36; cf. 8.81). It is critical to see the extent to which Orlando's madness is but the fruition of seeds he himself has planted, to see the logic in the fact that a love that is from the outset a form of self-betrayal should end in betrayal by the loved one. Orlando's insanity manifests itself as a disjunction between appearances and reality (23.126–28), but as such his madness simply dramatizes what has been implicit from the moment he set out in pursuit of Angelica "Without considering that images may be false when one dreams in fear and in desire" (8.84). Orlando's vision of catastrophe in canto 8 is both predictive and determinative. The lesson, then, is not simply that disillusionment is inevitable and that one should never put his hope in love (although this is the conclusion drawn by both Orlando, st. 128, and the narrator, 24.1–2); such a reaction to Orlando's story ignores his responsibility for his own fate.[11] The narrator's efforts at the beginning of canto 24 to offer Orlando as an illustration of the need for prudence and restraint in the matter of love amount to an evasion of the moral issue involved where love has been misconstrued as a debilitating passion:

> Chi mette il piè su l'amorosa pania,
> cerchi ritrarlo, e non v'inveschi l'ale;
> che non è in somma amor, se non insania,
> a giudizio de' savi universale:
> e se ben come Orlando ognun non smania,
> suo furor mostra a qualch'altro segnale.
> E quale è di pazzia segno piú espresso
> che, per altri voler, perder se stesso?   [24.1]

[He who sets his foot on the bird lime of love should try to draw it back and should not get his wings sticky there, because in the universal judgment of wise men love is, in brief, nothing except insanity, and even though everyone does not go crazy like Orlando, his frenzy is shown by some other sign. And what sign of madness is clearer than losing oneself through desire for another?]

Orlando's pursuit of Angelica is in effect the Augustinian quest for integration of the self brought to the opposite conclusion. As in the *Confessions* (8.12), the quest turns on an encounter with a text, but Orlando reads Medoro's amorous graffiti rather than Paul's Epistles, the testimony of lust indulged rather than an admonition against it.[12] Orlando literally falls apart:

> "Non son, non sono io quel che paio in viso:
> quel ch'era Orlando è morto et è sotterra;
> la sua donna ingratissima l'ha ucciso:
> sí, mancando di fé, gli ha fatto guerra.
> Io son lo spirto suo da lui diviso,
> ch'in questo inferno tormentandosi erra,
> acciò con l'ombra sia, che sola avanza,
> esempio a chi in Amor pone speranza."   [23.128]

["I am not, I am not the one my face makes me seem; he who was Orlando is dead and is buried; his most ungrateful lady has killed him; she has so made war on him in her lack of fidelity. I am his spirit separated from him, which wanders in torment in this hell, so that with my shade, which alone is left, I may be an example to him who puts any hope in Love."]

Orlando's "I am not the one my face makes me seem" recalls all those Renaissance utterances of self-denial—Petrarch's "era in parte altr' uom da quel ch' i' sono" (*Rime* 1), Sidney's "I am not I, pitie the tale of me" (*Astrophil and Stella* 45), even Iago's "I am not what I am"—behind which one hears the divine self-assertion of Exodus 3.14, "I am that I am," alerting us to the moral dimension of the problem of the divided self.

The narrator of canto 23, to be sure, seems willing to elicit the reader's sympathy for Orlando at every turn. The narrator does what he can to portray Orlando as a Petrarchan lover cheated of happiness by his lady's and not his own violation of the prescribed code of behavior. But having noted the narrator's compassion we should observe as well that he is not motiveless in his bias. He is himself a victim of the "malady" of love (24.3), one who has experienced "the sorrow that surpasses all the others" (23.112). And his admissions serve to draw him into the light for our scrutiny. In effect the narrator abandons his claims to omniscience and objectivity with his personal asides. He ceases to speak in the public, "choric" voice of the epic poet, the voice that expresses the accepted values of its audience.[13] Indeed, to the extent that he insists on his resemblance to his hero, the speaker seems prepared to accept passion and madness as qualities of his art. "The lunatic, the lover and the poet," in the words of Shakespeare's Theseus, "Are of imagination all compact."[14] The narrator disavows rational control over his plot (justifies transitions with an arbitrary assertion of authorial will[15]) and, more importantly, undermines our faith in his moral judgment. As readers we are asked to recognize the speaker's characterization of himself as part of a rhetorical strategy designed not to seduce us into sharing his view of the world but to evoke from us a critical response to that world view.[16] We are invited to engage the speaker in a dialogue like that we overhear in the opening stanzas of canto 24:

> Ben mi si potria dir: "Frate, tu vai
> l'altrui mostrando, e non vedi il tuo fallo."   [24.3]

[It may well be said to me: "Brother, you go on showing another man his error and do not see your own."]

The word *fallo* ("error") need not be uttered in a spirit of self-righteous piety, but we should also not ignore its meaning. Ariosto, to distinguish him from his narrating persona, has a fundamentally moral concern throughout his poem.

The cure for Orlando's madness, in keeping with the nature of all romance incident, seems exasperatingly arbitrary. The English knight Astolfo, who moves with a special facility through the romance world, travels to the moon on a hippogriff, finds Orlando's lost wits, and restores them to their owner (canto's 34, 39). But if we see here the romance poet exercising his prerogative to manipulate his plot however he will to achieve the desired outcome, we also see romance *maraviglia* brought into proximity with Christian mystery. We are shown the truth by which romance action is to be evaluated. Astolfo's guide on his journey to the moon is St. John, who insists that the hand of Providence has been directing Astolfo's movements all along, unbeknownst to him (34.55). The presence of the Evangelist invites us to see the miraculous recovery of Orlando as a romance version—a parody—of the Christian miracle of salvation by grace. It has been argued that St. John of the Gospels has undergone a burlesque transformation in becoming the St. John of Ariostan romance, that in taking Astolfo to the moon John leads the English knight not to a higher realm of truth beyond the poem but to a landscape that merely reflects the folly and futility of the sublunar world (34.70–83), and that in describing himself as a writer who served Christ in the capacity of a poet serving his patron (35.28–29) John indicts himself (and Ariosto) with the charge of falsehood he earlier aims at the classical epic poets:

"Non sí pietoso Enea, né forte Achille
fu, come è fama, né sí fiero Ettorre;
e ne son stati e mille e mille e mille
che lor si puon con verità anteporre:
ma i donati palazzi e le gran ville
dai descendenti lor, gli ha fatto porre
in questi senza fin sublimi onori
da l'onorate man degli scrittori."   [35.25][17]

["Aeneas was not so pious nor Achilles so strong nor Hector so valiant as rumor makes them, and there have been thousands and thousands and thousands who can with truth be put before them; but the palaces and the great villas given by their descendants have caused the honored hands of the writers to bring them to these high and endless honors."]

But it would be a mistake, especially in the context of a discourse on the deceitfulness of poets, to take Ariosto at his word, to hear him uttering wry blasphemies *in propria persona*. The irony of the poet of the Orlando plot consistently cuts against its author. That the figure of the Evangelist is traduced as he is incorporated into the romance narrative should lead more readily to insights into the nature of romance, I believe, than to the conclusion that Ariosto means to impugn the authority of Scripture. But we have only half of Ariosto's discourse on poetry and truth until we examine the *Furioso's* other major plot.

II

The *Furioso* becomes a different poem and Ariosto a different poet when he changes the subject from Orlando to Ruggiero and Bradamante. If the Orlando plot seems to exist only to frustrate any expectations one might have of coherence and meaning, the Ruggiero story is the opposite, an orderly account of the hero's progress from an initial state of moral delinquency to spiritual regeneration through baptism (41). If the Orlando narrative everywhere turns inward upon itself, betraying its essential artificiality and unreality, the Ruggiero–Bradamante plot, with its conclusion in dynastic marriage (46), provides the link that connects the world of fiction to that of fact, the Carolingian and Arthurian past to the Estense present. If in the Orlando narrative we are aware of the *Aeneid* only as it has been turned inside out by a hero who has chosen to pursue his passions rather than his civic duty, in the Ruggiero–Bradamante narrative we find Ariosto successfully mediating the *Aeneid*, adapting its language and its action to a new cultural context. And if the poet who tells the story of Orlando confesses himself incapable of sufficient critical distance from his subject to govern it rationally, the other poet speaks with Godlike detachment, asserting his authorial control over his creation. He compares himself to the "good musician on his harmonious instrument" who "often changes strings and varies the sound, seeking now the low, now the high" (8.29). Behind the variety and multiplicity of his narrative, he implies, lies a plan, a notion of harmony.[18] The Orlando poet gestures privately toward his *donne*, alluding to his own victimization by love in occasional asides to his audience of courtly lords and ladies; the other poet speaks in a public voice directly to his patrons Alfonso and Ippolito d'Este. His tone is formal; his mask is that of the Virgilian *vates*, the poet-prophet:

> Chi mi darà la voce e le parole
> convenïenti a sí nobil suggetto?
> chi l'ale al verso presterà, che vole
> tanto ch'arrivi all'alto mio concetto?
> Molto maggior di quel furor che suole,
> ben or convien che mi riscaldi il petto;
> che questa parte al mio signor si debbe,
> che canta gli avi onde l'origine ebbe.　　　[3.1]

[Who will give me voice and words fitting so noble a subject? Who will lend wings to my verse, that it may fly so high as to reach my lofty conception? It is necessary now that fury much greater than that to which I am used should make my breast hot, because this part is the due of my lord, for it sings the ancestors whence he had his origin.]

This stanza signals one of the changes of key of which Ariosto in his role as "good musician" claims to be capable. The first line is an allusion to Boiardo's *Orlando Innamorato* (1.27), but beyond that the passage amounts to a reassertion of the poem's Virgilian, dynastic theme. More specifically, the passage recalls the moment in the seventh book of the *Aeneid* (37–45) in which Virgil himself restates his purpose in a new invocation to his muse and so marks the transition from the Odyssean to the Iliadic half of his poem: "Greater is the story that opens before me; greater is the task I essay" (44–45). For Ariosto, as the modulation from the *Innamorato* to the *Aeneid* suggests, the equivalent transition is from romance to epic narrative. What follows in canto 3 is one of

Ariosto's most prolonged and precise imitations of Virgil, the account of Bradamante's descent into the underworld to receive from Merlin a prophecy of the rise of the house of Este. As Bradamante, the Carolingian heroine, is informed by Merlin, the Arthurian mage, of her posterity in a Virgilian prophecy, we find ourselves at the point of convergence of the three categories of "historical" matter traditionally deemed suitable for adaptation by the epic poet, the matière de France, the matière de Bretagne, and the matière de Rome.[19]

The Furioso, as I have said, is a dialogue between a romance poet and an epic poet in which the latter proclaims himself the only true instrument of historical revelation. That he does so in Virgil's voice, however, may be misleading because in the last analysis neither Ariosto's conception of epic nor his view of history is Virgilian. For Ariosto, history is the will of God revealing itself in time, as the circumstances of Bradamante's descent into the underworld imply. She is brought to Merlin's cave, dropped into it rather, by the treacherous Pinabello, who is moved to his act of villainy by a longstanding enmity between his family and hers. As he leaves her for dead he utters a curse in the form of a wish, which comes true, although not as he intends: "Would that all your kin were here with you!" Indeed they are, Bradamante discovers, but in the form of Merlin's prophecy of a glorious posterity, not, as Pinabello would have it, in death. The irony at work here attests to the existence of Providence as Augustine conceives it, capable of using evil in the service of good. Pinabello presumably goes off congratulating himself on his misdeed but from inside the cave we learn to read the situation differently. Bradamante has been expected; Pinabello has merely been the instrument of the Great Mover. It is with this understanding of the nature of Providence, as we shall see, that Ariosto redefines Virgilian epic even as he imitates it.

It is clear that Ariosto writes canto 3 with a copy of the Aeneid opened at book 6, consciously attempting to emulate Virgil's style. But it is also clear that Ariosto intends to revise Virgilian prophecy from the standpoint of his Christianity. Virgil's Anchises begins by saying he has anxiously awaited Aeneas's arrival, fearing that some harm might have befallen him (6.687-94). Ariosto's Melissa, Merlin's assistant, has similarly anticipated the arrival of Bradamante, but confidently, in the knowledge that the event has been preordained by the divine will (3.9). Anchises prods Aeneas into shouldering his destiny with the insinuation that it is fear that holds him back (806–07); Merlin assures Bradamante that Providence, which has decreed that she will marry Ruggiero, will remove all obstacles in her way (19).

Merlin constructs his prophecy of the Estense dynasty out of Virgilian materials: a pageant of heroes, the greatest of which restores the Golden Age (*Aen.* 6.791–97; *OF* 3.18, 51), and an imperial city that will "bound her empire by earth, her pride by heaven" (*Aen.* 6.782; cf. *OF* 3.44). For Merlin as for Anchises, prophecy culminates with the emergence of the great contemporary *conditor urbis* and a city that embodies an ideal of justice. The difference between the two visions of history becomes apparent when we recall the pains taken by Virgil to avoid implicating Augustus in the civil strife of the period of Roman history immediately preceding his full ascension to power. Ariosto registers no equivalent hesitancy in projecting the advent of the Estensi, Alfonso and Ippolito, as an apocalyptic culmination of dynastic history. Their *imperium* is pictured as a providential vindication of their moral rectitude:

> "Avrà il bel regno poi sempre augumento
> senza torcer mai piè dal camin dritto;
> né ad alcuno farà mai nocumento,
> da cui prima non sia d'ingiuria afflitto:
> et è per questo il gran Motor contento
> che non gli sia alcun termine prescritto;
> ma duri prosperando in meglio sempre,
> fin che si volga il ciel ne le sue tempre."   [44]

["The fair kingdom then will always increase without ever turning aside its foot from the straight road, and never will it do violence to one by whom it is not first tormented with harm; and because of this, the Great Mover is content that for it no bounds shall be set down, but it shall continue prospering ever more while the sky circles round in its spheres."]

Ariosto, moreover, is apparently willing to alter, even to fabricate historical facts in order to make them conform to his scheme.

Thus Ruggiero's son Ruggierino (24), for instance, is an imaginary figure introduced to exact a just revenge on the Maganzesi, who are to murder Ruggiero; an imperial marriage between Alberto Azzo II (26) and the daughter of Emperor Otto is invented, as are the rescue by their son Ugo of the pope and the emperor (27) and the victories of Bertoldo (29) and Rinaldo (30), all to establish both a heroic precedent and some important connections to papal and imperial authority early in Estense history. In general, Ariosto seems to wish to shape dynastic history in such a way as to permit at any given moment an interpretation of the complex shifting of allegiances of the contemporary Estensi between church and empire (52–58) as just retribution for betrayals of previous acts of loyalty.

The main theme of Merlin's prophecy, then, is the advent of a reign of perfect justice. The theme is announced at the outset of the genealogical survey:

> "Quindi terran lo scettro i signor giusti,
> che, come il savio Augusto e Numa fenno,
> sotto il benigno e buon governo loro
> ritorneran la prima età de l'oro."　　　　　[18]

["Just rulers from among them will hold the scepter in such fashion as did the wise Augustus and Numa, for under their good and benignant government they will bring back the first age of gold."]

And the theme comes to a climactic conclusion in the person of Alfonso, under whose reign Astraea, the goddess of justice, will return to earth (51). Merlin's prophecy of a reign of justice returns us to Anchises, who concludes his prophecy on a similar note, exhorting the future Romans to practice above all other arts that of lawful and peaceful government (851–53). The difference remains, however, that Ariosto, in his greater assurance of a providential mandate for his dynasty, proclaims the fulfillment of an ideal that Virgil seems still to be anticipating as his survey of history concludes.

The concern with justice in Merlin's vision of the future may partly account for its most striking revision of its model, the substitution in a parallel passage of Alfonso's treasonous brothers

Ferrante and Giulio for the tragic figure of Marcellus, the adopted son and designated heir of Augustus. At first glance the change seems to cast a shadow over the dynastic future. When Merlin has completed his presentation, Bradamante, in imitation of Aeneas (860), sees two figures hanging their heads in sorrow and asks who they are. Where Aeneas hears of a youth who might have attained the heights of glory had he lived, Bradamante sees two traitors. But seen from another angle, the story of Ferrante and Giulio, who were discovered plotting against Alfonso and Ippolito and were sentenced to lifetime imprisonment after first having been condemned to death, is a final triumph of justice, tempered in the last moment with mercy (62). Moreover, the incident replaces one in the *Aeneid* that serves to remind us that Fate can frustrate human designs with one that implies instead destiny's endorsement of the success of the true ruler. The last note, however sour, is not one of pathos and disappointment but of authority and justice affirmed. The incident completes the pattern of retribution and vindication established from the outset of the prophecy.

This is history, then, in which morality plays a part. The triumph of the Estensi is a triumph of righteousness. It is with this introduction of a moral interpretation of historical processes that Ariosto overgoes Virgil. But Ariosto's moral perspective, one should note, is a sword capable of cutting two ways. It is an instrument that can as easily be used against his patrons as in their service. Inasmuch as it is not the triumph of the Estensi per se but that of Alfonso and Ippolito as exempla of good rulers that the prophet celebrates, he has painted an idealized portrait against which the actual lords of Ferrara can be measured. And a contemporary reader of Ariosto's encomium of the Estensi might well have found reason to question it. Such a reader, on hearing of the enmity between Ippolito and his brothers Ferrante and Giulio, for instance, might have recalled the time when Ippolito, the paragon of justice, had in a fit of jealousy had Giulio's eyes put out because Ippolito's mistress had admired them.[20] Irony, to be sure, has its place in Ariosto's portrait of the Estensi, but to see only irony is to see only one of the implications of Merlin's prophecy. It is possible at the same time to note the discrepancies between the actual and the idealized Estensi and to take seriously the implicit assertion that Merlin's vision of destiny as moral process—as Providence—penetrates to a truth beyond the capacity of Virgil's Anchises to see.

But what are we to make of the most obvious of Ariosto's revisions of Virgil, the fact that it is Bradamante rather than Ruggiero who plays the part of Aeneas in this episode? Ariosto has in fact divided the role of Aeneas between Ruggiero and Bradamante, giving their adventures the appearance of an Aristophanic quest of two halves of an originally integral being for reunion. Both Bradamante and Ruggiero are reminiscent of Aeneas in different phases of his career. Bradamante, as we have seen, recalls the Aeneas of book 6, receiving the dynastic prophecy from Anchises; Ruggiero in canto 7 returns us to the Aeneas of book 4, dallying with Dido in amorous delinquency. As we first see them, Ruggiero and Bradamante are antithetical in nearly every category in which characters are defined in the *Furioso*. Ruggiero is pagan; Bradamante is Christian. Ruggiero is the victim of the wizard Atlante's overprotection (Atlante seeks to forestall Ruggiero's fated conversion to Christianity and his subsequent death at the hands of the Maganzesi by imprisoning him in an enchanted palace [4.29–31]; Bradamante is usually unescorted and wholly capable of defending herself. Bradamante is militantly chaste; Ruggiero finds himself involved in adventures that suggest his susceptibility to cupidinous love, as when Atlante's hippogriff, which Ruggiero cannot at first control, carries him to the garden of pleasure that is Alcina's island (canto 6). Separately, each is a complementary inversion of a chivalric norm, an image of an imbalance that it would take the other partner to repair. Bradamante passes for a man in all her adventures, as well she might, given her masculine disguise and her proficiency with lance and sword.[21] Ruggiero, meanwhile, lapses into a state of effeminacy as he falls under Alcina's spell in canto 7. Bradamante plays the part of the pursuer in their relationship; Ruggiero is consistently portrayed as the beloved, the object for which Bradamante and Atlante contend (4.29–30). Thus Bradamante sees Ruggiero as a Ganymede as the hippogriff bears him away (4.47) and he is an Arethusa as he comes to rest on Alcina's island (6.19).

Ariosto, then, has differentiated Bradamante and Ruggiero in ways that imply their ultimate need for each other. But in order to complete their quests for union, both Bradamante and Ruggiero must overcome dilemmas in their respective virtues. Ruggiero, to whom Harington, Ariosto's Elizabethan translator, refers as "the verie Idea and perfect example of a true knight,"[22] can become that only after he deals with what might be interpreted as a problem of justice. He has sworn allegiance to the pagan lord Agramante but he also promises Bradamante that he will convert to Christianity in order to marry her. His problem will be how to decide between these conflicting obligations without violating his sense of honor. Bradamante will need to find a way to preserve her chastity and still satisfy her longing for Ruggiero.[23] Bradamante's notion of chastity and Ruggiero's sense of justice and honor are both virtues that come face to face with their limitations in the course of the poem, at which point those virtues must either be forsaken or redefined and expanded.

The effect of Ariosto's bifurcation of the Virgilian epic hero into two such halves is to shift the crisis of the dynastic quest from the establishment of a new race and a new city to the attainment of regenerate selfhood by the heroes. The subject of the *Furioso* becomes not so much a coming into Italy as a coming into being. The Virgilian theme of founding an empire is superseded by the Augustinian theme of self-discovery. In a sense the *Furioso* does not really begin to be an *Aeneid* until its end, when through the ceremony of their marriage Bradamante and Ruggiero resolve their respective dilemmas and so acquire a mutual wholeness. The moment they do so, however, their quest is over. Their beginning is their end; the moment of self-fulfillment and the moment of heroic achievement are one and the same. This reinterpretation of the nature of epic quest in turn implies a revision of the Virgilian concept of *imperium*. For Ariosto, empire is an extension of the state of wholeness attained on a personal level through marriage. Empire is forged with the resolution of all the dualisms Bradamante and Ruggiero embody, love and arms, passion and reason, charity and justice. Here, then, is Ariosto's most fundamental transformation of the *Aeneid,* in that the quest for empire entails not, as it seems to for Aeneas, a choice between these apparent opposites but the discovery of their interdependence, their oneness. This is empire defined in Augustinian terms, not an objective for which human love and selfhood must be suppressed but one in which they are fulfilled.

III

Let us turn then to Ruggiero, the other half of Ariosto's composite portrait of an epic hero. After his rescue from Atlante's enchanted palace by Bradamante in canto 4, Ruggiero is carried off by the hippogriff to Alcina's island, the locus of cupidinous desire. If we may know things by their effects, the hippogriff can be taken to represent desires Ruggiero is as yet unable to control.[24] The hippogriff is both literally and allegorically the cause of Ruggiero's arrival on the enchanted island, where the English knight Astolfo stands transformed into a tree, visible proof of the dangers of cupidity and truancy to the higher chivalric duty owed to France and Charlemagne:

> "Io mi godea le delicate membra:
> pareami aver qui tutto il ben raccolto
> che fra i mortali in più parti si smembra,
> a chi più et a chi meno e a nessun molto;
> né di Francia né d'altro mi rimembra:
> stavomi sempre a contemplar quel volto:
> ogni pensiero, ogni mio bel disegno
> in lei finia, né passava oltre il segno."   [6.47]

['I took delight in her delicate limbs; it seemed to me that here was gathered all the good that is scattered among mortals in many places, to some more and to some less and to nobody much. I did not remember France or anything else; I always stood idle, gazing on that face; every thought, every fine ambition of mine ended in her and did not go beyond that limit.']

Alcina's island is a version of the earthly paradise that figures prominently in Renaissance epic,[25] here representing the temptation to roll back history in an attempt to retrieve prelapsarian Eden. This, however, is a libidinous Eden, a refuge for "lithe and active" goats, rabbits, and fallow deer (22). To anyone accepting the illusion Alcina creates, time seems frozen in an eternal, blissful present. To the extent that Alcina's enchantments constitute

an effort to deny the effects of the Fall, this is an appropriate place
for Atlante's hippogriff to have carried Ruggiero because Atlante,
unlike Melissa, is motivated by a wish to prevent Ruggiero from
making the epic choice that would thrust him into the
mainstream of history:

> Ella non gli era facile, e talmente
> fattane cieca di superchio amore,
> che, come facea Atlante, solamente
> a darli vita avesse posto il core.
> Quel piú tosto volea che lungamente
> vivesse e senza fama e senza onore,
> che, con tutta la laude che sia al mondo,
> mancasse un anno al suo viver giocondo.   [7.43][26]

She was not easy on him nor so blinded by excessive love
for him that, like Atlas, she could set her heart merely on
giving him life. Atlas wished him to live a long time without
fame and without honor, rather than, with all the fame there
could be in the world, to miss one year of living delightfully.

Astolfo is an object lesson in cupidity from which Ruggiero
derives some benefit. He takes Astolfo's advice to avoid Alcina
and follow rather the difficult road toward her virtuous sister
Logistilla (6.53–55), and he shows that he has become aware of
the need for further moral education (literally, for a lesson in
horsemanship) by dismounting the hippogriff and leading it by
the bridle. But the rules of romance adventure do not permit such
an easy victory over error. Indeed—and this is more to the
point—neither do the rules of Christian pilgrimage: a fall is prerequisite to salvation; spiritual regeneration is not attainable by
intellect alone. Thus two maidenly emissaries from Alcina's
palace intervene and persuade Ruggiero to follow them there.
And there Ruggiero soon finds himself playing Aeneas to Alcina's Dido (and Antony to her Cleopatra [7.20]). He allows Alcina
to dress him in "soft and exquisite clothing" of her own making,
to hang his neck with a gemmed collar and his "once so manly"
arms with shining bracelets (53–54; cf. *Aen.* 4.261–64). He is reminiscent of Aeneas as Iarbas scornfully describes him, a "Paris
with his eunuch train" (*Aen.* 4.215). (The reference to Paris

clarifies the meaning of the effeminacy of Aeneas and Ruggiero: both have temporarily subordinated their true epic missions to their private passions; both thus betray the cities they should be serving.)

In this state of oriental decadence Ruggiero is discovered by Merlin's Melissa, who like Virgil's Mercury comes to recall Ruggiero to his epic duty. Melissa addresses Ruggiero in the language of the *Aeneid*, exhorting him to think of his descendants and their destined glory if not of his own.[27] But it is not, finally, through a simple revelation of the awesome authority of the gods that Ariosto moves his hero; to this he adds a romance touch, Melissa's magic ring, which has the power to dispel enchantments and unmask the ugly reality behind them. Suddenly Ruggiero sees the filth ("feccia") beneath Alcina's external beauty and begins to hate her as much as he had loved her before (70). It is not enough for Ariosto, apparently, to impress his hero with his duty to his race; Ruggiero must also be brought to despise his Dido. There will be no regret for what he leaves behind, no "Italiam non sponte sequor" when he turns away:

> Come fanciullo che maturo frutto
> ripone, e poi si scorda ove è riposto,
> e dopo molti giorni è ricondutto
> là dove truova a caso il suo deposto,
> si maraviglia di vederlo tutto
> putrido e guasto, e non come fu posto;
> e dove amarlo e caro aver solia,
> l'odia, sprezza, n'ha schivo, e getta via.   [71]

[As a boy who hides ripe fruit and then forgets where he has hidden it, and after many days is brought back where by accident he finds his store, is astonished to see it all rotten and worthless and not as it was laid away, and, though he had always loved it and been fond of it, he now hates it, scorns it, sickens at it, and throws it away.]

The stylistic issue raised by this exercise in Virgilian imitation is worth pursuing for a moment. Clearly Ariosto does not attempt to sustain the lofty tone of his source for long before descending into burlesque with the addition of the detail of Melissa's magic ring. He willingly sacrifices all the pathos of the original by reducing Alcina–Dido to a hag (72–73) and by reinterpreting Ruggiero's former love for her as the deluded infatuation of a schoolboy. How are we to take this parodistic treatment of Virgil, coming as it does within the context of the plot through which Ariosto seeks to assimilate his classical model? In another context Thomas M. Greene suggests that the comic manner of some of Ariosto's imitations of Virgil betrays an antihumanistic sensibility, a precocious readiness to take liberties with "an enshrined epic convention" that anticipates the mock-heroic mode of the eighteenth century.[28] But, I believe, the liberties taken with the Virgilian text here suggest something other than irreverence toward the classical past. The literary joke is determined by the same humanistic premise that guides Ariosto's imitation of Virgil in canto 3, the conviction that assimilating Virgil means overgoing him as well, reinterpreting him in the light of Christian morality. From this perspective it is not inappropriate that the Aeneas of book 4 is rendered in comic terms, because the Aeneas who dallies with Dido is himself a parody of the hero he will become after book 6. He is to his future self as Orlando is to the Aeneas of book 8.

The rotten fruit simile that Ariosto uses in the passage quoted above (71) is perfectly suited to his purpose, however far it takes us from the mood of book 4 of the *Aeneid*. For Ariosto's intention is not to generate Virgilian pathos, to make us feel the tragedy involved in Aeneas's choice of destiny over love, but rather to make us see the absurdity of any imagined impediment to the only viable pursuit, the quest for spiritual enlightenment. We are once again in the realm of Augustinian thought, where there is only one legitimate choice, one order of reality, and where any supposed alternative is illusory. To think otherwise would be to admit a Manichaean dualism, to confer substance on what is insubstantial. The rotten fruit image exposes the childishness of thinking that natural and temporal processes can be stopped, the absurdity of the dream of an amorous Eden preserved against the fact of the Fall. Neither this nor any of Atlante's schemes to evade reality, Ruggiero must learn, can substitute for the true grace God has provided through Christ. Thus for Ariosto, moral evaluation is a necessary component of literary imitation. Melissa's magic

ring, one notes, is an instrument of literary exegesis and an agent
of moral enlightenment at the same time:

> Giovane e bella ella si fa con arte,
> sí che molti ingannò come Ruggiero;
> ma l'annel venne a interpretar le carte,
> che già molti anni avean celato il vero.   [74]

[By means of art she makes herself so young and beautiful
that she deceived many as she did Ruggiero; but the ring came
to interpret the pages that had for many years before concealed the truth.]

The stanza is an allusion to Petrarch's *Rime* 4, where Christian
revelation is explicitly the issue:

> Que' ch' infinita providenzia et arte
> mostrò nel suo mirabil magistero,
> che criò questo et quell'altro emispero,
> et mansueto più Giove che Marte,
>
> vegnendo in terra a 'lluminar le carte
> ch' avean molt'anni già celato il vero,
> tolse Giovanni da la rete et Piero
> et nel regno del ciel fece lor parte.

[He who showed infinite providence and art in His marvelous
workmanship, who created this and the other hemisphere,
and Jove more mild than Mars, who, coming to earth to il-
luminate the pages that for many years had hidden the truth,
took John from the nets and Peter, and gave them a portion of
the Kingdom of Heaven][29]

The next station in Ruggiero's journey is the realm of Logistilla. With his arrival it becomes increasingly clear that his
movements follow a plan. Logistilla, as her name suggests, represents Reason, the power that we retrospectively understand
Melissa's ring to symbolize (8.2). With his arrival at Logistilla's
palace Ruggiero advances a stage in his moral education. The
materials of which Logistilla's castle is constructed are of supernatural origin and possess the illusion-dispelling properties of
the ring. More specifically, the castle walls instill in anyone who

looks on them rational self-knowledge, making him invulnerable
to false praise and undeserved blame (10.59). This is reason befit-
ting a good governor—or the aristocratic audience of a dynastic
poem.[30]

Superficially the realm of Logistilla bears some resemblance to
that of her sister Alcina.[31] The gardens of Logistilla, like those of
Alcina, are perpetually fresh and beautiful, but this timelessness,
one feels, proceeds from interior serenity and careful self-
management rather than craft or guile:

> Ma quivi era perpetua la verdura,
> perpetua la beltà de' fiori eterni:
> non che benignità de la Natura
> sí temperatamente li governi;
> ma Logistilla con suo studio e cura,
> senza bisogno de' moti superni
> (quel che agli altri impossibile parea),
> sua primavera ognor ferma tenea.   [63]

[But here perpetual was freshness, perpetual the beauty of
the immortal flowers; not that Nature's good will governs
them so equably,but Logistilla, without need of the celestial
motions (something that to others seemed impossible), by her
labor and care kept their spring always constant.)

It is not, after all, in the dream of an earthly paradise itself that
romance heroes transgress but in the illusion that such a gift is
within the power of the deity of desire to bestow. Reason requires
not abstention from the pleasures associated with Alcina but their
control. Thus Logistilla does not shackle the hippogriff that
transported Ruggiero to Alcina's island; she teaches him to make
it obey his commands. He becomes the horseman of Plato's
Phaedrus, rationally checking and directing his desires. The reward of rational self-government for Ruggiero is emergence into
historical reality. The hippogriff now carries him at his command
over the map of Europe (70–73) and brings him to London, where
he witnesses a pageant of English forces gathering to come to the
aid of Charlemagne (74–89; cf. *Aen.* 7.641–817). He will move in a
world whose authenticity is assured by names like Lancaster,
York, Norfolk, and Winchester, at least until he loses Melissa's

illusion-dispelling ring and becomes an inmate once again in Atlante's second enchanted palace (11.16, 12.17, 22.31).[32]

Under Logistilla's tutelage Ruggiero becomes acquainted with the four cardinal virtues, Fortitude, Prudence, Justice, and Temperance (10.52), knowledge of which qualifies him as the type of a good governor and thus the primogenitor of the Este dynasty. Logistilla brings Ruggiero to the level of enlightenment that Virgil's Christian allegorists believed the *Aeneid* could foster: Logistilla teaches moral philosophy and rhetoric (47), the highest attainments of human wisdom deprived of the benefit of Christian revelation. Logistilla has given Ruggiero what lies within the power of natural reason to endow, self-sufficiency, inner harmony, and a knowledge of the world, but it now remains for Ruggiero, if he is to complete his epic journey in the terms laid down by Christian allegory, to advance from reason to grace.

This he will do in canto 41, by which time it has become evident that the cardinal virtues alone are insufficient to deal with the problems Ruggiero confronts. Ruggiero, as I have said before, finds himself faced with what are for him insoluble dilemmas involving justice and honor. He promises Bradamante that he will be baptized out of love for her (22.35), but then the thought that his conversion would constitute betrayal of his sworn allegiance to the pagan king Agramante begins to torment him (25.81). The situation becomes more complicated when in canto 36 Ruggiero learns that his father had in fact been a Christian (romance typically arranges history so that instances of reform and conversion are really returns to an original state), that the father and grandfather were killed by Agramante's uncle, and that Ruggiero himself is connected by blood to Charlemagne (70–76). He is thus equipped with what seem more than adequate justifications for turning against Agramante. Still Ruggiero balks at the idea of converting, recalling that Agramante had, after all, "put the sword by his side" (80), and decides to await an occasion when he might with just cause ("giustamente") forsake his pagan lord (82). Ruggiero's condition of moral paralysis is the effect of an incomplete understanding of the virtues with which he associates himself. Justice and honor are by nature public virtues, to be sure, but fully conceived they are the public manifestations of truth. Ruggiero is concerned too narrowly with the fact of their public manifestation alone, with appearances. He cannot leave Agramante now that fortune has turned against him, Ruggiero ruminates, because no one would believe his conversion had been genuine rather than a change of heart prompted by cowardice (25.82). He reasons that he owes it to Bradamante as his future wife to preserve his good name (25.87), but such reasoning ironically keeps them apart. Bradamante, for her part, sees things from what is as yet the antithetical perspective of her love:

> "Ohimè! Ruggiero, ohimè! chi aría creduto
> ch'avendoti amato io piú di me stessa,
> tu piú di me, non ch'altri, ma potuto
> abbi amar gente tua inimica espressa?"   [30.82]

["Oh me! Ruggiero, oh me! who would have thought that when I loved you more than myself you would have been able to love more than me not merely another but one who is your open enemy?"]

In terms of Ruggiero's moral enlightenment, the events of canto 41 represent the superseding of reason by grace. Here Ruggiero undergoes his conversion to Christianity, to a doctrine in which both his concern for righteousness and Bradamante's love are comprehended. Here too the lines of the Virgilian and Christian quests fully converge. Ruggiero, on his way to Africa to rejoin Agramante, finds himself caught in a sea storm distinctly reminiscent of that which throws Aeneas onto the shores of Carthage in the first book of the Aeneid (OF 41.8–23; cf. Aen. 1.81–123). But it quickly becomes evident that Ariosto's storm is a double allusion, to that in the Aeneid but also to that which besets St. Paul on his voyage to Rome (Acts 27). Given the direction Ariosto's narrative now takes, it is worth recalling that in the tradition of medieval commentary that interprets the first six books of the Aeneid as an allegory of man's progress through six ages of life the storm of book 1 is taken to represent the trauma of birth.[33] The implications of this for Ruggiero become clear as the focus of Ariosto's double allusion shifts from the Virgilian to the Pauline text, where birth is the metaphor of baptism. The shipwrecked Ruggiero sees the point as he struggles toward the shore:

Teme che Cristo ora vendetta faccia;
che, poi che battezzar ne l'acque monde,
quando ebbe tempo, sí poco gli calse,
or si battezzi in queste amare e salse.   [41.47]

[He fears that now Christ is taking vengeance, that, because
baptizing in pure water concerned him so little when he had
time, now he is being baptised in this that is bitter and salt.]

Scripture replaces the *Aeneid* as the subtext of Ariosto's narrative
as Ruggiero climbs out of the sea and finds himself in the presence of an ancient hermit,

che, come gli fu presso: "Saulo, Saulo
(gridò), perché persegui la mia fede?
(come allor il Signor disse a san Paulo,
che 'l colpo salutifero gli diede).
Passar credesti il mar, né pagar naulo,
e defraudare altrui de la mercede.
Vedi che Dio, c'ha lunga man, ti giunge
quando tu gli pensasti esser piú lunge."   [53]

[who when he was near him: "Saul, Saul (he cried out),
why persecutest thou my faith? as our Lord said to Saint Paul
when he gave him the salvation-bringing blow. Have you
believed you could cross the sea without paying fare and de-
fraud Another of his wages? You see that God, who has a long
arm, reaches you when you have thought you were farthest
away from him."]

The hermit quotes from Acts 26.14–18, where Paul recounts his
miraculous conversion on the road to Damascus.[34] Like Paul, the
Pharisaic zealot, the "Hebrew of Hebrews" dedicated to perse-
cuting the Christians who becomes an equally dedicated advocate of Christ, Ruggiero now undergoes a sudden and complete
reversal of his loyalties.

The immediate consequence of Ruggiero's conversion is his
initiation into historical self-awareness by means of Virgilian
prophecy. Ariosto's point cannot be missed: Ruggiero's inauguration as a Virgilian epic hero is contingent on his reception of
Christian faith; the hero's encounter with history depends upon

his first accepting the God by whom history has been shaped. Ruggiero learns from the hermit that he is destined to die seven years from the date of his baptism but that his sister Marfisa and Bradamante will avenge his death. Bradamante will bear a son named Ruggiero, whom those of Trojan blood will recognize as one of their own and choose as their lord. This Ruggiero will receive in grant from Charlemagne the region that will become Ferrara. The chief irony of the hermit's prophecy is that it fixes the date of Ruggiero's death from that of his baptism, his spiritual rebirth. We may contrast the hermit and Ruggiero's misguided guardian Atlante in terms of their respective perceptions of this irony: Atlante's error lies in his inability to see beyond the apparent tragic implications, beyond the fact of Ruggiero's mortality to the consolation of historical and spiritual fulfillment envisioned by the Pauline hermit.

In the account of Ruggiero's conversion we hear once again the Christian poet's assertion that his access to divine revelation permits him to overgo Virgil. As elsewhere, however, this is not to say that Ariosto claims to have done so on Virgil's terms. There is clearly no evidence of Virgil's poetic skill or of his depth of feeling in canto 41. Ariosto does not meet Virgil on his own ground, but then it is precisely Ariosto's belief that he stands on different ground on which he bases his claim to have surpassed Virgil. What is most compelling in the scenes in the *Aeneid* in which the hero confronts his future is the ambivalence with which Virgil treats the moment. On the one hand we sense Aeneas's reluctance to consign himself to destiny, or we are made aware of the sacrifice in human terms that history exacts; on the other hand we acknowledge the legitimacy of history's demands and the value of the goals being pursued. But for Ariosto there is no need for ambivalence and thus no occasion for the use of Virgilian poetic and dramatic skills. There is only the choice of grasping or not grasping the paradox of a perfect consolation for mortality. I am in effect speaking of the difference between an epic that dramatizes the education of its hero and one that finally substitutes conversion for education as the mode of the hero's transformation. The Aeneas of book 6 is led gradually by the teacher-prophet Anchises to an understanding of the laws of history and of the necessity of submitting oneself to them. The process of his education is arguably incomplete and bound to be so, given the incompleteness of history itself. But the knowledge imparted through conversion is instantaneous and perfect, for the matter in question is not primarily history but grace. For the Christian hero there is no place for residual regrets once destiny has been seen and accepted.

Critics have protested that the *Furioso* cannot qualify as genuine epic because it contains no real heroic agon, no confronting of human will and *virtus* with their limitations. Struggles are decided by external forces, chance or Providence, and not by an individual functioning within the limits of his character.[35] Ruggiero's conversion brings such objections into focus since it establishes him as a hero by virtue of his reception of Christian faith and not through any exercise of personal prowess. It will be God's glory, one feels, and not Ruggiero's own that any subsequent trial will affirm. Now in the long run one may wish to exclude the *Furioso* from the category of epic poetry, but one should be conscious of the risk of denying the possibility of Christian epic altogether in doing so. And before doing so one should weigh the Christian poet's claim that his religion can indeed accommodate epic, however unlike Virgil's it may be. Thus to the charge that moments like Ruggiero's conversion effectively obviate the testing of will and fortitude so crucial to epic, that an epic in which grace is the determining factor in the institution of the hero is an epic whose heroes are inevitably the passive instruments of a moral argument, the answer is that within the context of Christian belief human will and heroic valor are in fact released through spiritual enlightenment, not sacrificed to it. We are asked to accept the Augustinian paradox in which true freedom of will results from submission to God's will. Looking back from canto 41 we see only evidence of Ruggiero's immobility, his inability to decide between Bradamante and Agramante, his susceptibility to the escapist allures of Alcina and Agramante. Looking forward we see the proof of his heroic competency in his climactic and decisive battle with the pagan Rodomonte. His conversion, then, has not brought him into a state of passivity but redeemed him from one.

Ruggiero's conversion, to be sure, is a Pauline moment that has been transcribed in a comic medium, but the comic tone is no reason to construe the author as an iconoclast. Solemnity is not for Ariosto, as it may be for later post-Reformation poets, the measure of sincerity. Ruggiero's conversion is forced—a bargain struck with God by a drowning man hoping desperately to save himself (48-49)—but the suddenness of the experience, even the element of coercion in it, makes it no less like that of St. Paul. Ruggiero's baptism marks the turning point at which the problem of determining where righteousness and justice and honor lie is finally solved. The solution seems arbitrary[36] but so it must to the eyes of the uninitiate in truth. And in fairness to Ariosto we should note that he does not leave matters at that. He objectifies all the doubts one may have as to the validity of Ruggiero's choice in the person of the great pagan antagonist, Rodomonte, the embodiment of the old code of honor and the older, more visible brand of heroism Ruggiero now leaves behind. Rodomonte will challenge Ruggiero in the area of his greatest apparent vulnerability, his decision to break his oath of allegiance to Agramante, and Ruggiero's victory over Rodomonte will amount to a vindication of the new order of righteousness.

Ariosto's final comment on Virgilian epic takes the form of the wedding between Ruggiero and Bradamante in canto 46. From Pauline conversion we proceed to Augustinian marriage, the sacrament through which fleshly concupiscence is redeemed and reconciled to chastity.[37] Thus Ariosto brings epic themes to their conclusion as Maphaeus Vegius had done by celebrating the union of Aeneas and Lavinia in his "Thirteenth Book of the Aeneid." The final violent and unapologetically Virgilian action of the poem, the killing of the pagan Rodomonte by Ruggiero, may seem to indicate otherwise, but as Ariosto adapts it, the Virgilian episode reinforces the meaning of the Christian ceremony. Ariosto invests the last moment of his narrative with a turbulence reminiscent of that with which the Aeneid closes:

> E due e tre volte ne l'orribil fronte,
> alzando, piú ch'alzar si possa, il braccio,
> il ferro del pugnale a Rodomonte
> tutto nascose, e si levò d'impaccio.
> Alle squalide ripe d'Acheronte,
> sciolta dal corpo piú freddo che giaccio,

> bestemmiando fuggí l'alma sdegnosa,
> che fu sí altiera al mondo e sí orgogliosa.　　[140]

[And two or three times, in Rodomont's horrible face (raising his arm as high as he could) he hid all the steel of his dagger and freed himself from straits. To the foul banks of Acheron—loosed from the body colder than ice—blaspheming fled the disdainful spirit that was so haughty in the world and so arrogant.]

And so the narrative breaks off, leaving the anger and frustration of the unregenerate pagan hero to reverberate in the reader's mind. But if Ariosto has not changed the ending of the *Aeneid*, he has modified its context.

The battle between Ruggiero and Rodomonte unfolds in the shadow of Ruggiero's marriage to Bradamante. In fact from one point of view the combat may be read as a narrative dramatization of the ritual challenge integral to the marriage ceremony itself. (Recall, for instance, Archimago's attempt to obstruct the marriage of Una and the Red Cross Knight [*FQ* 1.12.24–37].) In any case the battle between Ruggiero and Rodomonte clarifies the ideal that marriage celebrates. Harington draws such a connection between the battle and the marriage in his allegorical interpretation of the canto:

> In that mine author brings in for the conclusion of his whole worke that *Rogero* immediatly upon his marriage to *Bradamant* killeth *Rodomont*, this is the Allegoricall sence thereof: that *Rodomont*, which is to be understood the unbridled heat and courage of youth (for in all *Rodomonts* actions you shall finde him described ever most furious, hastie, and impacient), *Rodomont*, I say, is killed and quite vanquished by marriage, and how soever the unrulinesse of youth is excusable in divers kinds, yet after that holy state of matrimonie is entered into, all youthfull wildnes of all kinds must be cast away.

The battle is carefully orchestrated to make its point: Ruggiero is a skillful and clever fighter; his opponent is physically more imposing but unrestrained and impatient (133). Ruggiero's bearing throughout the struggle attests to the integrity, the harmonious wholeness of being that has resulted from his marriage to Bradamante:

> Ruggier sta in sé raccolto, e mette in opra
> senno e valor, per rimaner di sopra.   [133]

[Ruggiero keeps collected and puts his brains and strength to work, in order to come out ahead.]³⁸

In the end Rodomonte makes a desperate attempt to wound Ruggiero in his loins; Ruggiero dispatches his enemy with blows to the head. Their respective targets imply the faculties with which each combatant is associated.³⁹ Ruggiero's struggle is in a sense with his former self, or, in Pauline terms, with the *vetus homo* that dies at the moment of his baptism (Rom. 6.6–11, Col. 3.7–10, Eph. 4.22–23). In one of his aspects Rodomonte is Ruggiero's old carnality; in another Rodomonte is Ruggiero's former adherence to justice in its Old Law formulation as righteousness without charity. Like Ruggiero before his baptism, Rodomonte sees only the literal dimension of justice and so challenges Ruggiero on the grounds that he has betrayed his sworn allegiance to the pagan cause. Rodomonte himself accepts death unhesitatingly rather than stain himself with the supposed dishonor of submission (137). His epitaph might be taken from 2 Corinthians 3.6: "For the letter killeth, but the Spirit giveth life."

As in Spenser, marriage in the *Furioso* opens out on history. Thus the nuptials of Bradamante and Ruggiero occasion the poem's most sweeping Virgilian prophecy of imperial continuity, connecting Homeric Troy through Carolingian Paris to contemporary Ferrara (67–99). The enchantress Melissa imports for the ceremony a pavilion in which Constantine (the fictional Emperor of the East of cantos 44–46, not the historical Constantine) has been encamped. The pavilion is embroidered with scenes prophetic of Ippolito d'Este but the history of the pavilion itself is as important as the story it tells. Made for Hector by the prophetess Cassandra, it passes to Menelaus at the fall of Troy. Menelaus in turn barters it for Helen in Egypt,⁴⁰ and the pavilion remains with the Ptolemys until Agrippa takes it from Cleopatra to Rome. There it remains until Constantine (the historical one this time) removes it again:

> quel Costantin di cui doler si debbe
> la bella Italia, fin che giri il cielo.
> Costantin, poi che 'l Tevero gl'increbbe,
> portò in Bisanzio il prezïoso velo.   [84]⁴¹

[that Constantine because of whom fair Italy must feel sorrow as long as the sky turns round. Constantine, after he grew sick of the Tiber, carried the precious cloth to Byzantium.]

By now it is evident that the cloth is a symbol for empire and that the movements of the pavilion retrace the translation of *imperium* from Troy to the west and from pagan to Christian culture. In this moment of epic dilation, empire is conceived as a transhistorical entity that survives a series of falls and reincarnations. The history of the pavilion, moreover, recapitulates literary as well as imperial history, recording the westering of epic from Homer to Virgil to Carolingian romance and the present poem. As the *Aeneid* does in the moment Aeneas receives his shield in book 8, the *Furioso* here catches sight of itself in several configurations of time. But this is the Virgilian topos transformed, for history is represented now not by an implement of war but "in the beautiful embroideries gay with gold and various silks" of the nuptial tent (81). We are reminded that love is an element in Ariosto's conception of empire.

On the walls of the pavilion, we are asked to believe, the prophetess Cassandra has embroidered images foretelling the life of Ippolito d'Este. Here the court poet discharges his obligation to praise his patron but does so in such a fulsome manner that the encomium is undermined through overstatement. Such is almost certainly Ariosto's intent.⁴² The result is a portrait of Ippolito in formal dress as an exemplum of an ideal, not, we may believe, as he was in life.⁴³ Ippolito's youthful training amounts to a prospectus for the balanced educational program that proliferates in the pages of Renaissance humanist literature. He studies classical literature and moral philosophy (89); he impresses his teachers with his eloquence (90); he excels at chivalric sports (91) and he learns natural philosophy, music, dance, and poetry in the setting of a humanist court. He is the fulfillment of the promise of a ruler embodying the four cardinal virtues (Harington notes what is perhaps the most plausible justification for this compliment in the pun on Ippolito's ecclesiastical title: "he prayseth a Cardinals vertues"), to which Ariosto appends a fifth, the virtue of generosity: "la virtú che dona e spende" (93). Given Ariosto's documented resentment of Ippolito's ingratitude and parsimony,[44] the tribute is surely an empty one. As the encomium turns even more toward hyperbole Ippolito's position seems correspondingly less tenable. Christian and Roman imperial matrices converge in the portrait. The scene of Ippolito's birth iconographically suggests Christ's nativity, mediated, perhaps, through Virgil's Fourth Eclogue (85-86). The child is adored as a god (87); he amazes his elders in the Vatican consistory with his wisdom and eloquence (90). His role in the campaign against the Bentivoglio (1507), which served the interests of the papacy, associates him with Caesar: "Sí che può dir, che viene e vede e vince" (96) ("So it can be said that he comes and sees and conquers").

This conflation of spiritual and temporal ideals is appropriate, within the convention of idealized portraiture, not only because Ippolito was a cardinal as well as a soldier but also because such a combination is implicit in the concept of heroism toward which Ippolito's chivalric ancestor Ruggiero has evolved. Ruggiero, as he incorporates both Aeneas and St. Paul, evokes an ideal of secular and spiritual *imperium* whose standard Ippolito is now said to uphold.

There is a clear discrepancy between the real Ippolito and Ariosto's idealized portrait of him—a discrepancy greater by an order of magnitude than any evident in Virgilian prophecies of Augustus. It would be a misconstruction of Ariosto's irony, however, to see in it a cynicism that extends to the ideal by which the shortcomings of the real Ippolito are exposed. Reading between the lines, we may conclude that Ariosto's purpose is to leave his audience with the distinct impression that Ippolito is no Augustus, but we should realize at the same time that Ariosto's irony is the product of a moral consciousness of a kind that Virgil does not possess. The ideal, at least, that Ippolito is said to represent is held to be higher than the one that Virgil could envision by virtue of the inclusion of a Christian component.

The dubious encomium to Ippolito, however, is not Ariosto's

only means of bringing his dynastic theme to closure. In the same canto, and with no audible dissonance in his voice, he announces his heroes' and his own emergence from the "selva oscura," the "boscherecci labirinti," the dark woods and mazes of the romance landscape into the cosmopolitan environment of court and city. He guides the poem from the narrow enclosures of romance into the expanded space of the real world. The marriage of Ruggiero and Bradamante takes place in a Paris teeming with "countless strangers," lords and embassies from every nation (75).[45] This city is not only the setting for the marriage but a reflection of its meaning as well. The entrance into Paris, the antithesis of those illusory romance courts and palaces in which knights and ladies are imprisoned by their own false desires, signals the release from solipsism and the triumph over cupidity that marriage celebrates. At the same time Ariosto imagines himself returning from the sea voyage that has been his poem (46.1-2) to the resounding welcome of the citizens of another sort of city, the general community of the actual lords and ladies and humanist scholars and poets of his contemporary Italy (1-19). With the long catalogue of their names at the opening of the canto Ariosto creates an image of a society in which the real and the ideal are harmonized. This city too is in a sense a product of the marriage of the dynastic heroes. The community of poets and patrons, assembled here in the true spirit of patronage to recognize and pay homage to one of their own (a contrast with Ippolito as he was in life is implicit), is an extension of the ideal of reciprocity that the marriage of Bradamante and Ruggiero establishes. Here Ariosto's fifth cardinal virtue, generosity (93)—a secular manifestation of grace—finds its true context.

The *imperium* that Ariosto's poem celebrates, then, is something more than his contemporary Ferrara. Unlike Virgil, for whom destiny is defined in terms of historical Rome, Ariosto conceives of his Ferrara as one particular embodiment of a transhistorical and suprahistorical imperial ideal. The marriage of Bradamante and Ruggiero, by the same token, is for Ariosto more than the starting point for a genealogical chart connecting the Estensi to the Carolingian past. Their union has a symbolic meaning that may be inferred from what we have seen of Bradamante and Ruggiero as they exist apart from each other. Bradamante is compelled by love; Ruggiero's domain is generally that of the cardinal virtues, which the Renaissance poet habitually recommends to figures of public office. The marriage implies a belief on Ariosto's part in the interdependence of these two orders of virtue in the ideal *imperium*.

Spenser, always the best of Ariosto's allegorizers, gives us what may be read as the definitive commentary on the events of canto 46 as he narrates the liberation of a city called Eden and the betrothal ceremony of Una and the Red Cross Knight in the last canto of the first book of *The Faerie Queene*.[46] For in the last analysis it is not enough to note that Ariosto's narrative overgoes and completes Virgil's without also noting that Ariosto's does so as it converges with Christian myth. The story of Ruggiero and Bradamante, like that of Una and Red Cross, finally takes its meaning from the story of the Fall. Bradamante's chaste and self-less love for Ruggiero succeeds in repairing the damage done by Eve's cupidity. Ruggiero, for his part, regains something of the dominion Adam lost by subordinating his reason to Eve's will. In canto 45 Ruggiero establishes his supremacy over Bradamante in a trial of arms (64–82) and thus, although she resists him, thinking him to be someone else, wins what she has long sought to grant him:

> "A voi, Ruggier, tutto il dominio ho dato
> di me, che forse è piú ch'altri non crede.
> So ben ch'a nuovo principe giurato
> non fu di questa mai la maggior fede."   [44.63]

["To you Ruggiero, I have given all the dominion over myself, which is perhaps more than others believe. I am sure that fidelity greater than this never was sworn to new prince."]

Their union represents a restoration of the human integer that consisted of Adam and Eve in their prelapsarian state, his rational virtue perfected by her charitable one, her love completed by his reason.

The *imperium* at issue with the marriage of Ruggiero and Bradamante, then, is Edenic at one extreme on the spectrum of its meaning. For Ariosto as for Spenser, recovery of the Edenic kingdom depends on reestablishing through marriage the har-

mony between man and woman lost with the Fall, for that harmony is the basis of a true society. This is not to say that at the last
moment Ariosto's and Spenser's allegories turn their backs to
history, seeking to circumvent it by projecting a return to
Paradise; the point in both cases is rather that only when history
has been understood in terms of Christian myth can history truly
be engaged. A return to Eden in spirit is the prerequisite of a
return to the society of men, where both Spenser's and Ariosto's
heroes conclude their adventures. The Red Cross Knight is designated heir apparent to the throne of Una's Eden (1.12.20); Ruggiero is crowned king of the Bulgarians (46.71). For each the role
of governor is an extension of the role of bridegroom.

Such a conception of *imperium* permits Ariosto a degree of
closure inaccessible to Virgil. Virgil, for one thing, never really
enters his Rome, never completes his poetic voyage as Ariosto
does in his last canto (and Spenser in his [1.12.1]). The Roman
future is always glimpsed as a distant prospect, and sometimes as
a vaguely ominous one. Thus Evander, for instance, awestruck at
the "dread sanctity" of the place as he stands on the primitive,
pastoral site of the future Roman capitol, betrays Virgil's characteristic ambivalence toward historical processes: "Even then they
shuddered at the forest and the rock. 'This grove,' he cries, 'this
hill with its leafy crown,—though we know not what god it is—is
yet a god's home'" (8.350–52). These woodlands are not the
"selve oscure" or the "scuri boschi" from which the Ariostan
hero triumphantly emerges; the groves of Latium recall an earlier
era of virtuous simplicity whose passing is to be lamented. Between the poverty and humility of the past and the material
splendor of the Roman future there is a tension that Virgil never
dissipates. It is with an unqualified sense of relief, however, that
we hear Ariosto's announcement of his arrival at his destination
in the last canto of his poem. The distance between the images of
courts or the pastoral settings in the body of his poem and the
image of society projected in canto 46 is not simply temporal; it is
the distance between falsehood and truth, illusion and reality,
the palace of Atlante or Alcina's island and the community of
contemporary Italian humanists, and it is a distance that can disappear in a moment of enlightenment. In the end we are left not,
as in the *Aeneid*, with an impression of the great struggles yet to

be undertaken before the Augustan Golden Age can become a reality but with a feeling of having arrived, indeed, of having been there all along. The crucial moments in the *Furioso* are not those in which we look down the long corridor of history but moments of discovery and self-recognition and emancipation. The central crisis of Ariosto's poem, after all, concerns not so much the founding of a city as the liberation of one. The lords and ladies, patrons and patronnesses, scholars and poets catalogued in the opening stanzas of the canto may in this light be seen as the *donne* and *cavallieri* of the romance narrative with their masks dropped. The Paris that is rescued from the assault of Agramante, contemporary Ferrara, and the community of humanists are all finally reflections of the same city. It takes only a clearing of the eyes to see the reality that otherwise lies obscured in the romance terrain.

Virgil reinterpreted from the perspective of Christian morality, as we have seen, is Virgil transformed. And yet the Renaissance dynastic poem continues to represent itself as Virgilian epic. It is in fact by transforming the *Aeneid* that the Renaissance poet seeks to preserve what is essential to it. The *Aeneid* is concerned with history and with man's status as a historical being; so too is the Renaissance epic poem. But the Renaissance poet bases his claim to have disclosed the truth of history on his conviction that historical awareness is contingent on moral awareness. Ariosto retains as his objective the Virgilian one of proclaiming the advent of a historical *imperium* as he celebrates the Estense court at Ferrara, but Ariosto holds that this empire becomes visible only by virtue of a prior perception of the ideal of which Ferrara is a manifestation. It is not Augustine's City of God but an earthly city to which Ariosto finally takes us, and to this extent his poem remains faithful to its model. But on the other hand, it is only because we have glimpsed something like the heavenly city, an *imperium* in which love is a component along with fortitude, temperance, prudence, and justice and one in whose service its heroes and citizens find fulfillment, that entrance into the earthly city becomes possible.

What has made critical assessment of the *Furioso* particularly difficult is the fact that Ariosto makes his appeal to moral consciousness without sacrificing his instinctive urbanity and his sense of humor. The problem surfaces in the cinquecento in the form of the protracted literary debate between the admirers of Ariosto and those who defend Tasso as the true epic poet. Tasso himself judges the *Furioso* a failure as an epic by the standards he derives from Aristotle. But Aristotle, I suggest, is ultimately a less important factor in assessing the relationship between the two Renaissance poets than is the bond that unites them, their Christian humanism. Ariosto and Tasso, to be sure, are temperamentally different from each other: Ariosto is less dogmatic and more inclined to include statements of principle within the compass of wit. But if he does not strain so hard as Tasso to articulate his convictions, it should be remembered that Ariosto's Christianity was not, as Tasso's was, under pressure either to justify or to reform itself.

CHAPTER FOUR

TASSO:
Romance, Epic, and Christian Epic

The dynastic couple in Tasso's *Gerusalemme Liberata* consists of Rinaldo, the strong right arm of Goffredo, commander of the Christian forces in the First Crusade, and Armida, who until her sudden conversion in the poem's closing stanzas plays the part of the meretrix, the principal agent of the demonic plot (instigated by Pluto himself) to subvert the Christian cause. Armida may seem a surprising choice for the role of progenitress of the House of Este,[1] but Tasso could not have found a more effective means of illustrating the scope of Christian deliverance, the theme of his poem. Tasso's dynastic heroine is no Bradamante, no championess of chastity, fundamentally virtuous if initially incomplete, but something of a Mary Magdalen, a creature in whom the precept that grace ultimately extends to all of fallen nature finds one of its most dramatic confirmations. Tasso's Rinaldo, too, falls further than does his counterpart in Ariosto's poem. In canto 16 Rinaldo is found, like Ruggiero before him, in the locus amoenus of romance truancy, Armida's garden, but to the faults of Ruggiero Rinaldo adds those of an Orlando. In canto 5 he commits an act of irascible passion in killing Gernando and, disdaining to submit himself to Goffredo's justice, deserts the Christian camp. At the other pole of his experience, however, Rinaldo undergoes a Christ-like transfiguration (canto 18). In the *Liberata*, then, Tasso projects the basic plot of redemption in its largest possible

A version of chapter 4 was published in *PMLA* 93 (1978) as "Tasso's Epic of Deliverance."

compass. His heroes touch the extremes of depravity and regeneration in the course of their careers.

Tasso's choice of redemption as a theme is perfectly suited to his purpose of constructing a true Christian epic, a poem based on Christian principles but one that also possesses the formal properties of the *Aeneid*, wholeness, magnitude, and unity of plot and character.[2] Regeneration, as Tasso conceives it, implies such unity. His theme permits him, for instance, a single heroine where previous poets had offered two, an Armida who by virtue of the transforming power of grace can fulfill the roles of both Virgil's Dido and his Lavinia, Ariosto's Angelica and his Bradamante. Indeed, as the character of Armida suggests, Tasso's theme allows him to overgo (in effect, to redeem) both Virgil and Ariosto, each for a different reason. Virgil could not, Tasso seems to say, and Ariosto could have but did not, follow to their end the implications that Christianity's doctrine of deliverance held for epic poetry. Virgil could not reverse Dido's tragic fate: the world of the *Aeneid* is irremediably one of painful choices. Ariosto knew otherwise; his moral vision was not fundamentally different from Tasso's. But Ariosto had not succeeded, as Tasso meant to, in reflecting the unity of creation in the medium of poetic form.

That Tasso believes romance stands in need of a kind of redemption is made clear in his *Discorsi del Poema Eroico*. Romance, of which *Orlando Furioso* is for Tasso the principal exponent, is described as a rambling, disjointed, fanciful narrative intended primarily to delight rather than instruct its audience. As such it violates the classical canons for epic, which require it to be a work of great formal integrity and high moral purpose. True epic describes a single action carried to full closure, undertaken by a single hero rather than several.[3] If Tasso seems to have disregarded his own theoretical precept in dividing the Aeneas figure of his poem into two, Rinaldo and Goffredo, he argues otherwise in the *Allegoria* he appends to the *Liberata*:

> The *Army* compounded of diuers Princes, and of other Christian souldiers, signifieth *Man*, compounded of soule and bodie. . . . *Godfrey*, which of all the assembly is chosen

Chieftaine, stands for *Vnderstanding*, and particularly for that vnderstanding, which considereth not the things necessarie, but the mutable and which may diuersely happen, and those by the wil of God. . . . *Rinaldo, Tancredi,* and the other Princes are in liew of the other powers of the soule; and the *Bodie* here becomes notified by the souldiers lesse noble.[4]

The *Liberata*, then, is superficially a romance fable involving the apparently separate actions of Goffredo, Rinaldo, and a number of others, but the completed poem is meant to project an image of the reintegrated human form compounded of its diverse faculties and hence to convert romance multiplicity into epic unity:

Finally, to come to the conclusion, the army wherein *Rinaldo* and the other Woorthies by the grace of God and aduise of Man, are returned and obedient to their chieftaine, signifieth man brought againe into the state of naturall Iustice and heauenly obedience: where the superior powers do command, as they ought, and the inferiour do obey, as they should.

This is romance reconciled to the rules of classical epic and epic in turn conceived within the framework of Christian Neoplatonism.

Implicit in Tasso's criticism of romance conventions is a moral indictment, which comes to the foreground in the *Liberata*. Here we experience the confusion and unreality of romance as anarchy and illusion, as projections of that state of mind in which nothing seems stable or sure. In a poem in which order is meant to be a manifestation of moral value, romance disorder becomes a metaphor for spiritual privation, for cupidity and heresy. And in a poem that is meant to move in the world of human history, the images of confinement and isolation in the romance landscape betray the hero's inability to see beyond himself.

Yet seen from another angle, romance represents nothing more than a failure of the imagination to complete its epic (and Christian) quest, to go far enough in pursuit of truth: we see the part but not the whole, the effect but not the cause, the incessant movement of the phenomenal world but not the permanence beyond it. The urges of romance, in other words, are essentially continuous with those of epic and with those of Christianity as well. Romance magic, for all its associations with deception and illusion, may finally be seen as a vehicle for Christian mystery.[5] We have only to look far enough to see the completion of the one in the other. The nature of redemption, as the concept is implied in the critical argument of the *Discorsi*, embodied in the *Liberata*, and stated in the *Allegoria*, demands not that the genre of romance literature be rejected but that it be enfolded into epic, that the romance impression of multiplicity and discontinuity be replaced by the epic vision of wholeness and unity. Romance diversity, in fact, occupies a crucial place in the total design of Christian epic. Just as Rinaldo must first be truant to his cause before he can be redeemed, so the poem must first represent itself as a romance before its epic structure can be discerned. Both the plot and the form of the *Liberata* are thus manifestations of the paradox of Christian salvation that ordains that one must be lost before he can be found.

Tasso belongs to the tradition of humanist thought that strives everywhere for a theoretical reconciliation of the various currents by which it is nourished: philosophy and religion, reason and faith, nature and grace, classical and vernacular literature. He is among the most undaunted of synthesizers in an era increasingly aware of the diversity of its cultural sources. His critical theory is shaped in part by the widespread resurgence of Aristotelian theory following the 1536 Latin translation of the *Poetics*, and perhaps equally by the Neoplatonism of Ficino and others,[6] but it is in the last analysis a product of his Christianity. In its narrowest dimension Tasso's conception of poetic unity may be traced to a Counter-Reformation bias toward centralization, conformity, and authoritarianism. At its best it is an inclusive and a creative response to problems of literary form. The conciliating impulse that unites epic and romance is finally best expressed in the *Liberata* itself but it may be useful to approach the epic by the avenue Tasso provides in the *Discorsi*.[7]

I

The *Discorsi del Poema Eroico* (1594), enlarged from the earlier *Discorsi dell'Arte Poetica*, may be read in part as Tasso's attempt to defend the *Liberata* in the critical debates that followed its printing in 1581.[8] His emphasis on unity and his deference to Aristotelian rules of composition represent his efforts to find for the *Liberata* a place in what he hoped would be a continuance of the classical tradition of epic poetry. He shares with other humanist poets the ambition to produce a contemporary *Aeneid,* or at least to elevate contemporary language and literature to a higher status by attaching to them a comprehensive theory of diction and composition. What the *Liberata* is meant to embody, the *Discorsi* attempt to document by extending to cinquecento Italy the principles of Aristotelian, Horatian, Platonic, and Neoplatonic poetic analysis.

The scope of Tasso's success is measured in his ability to reconcile several strands of poetic theory. His method is Aristotelian to the extent that it derives its categories of generic definition deductively from analysis of an exemplary masterpiece (*Discourses,* p. 6). But Tasso admits a Neoplatonic qualification of this method by taking as his "exemplar" an abstraction instead of a specific poem or poetry. If Aristotle could look to the works of Homer to find the model for epic poetry, Tasso would look to an "idea of the most excellent kind of poem" compounded of examples of "beauties and perfections" from many admittedly imperfect works. It is a felicitous compromise since it obviates the necessity of locating among modern works a single ideal heroic poem. At the same time it permits Tasso to select poetic examples from various contemporary sources, which thus share space with Homer and Virgil in an ongoing literary tradition.

Even so it may seem strange that there are no explicit references to the *Liberata* in the *Discorsi.* The *Liberata* goes unannounced and largely unacknowledged except as its theme and subject may be inferred from the description of the ideal epic. The *Discorsi,* whose stated purpose is to erect a generalized theory of epic poetry, approach the *Liberata* by "argument, authority, and example" (p. 5) but never arrive there. Tasso's reluctance to include the *Liberata* among the exempla of heroic poetry is significant. It is for one thing a clue to the strategy of the *Discorsi,* which must, insofar as they are cast in the mold of a classical treatise on poetics, approach Christian epic inductively and indirectly. The *Discorsi* are a deliberate exercise in obliquity calculated to demonstrate Tasso's conviction that classical poetic theory is continuous with and is finally completed in Christian doctrine.

The literary ideal to which our attention is drawn in the *Discorsi* is thus a disembodied one, yet one whose appearance we are led to anticipate through the ineluctable logic of Tasso's syllogisms. The proper subject for epic poetry, he begins, is one taken from history rather than one wholly invented by the poet because pure fiction does not so fully engage the minds of its readers: "Men do not await the end of the story with the same expectation as when they deem it true entirely or in part" (p. 26). History rather than legend, then, should be the basis of epic plot—history remote enough to permit the poet certain mimetic liberties but not so remote as to involve archaic customs, "which those whose taste is used to the gentleness and decorum of this age shun as obsolete and stale" (p. 40). "But history," Tasso reminds us, "involves a religion either false or true" (p. 34), and so, striking a posture of broad-mindedness and equanimity, Tasso contemplates the relative merits of each choice. He concludes that true religion is to be preferred as the subject of epic on the grounds that its prodigies and miracles are more probable than those of false religions and so make compliance with the Aristotelian requirement of verisimilitude more feasible (pp. 34–37).

If it is not yet clear that Tasso is steering his Aristotelian discourse in the direction of Christian epic, it becomes more so when he discusses the nature of the action appropriate to epic. It should be "noble, illustrious, and great" (p. 42), to be sure, but within these categories Tasso finds room to debate whether wrath or love is the subject for the nobler action. The weight of classical authority seems to fall on the side of wrath, the subject of the *Iliad*. It can be argued, moreover, that the *Odyssey* hardly mentions love (p. 44) and thus that the epic poet whom Aristotle considered "preeminently heroic" was unconcerned with the matter. Nor does Virgil say as much as he might have about the loves of Aeneas, Iarbas, Turnus, and Lavinia (p. 45). Love, furthermore, might more properly be assigned to comedy (p. 45), and epic, according to Aristotle, more closely resembles tragedy than comedy in the actions it imitates (pp. 42–43). For Tasso, however, such reasoning is problematic. Neither the subject of wrath nor the assumption of an affinity with tragic rather than comic perspective is appropriate where the objective is Christian epic. And so with considerable dexterity he maneuvers around the obstacles. Aristotle, he maintains, has "with that obscurity habitual to him" (p. 43) left it unclear whether tragic and epic poets are to be considered entirely alike in what they imitate:

> If epic and tragic actions were of the same nature, they would produce the same effects, because identical causes produce identical effects. But since they give rise to different passions, it follows that their nature is different. Tragic actions move horror and pity; . . . the epic poet does not generally make us sad in that way, nor is he required to as a necessity.   [p. 43]

Continuing to move in the shadow of Aristotelian discourse, or rather Aristotle mediated through Plato, Tasso goes on to argue that a greater degree of nobility attaches to the subject of love than to wrath:

> All beautiful things are suitable to the heroic poem, and love is indeed beautiful, as Phaedrus says in Plato. It cannot be denied that love is a passion suitable to heroes, since, as Proclus, the great philosopher of the Platonic school, says, they were especially subject to two feelings, wrath and love. If one of these is appropriate to the heroic poem, the other surely cannot be inappropriate.   [p. 45]

From "not inappropriate" Tasso moves toward the proposition that love is in fact a superior subject for epic in the next stage of his argument and so brings us closer to seeing the *Liberata* as the ideal heroic poem. Plato, Tasso admits, ranks love below wrath in his arrangement of the three faculties of the soul, reason, the irascible appetite, and concupiscence:[9]

> Reason is surely the noblest, queen as it were of the others, while concupiscence rather resembles a popular uprising, which, swelling and raising havoc in the mind, refuses to grant obedience to reason, whereas the irascible faculty is the soldier and minister of reason in curbing its opponent.   [p. 47]

But Plato is speaking of concupiscence. There is another kind of love, Tasso reminds us, of which we hear if we turn from Plato to Aquinas:

But if love is not merely a passion and a movement of the sensitive appetite, but a highly noble habit of the will, as St. Thomas held, love will be more praiseworthy [than wrath] in heroes and consequently in the heroic poem. This kind of love the ancients either did not know or did not wish to describe in their heroes, but if they did not honour it as a human virtue, they worshipped it as virtually divine; they should therefore have esteemed no other [passion] more appropriate for heroes.   [p. 47]

With this last turn of thought Tasso arrives (ostensibly by clarifying the ambiguities and extending the logic of classical poetic doctrines) at a justification for his poem's concern with love, or caritas, that motion of the soul toward God that signals deliverance. Charitable (as opposed to cupidinous) love is a higher passion than Plato's irascible appetite: "Hence we may regard actions performed for the sake of love as beyond all others heroic." An example of such an action, he then suggests, can be found with "those who risk their lives for Christ." Thus Christian history supplies the subject that classical poetic theory needs and lacks as it seeks to formulate the perfect heroic poem.

Other major lines of Tasso's theoretical discourse point to the same conclusion: Christian epic is the logical culmination of classical poetic theory. Tasso's discussion of verisimilitude, for instance, opens with Aristotle but finally comes to rest, once again, with St. Thomas. Tasso begins with the Aristotelian assertion that poetry should be truthful in quality if not in substance and in universals if not in particulars. The poet need not be a literalist in his interpretation of history; utter fidelity to historical detail is the province of historians, not poets. Indeed an overly narrow construction of verisimilitude limits the poet's capacity to represent the higher truths with which he ought primarily to be concerned. Thus "if Lucan is not a poet, it is because he binds himself to the truth of particulars with little regard to the universal" (p. 61). But neither should the poet wholly disregard historical fact. To make this point Tasso—everywhere inclined to propound a synthesis of the two principal strands of classical philosophy—shifts his focus from Aristotle to Plato, or rather to the misconstruction of Platonism he discovers in Mazzoni.[10] In an effort to defend poetry (particularly Dante's *Commedia*) as mimetic art, Mazzoni distinguishes between "phantastic" and "icastic" imitation, "following Plato's doctrine in the *Sophist*" (p. 29): "He calls the kind that imitates things present or past icastic and the kind that imitates non-existent things phantastic. And this latter he chooses to call perfect poetry, which he places under the sophistic faculty, whose subject is the false and the non-existent." In doing so, he removes reality and probability as standards of poetic imitation. Tasso, who sees the danger of restricting poetry's claim on truth by divorcing so completely the functions of the poet and the historian, insists on counting poetry among the sciences of probable and demonstrable reality: dialectic, metaphysics, and theology. Plato is to be credited with understanding that reality lies in the realm of the intelligible rather than the visible (p. 32), that "visible things [belong] in the genus of non-being and only the intelligible in the genus of being" (32), but he is misinterpreted when he is thought to endorse imitation of something unreal. "Poetic imitation is thus rather icastic than phantastic: and even if it were the work of phantasy, it would be in the sense of an intellectual imagination which cannot be differentiated from the icastic" (p. 33).

What Plato, properly understood, does contribute to Tasso's conception of verisimilitude is a justification for the claim that truth does not reside in the region of human experience and historical accident: "Thus the images of the angels that Dionysius describes are of existences more real than all things human" (p. 32). Tasso, like Augustine, attributes to Plato the perception that truth is something incorporeal (*Conf.* 7.20), but at this point, again like Augustine, Tasso turns from Platonism to Christian doctrine for fuller knowledge of the nature of truth:

> To prove that the poet's subject is rather the true than the false we can offer yet another argument, derived from the teaching of St. Thomas in the *Summa* and other works of his, according to which the good, the true, and the one are interchangeable, and the true is the good of the intellect; besides, he asserts that evil is not "a nature." Evil, therefore, not being in nature, must be founded in goodness or some good thing, since no

entirely wicked or evil thing can exist. In the same way, every multiplicity is based on unity, nor is there any multiplicity which does not participate in unity; and every falsehood is founded on truth. Thus what is totally false cannot be the subject of poetry, indeed it does not exist.   [p. 33]

Once again Tasso invokes the authority of St. Thomas at the moment Aristotelian and Platonic logic converge. He might as easily have called upon Boethius or Augustine since the notion of the coequality of truth, oneness, and goodness is central to orthodox Christian belief. [11]

As Tasso applies this principle of Christian thought to poetics, the claim for the truthfulness of epic poetry, specifically for its credibility as a record of the universal and intrinsic truth of history, is equally a claim for wholeness. What is real is also necessarily an integral part of the unity that characterizes divine creation; what the poet would make truthful he must also make whole. Thus verisimilitude, the issue of poetic matter, is inextricably bound up with unity, the issue of poetic form, and both are subsumed under the larger issue of morality. For Tasso a manifestation of truthfulness and oneness in literature is by the same token a manifestation of goodness, and, conversely, irreality and diversity or incompleteness in literature signal moral depravity. In other words Tasso's discussion of the formal requirements of epic follows the course already plotted in the discussion of imitation. Unity, or more precisely the three conditions of oneness, wholeness, and "appropriate magnitude" or length, are first identified as the attributes Aristotle assigns to true epic (p. 62, following *Poetics* 7), but it is finally the Thomistic precept that "every multiplicity is based on unity" toward which Tasso's discourse bends.

For both Aristotle and Tasso the idea of unity implies limit and restraint but it is also an inclusive concept, an idea whose complexity Tasso conveys through organic and syntactic metaphors:

We call one the form of elements that is simplest, of single power and operation; so too we call one the composite form of plants and animals that results from the forms of elements gathered together, blunted, and modified, with the powers and qualities of each shared. We call a letter or word one; and we call a speech composed of many letters and words one, as Aristotle teaches in his work *On Interpretation.*   [p. 79]

The principle may be Aristotelian but the habit of drawing an analogy between words and things, between the word and the world, is also fundamental to Christian thought. Tasso's metaphor is reminiscent of Augustine's comparison of the world to a psalm (*Conf.* 11.28). Tasso's most famous statement on the subject further illustrates the essential interdependency of the subject of unity and verisimilitude:

> For just as in this marvellous domain of God called the world we behold the sky scattered over and adorned with such variety of stars, and as we descend from realm to realm, we marvel at the air and the sea full of birds and fish, and the earth host to so many animals wild and tame, with brooks, springs, lakes, meadows, fields, forests, and mountains, here fruits and flowers, there glaciers and snow, here dwellings and ploughed fields, there desert and wilderness; yet for all this, the world that contains in its womb so many diverse things is one, its form and essence one, and one the bond that links its many parts and ties them together in discordant concord, and nothing is missing, yet nothing is there that does not serve for necessity or ornament; just so, I judge, the great poet (who is called divine for no other reason than that as he resembles the supreme Artificer in his workings he comes to participate in his divinity) can form a poem in which, as in a little world, one may read here of armies assembling, here of battles on land or sea, here of conquests of cities, skirmishes and duels, here of jousts, here descriptions of hunger and thirst, here tempests, fires, prodigies, there of celestial and infernal councils, there seditions, there discord, wanderings, adventures, enchantments, deeds of cruelty, daring, courtesy, generosity, there the fortunes of love, now happy, now sad, now joyous, now pitiful. Yet the poem that contains so great a variety of matters none the less should be one, one in form and soul; and all these things should be so combined that each concerns the other, corresponds to the other, and so depends on the other necessarily or verisimilarly that remov-

ing any one part or changing its place would destroy the whole. And if that is true, the art of composing a poem resembles the plan of the universe, which is composed of contraries, as that of music is. For if it were not multiple it would not be a whole or a plan, as Plotinus says.   [pp. 77-78]

Here is the *Discorsi*'s most eloquent tribute to Neoplatonic thought, revealing both in its statement and in its composition a sense of discordia concors and a vision of the world unified in its diversity. It is the cornerstone of Tasso's theories of decorum and verisimilitude. Yet despite its eloquence this passage is perhaps more revealing for what it leaves unsaid; here, too, one can see the limits by which Tasso's thought in the *Discorsi* is confined. There is no mention, for instance, of the *Liberata* although by inference the catalogue of plausible epic actions and the call for a oneness of form and essence, form and soul, may be read as one of the clearest allusions to the poem to be found in the *Discorsi*. If the *Discorsi*'s implicit subject is the *Liberata*, it remains concealed behind an arras, the ideal poem for which the *Discorsi* are a quest but which cannot be fully unveiled in the context of a treatise that generally restricts itself to classical poetic theory.

There is a further omission in Tasso's hymn to unity to which one might be alerted by Tasso's pointed reference to Plotinus. Although Plotinus undertakes the first major systematic revaluation of Platonic philosophy, he would not have been thought by Tasso to have had the last word. If Boethius, to whom Tasso alludes several times in passages immediately preceding this one, had been the acknowledged conduit of this Platonic conception of unity, we might have heard in Christian terms of a unity coextensive with both divinity and goodness. [12]

Perhaps the best evidence of the inclusiveness of Tasso's poetic theory emerges in his discussion of Ariostan chivalric romance. The substance of Tasso's quarrel with Ariosto is implicit in what has already been said about verisimilitude and unity. *Orlando Furioso* manifestly violates both requirements. The *maraviglie*, the prodigies and marvels of the *Furioso*, far exceed the limits of plausibility; the work cannot be considered formally whole since it is a continuation of Boiardo's *Orlando Innamorato:* "The *Furioso* lacks a beginning, the *Innamorato* an ending" (p. 63).

Even if they were to be taken together as a single poem they would not fulfill Tasso's requirements for magnitude and integrity. They would constitute a poem of excessive length, but more importantly, they lack shape. They involve an unmanageable multiplicity of fable and their episodic narratives seem to refuse closure. This amounts to an assault on verisimilitude as well as on unity since nature, which art should imitate, does not behave in the manner of Ariostan romance:

> If art is an imitation of nature, since nature does nothing episodically, as Aristotle says in the *Metaphysics*, neither should art. And surely, if using episodes means going beyond the original purpose, neither art nor nature does anything episodically, since both act toward a determined end.   [p. 83]

In addition to these failures, Tasso argues, romance subordinates the epic obligation to instruct and enlighten its audience to the motive of pleasing it. Romance elects multiplicity of action on the grounds that diversity is more delightful than unity.

In all respects the judgment Tasso pronounces on romance is a moral one. A poem devoid of unity and verisimilitude is also devoid of goodness if, as St. Thomas tells us, "the good, the true, and the one are interchangeable" (p. 33). But the same article of Christian doctrine contains the logic that will permit Tasso to argue the reformation rather than the rejection of romance. If romance, given its irreality and multiplicity, is to be associated with evil, let us recall that evil, according to Augustinian, Boethian, or Thomistic thought, has no being in nature. "In the same way, every multiplicity is based on unity, nor is there any multiplicity which does not participate in unity." Extending this logic to the subject of romance, Tasso arrives at the conclusion that romance has no generic status independent of epic.[13] Tasso's purpose in the *Discorsi* is not to counterpose romance and epic as antithetical literary forms but to argue their identity, to draw romance into the shadow of epic.[14] "Romance and epic," he asserts, "imitate the same actions, that is illustrious ones"; they imitate in the same manner, narrating rather than representing things dramatically; and they use the same means to imitate (69):

From the bond of the actions they imitate and of their means and manner of imitating, it follows that the poetry called epic and the poetry called romance are one and the same poetic genre.   [p. 70]

As the issue of poetic form is resolved, so is the issue of poetic matter. The charge that romance maraviglia is not verisimilitudinous can be dropped if marvels can be seen as miracles—if they are understood to emanate not from the necromancer but from that being of which he is a parody, from God. What is required is that romance maraviglia be seen from the higher perspective that includes a knowledge of first causes:

One same action can then be both marvellous and verisimilar: marvellous when regarded in itself and confined within natural limits, verisimilar when considered apart from these limits in terms of its cause, which is a powerful supernatural force accustomed to performing such marvels.   [p. 38]

The case against romance lies in the narrowness of its vision. What is experienced as aberrant nature within the confines of the romance landscape may be perceived differently by the visionary who is not restricted to the realm of corporeal and visible things. Romance is the experience of effects where causes are unknown, of movement without a sense of direction; its events seem to be discrete and random accidents because they are not perceived sequentially. But the "world" of romance is the same as that of epic even if its appearance is different, because there is only one world.

Romance, then, is epic whose multiplicity has not yet been seen as unity and whose marvels are still perceived as distortions of nature rather than acts of supernature and "existences more real than all things human." Tasso's treatment of romance is more than an ingenious theoretical equivocation. His argument that apparently antithetical genres are in the last analysis one and the same comes from the core of his Christian belief. It is an expression in critical theory of Augustine's perception that the solution to the dilemma of Manichaean dualism is that one of the terms of this dualism simply does not exist. Such logic, the logic

of salvation, informs every aspect of Tasso's poem, its form—
which may be described as romance subsumed by epic and classical epic overgone by Christian epic—as well as its theme, deliverance.

The ideas that are peripheral to, or at best implicit in, the
Discorsi are more directly expressed in Tasso's *Allegoria del Poema*,
drafted in 1576 and appended to most early editions of the *Liberata*
as an interpretive guide to the poem. In his gloss on the role of the
Wise Man in the *Liberata* Tasso gives us a picture of natural wisdom superseded by grace:

> It is fained, that this wise man was by birth a Pagan, but being
> by the *Hermite* conuerted to the true faith, becommeth a Chris-
> tian, and despising his first arrogancie, he doth not much
> presume of his owne wisedome, but yeeldeth himselfe to the
> iudgment of his master, albeit that *Philospophie* be borne and
> nourished amongst the Gentiles in Aegypt and Greece, and
> from thence hath passed over vnto vs, presumptious of her
> selfe, a miscreant bold and proud aboue measure: but of *Saint
> Thomas* and the other *holy Doctors* she is made the disciple and
> handmaid of Diuinitie.

The relation of the Wise Man to the Hermite is like that of Plotinus
to Boethius, St. Thomas, "and the other holy Doctors" and in
many respects like that of the *Discorsi* to the *Liberata* itself. Classical philosophy adumbrates Christian doctrine. This reflects a notion of redemption that the *Liberata* is meant to extend to the
Aeneid by converting epic to crusade, and the *imperium* of Rome to
Christianitas. As Goffredo says, in the accents of Pauline exhortation,

> "Non edifica quei che vuol gl'imperi
> su fondamenti fabricar mondani."   [1.25]

> ["He does not build truly who wishes to construct his empire
> on worldly foundations."][15]

This is the act of deliverance that will be repeated in form and
essence ("una la forma e l'anima sua") throughout the epic.

II

The case against romance in the *Liberata* may be stated best in terms of the poem's central action. The historical subject of the epic is the First Crusade, the eleventh-century campaign of Geoffrey of Boulogne to liberate Jerusalem from pagan control. But the thematic subject (whether we hear it from the *Allegoria* or from the poem itself) is the spiritual progress of Christian man toward the other Jerusalem, "*Ierusalem* the strong citie . . . situated vpon the top of the Alpine and wearisome hill of virtue" (*Allegoria*). This crusade, moreover, is prerequisite to the literal one. Goffredo's army cannot enter the city until movement in that direction is understood in both senses—until, that is, the moral regeneration of the Christian community is complete. It is where movement lacks moral direction, where Goffredo's knights pursue the lesser, phantom goals of their own cupidity—Baldovin, his ambition ("l'umane grandezze"); Tancredi, vain love ("vano amor"); Boemondo, empire; and Rinaldo, his personal honor (1.8–10)—that we find ourselves in the confused, interior, and illusory regions of romance. It is no accident that Tasso chooses an epic action in which the moral and historical dimensions are isomorphic, or, to put it in the more circumspect terms of the *Discorsi*, an action drawn from both "true history" and "a religion that is not false" (p. 39).

In the *Liberata* romance variety, formlessness, and fantasy become, with a slight shift of perspective, the labyrinthine nightmare of sensuous, Ovidian nature and unregenerate selfhood, an image of the world unredeemed from mortality and mutability:

> Sorge non lunge a le cristiane tende
> tra solitarie valli alta foresta,
> foltissima di piante antiche, orrende,
> che spargon d'ogni intorno ombra funesta.
> Qui ne l'ora che il sol più chiaro splende,
> è luce incerta e scolorita e mesta,
> quale in nubilo ciel dubbia si vede,
> se 'l dì a la notte, o s'ella a lui succede.   [13.2]

[From Godfrey's camp a grove a little way,
  Amid the valleys deep, grows out of sight,
Thick with old trees, whose horrid arms display
  An ugly shade, like everlasting night:
There, when the sun spreads forth his clearest ray,
  Dim, thick, uncertain, gloomy seems the light;
As when, in ev'ning, day and darkness stive
Which should his foe from our horizon drive.]

Fairfax's translation makes explicit, with its mention of "everlasting night," a metaphor underlying Tasso's conception of romance. The romance landscape is cut off from the visually and spiritually clarifying light of the sun. The light we do find there is the reflected, interior light associated with the enchantress Armida—"her burning face" ("suo infiammato viso," [16.18]) or the "burning thoughts" (the "mente accesa" and "pensier ardenti" [5.7-12]) of those in her power. Her smile is like sunlight ("Qual raggio in onda, le scintilla un riso" [12.18]) but the parallel is a false one.

The romance world is temporally indefinite as well as visually indistinct, timeless in a sense, but not in an eschatological sense. At one end of its imaginative spectrum we hear the carpe diem song of Armida's enchanted island (16.14-15), appealing for an arrest of natural time in an ongoing present. Romance is an endless continuum of flight, pursuit, and entrapment—chivalric activity, that is, from which all sense of purpose and direction has been withdrawn.

In the pagan heroes of the *Liberata* we discern an attitude to time philosophically alien to providential historiography. The first articulate spokesmen of the pagan viewpoint are Aletes and Argante, emissaries from the Egyptian camp to Goffredo in canto 2. Theirs is chiefly a rhetorical skill, supplied with aphoristic, cautionary wisdom garnered, presumably, after many turns on fortune's wheel:

> "Giunta è tua gloria al sommo; e per l'inanzi
> fuggir le dubbie guerre a te conviene:
> ch'ove tu vinca, sol di stato avanzi,
> né tua gloria maggior quinci diviene;
> ma l'imperio acquistato e preso dianzi,

e l'onor perdi, se 'l contrario avviene.
Ben gioco è di fortuna audace e stolto
por contra il poco e incerto il certo e 'l molto."   [67]

["Thy sun is in his Apogaeon placed,
    And when it moveth next must needs descend;
Chance is uncertain, fortune double-faced,
    Smiling at first, she frowneth in the end;
Beware thine honor be not then disgraced,
    Take heed thou mar not, when thou think'st to mend,
For this the folly is of fortune's play,
'Gainst doubtful, certain; much, 'gainst small, to lay."]

Aletes counsels Goffredo on behalf of the king of Egypt to settle
for the partial victory he has already won (65). His advice to the
Christians to stop while they are ahead is an appeal for a sober
and an apparently humane realism sweetened with a gesture of
concord (64). Goffredo, however, sees the advice and the offer of
peace as pernicious, not necessarily because they may be delivered in bad faith but because they constitute the first steps of
seduction by a fundamentally fatalistic and materialistic philosophy:

"Ché non ambizïosi avari affetti
ne spronaro a l'impresa e ne fur guida:
(sgombri il Padre del Ciel da i nostri petti
peste sì rea, s'in alcun pur s'annida)."   [83]

["Not hope of praise, nor thirst of worldly good,
    Enticed us to follow this emprise:
The heav'nly father keep his sacred brood
From foul infection of so great a vice."]

According to the worldly wisdom of the pagans, time is a
repeated pattern of ups and downs to which men may adjust but
in which they should not expect the fulfillment of moralistic
ideals. What Aletes subtly proposes is a view of history un-
sanctioned by intelligible purpose, a continuum in which gains
must be weighed against prospects of equal loss at each new
juncture. But Goffredo recognizes in this a philosophy in which
the grounds for heroic action are eroded. Aletes' rhetoric, how-

ever attractive, is analytic reasoning applied in a void, oblivious to moral absolutes, and thus it opens a door on chaos.

Pagan heroes, rhetoricians, and seers are continually frustrated by the narrowness of their horizons in the *Liberata*. The pagan wizard Ismeno, for instance, confesses his inability to see into the future in canto 10 (the same canto in which the Christian hermit Piero does so on Rinaldo's behalf) and takes a stoic view of things:

> "Ciascun qua giù le forze e 'l senno impieghi
> per avanzar fra le sciagure e i mali;
> ché sovente adivien che 'l saggio e 'l forte
> fabro a sé stesso è di beata sorte."   [20]

> ["Our wit and strength on us bestow'd, I hold,
>   To shun th' evils and harms 'mongst which we dwell;
> They make their fortune who are stout and wise,
> Wit rules the heav'ns, discretion guides the skies."]

Like Aletes, Ismeno regards *fortuna* as the goddess of the temporal world and thus can salvage only that part of wisdom that is discretion, or such wisdom as can be attained within the limits of personal experience.

At its furthest extreme pagan logic deteriorates into demonic illogic. This extreme is reached with the poem's *descensus ad inferos* in canto 4, the canto, as Tasso tells us in one of his letters, from which all the episodes of the poem derive. Tasso's Pluto, like Milton's Satan after him and like the pagan heroes of whose cause he is author, suffers from the delusion of self-sufficiency. His vain attempt to assert his independence of the godhead ironically confirms the opposite, his status as parody. As he recapitulates history from his perspective he inadvertently reveals his limitations. Pluto recounts universal history as he remembers it, not from the moment of creation but from his fall (4.9). From this beginning history seems an agonistic process, a struggle between two opposed forces.

As with Milton's Satan, there is a semblance of heroism in the posture of defiance Pluto assumes, but it is a heroism grounded in the false notions that the universe is dualistic and antagonistic rather than unified and harmonious and that greatness consists in asserting one's personal will in hostile circumstances rather than in acceding to the will of God. Herein lie the limitations of the pagan heroes of the *Liberata*. And here is the logic by which Pluto and his associates seek to seduce the Christian heroes away from their chivalric obligations.

Pluto's program for the subversion of the Christian crusade amounts to a synopsis of the poem's romance subplots:

> "Sia destin ciò ch'io voglio: altri disperso
> sen vada errando; altri rimanga ucciso;
> altri, in cure d'amor lascive immerso,
> idol si faccia un dolce sguardo e un riso:
> sia 'l ferro in contro al suo rettor converso
> da lo stuol ribellante e 'n sé diviso:
> pèra il campo e rüini, e resti in tutto
> ogni vestigio suo con lui distrutto."   [17]

> ["Among the knights and worthies of their train,
>   Let some like out-laws wander uncouth ways,
> Let some be slain in field, let some again
>   Make oracles of women's yeas and nays,
> And pine in foolish love; let some complain
>   On Godfrey's rule, and mutines 'gainst him raise;
> Turn each one's sword against his fellow's heart;
> Thus kill them all, or spoil the greatest part."]

More specifically, Pluto (or his wizard Hidraort) unleashes the meretrix Armida against the Christians with a plot to distract them from their purpose. Her appeal is to human cupidity in its several forms, sensuality, pride, ambition, self-love, and whatever other forces move the heart or mind away from God. Armida's scheme is to redirect the chivalric instincts of Goffredo's knights toward herself, which is to say toward their own selves. Thus she fabricates a tale of personal injustice and calls on Goffredo for assistance. Her rightful place as heir to her father's kingdom, she claims, has been usurped by an unscrupulous uncle and his unchivalrous son, whom Armida would have Goffredo overthrow. Her device meets with at least partial success, we note, because the mission Armida advocates is closely analogous to that on which the Christians are already engaged. They are called upon to invade a kingdom and expell a usurping tyrant, although now for the sake of Armida and a romance order of chivalry rather than for the Christian faith.

But once again we are invited to see the higher providential truth that ironically circumscribes the romance plot. Armida's intentions are deceitful and the personal history she unfolds is entirely contrived, but like every demonic artifice her fable contains more truth than she knows. That she is genuinely exiled from her father's kingdom, although not the father she now has in mind, becomes clear in canto 20 as Rinaldo promises to restore her "to that throne whereof thy sire was lord" (135)—to comply with her original request, in effect, in a way she did not intend—if she will cease to be a pagan. In the light of her eventual realization that her father's kingdom is heaven, the anguish she feigns in canto 4 (72) at having been exiled and disgraced is justified beyond her awareness. To see the potential of the romance theme of restoration become an allegory of Christian salvation we have only to look ahead to the first book of Spenser's *Faerie Queene* or to see in the *Liberata* that it is the redemption of Jerusalem that finally subsumes and completes all romance questing.

Armida exercises her momentary spell over Rinaldo in canto 16 in her illusory paradise.[16] Armida's garden, a parody of Eden, is a clue to the nature of her perversity. She offers to satisfy a human yearning to reverse the temporal process begun with the Fall, to transfix time in an artificial eternity. The songs heard on the approaches to Armida's palace play on the dynastic dream of a restoration of the Golden Age and the epic longing for rest:

> "Questo è il porto del mondo; e qui è il ristoro
> de le sue noie, e quel piacer si sente
> che già sentì ne' secoli de l'oro
> l'antica e senza fren libera gente.
> L'arme, che sin a qui d'uopo vi fôro,
> potete omai depor securamente,
> e sacrarle in quest'ombra a la quïete:
> ché guerrier qui solo d'Amor sarete."   [15.63]

> ["This is the place wherein you may assuage
>   Your sorrows past, here is that joy and bliss
> That flourish'd in the antique golden age;

Here needs no law, here none doth aught amiss;
Put off those arms, and fear not Mars his rage,
   Your sword, your shield, your helmet needless is;
Then consecrate them here to endless rest,
   You shall love's champions be and soldiers blest."]

That the danger of yielding to the allures of Armida involves
truancy to true epic mission is implied through her association
with Dido (16.36–74), Cleopatra (5–7), and Omphale (3). The engravings on the castle portals are a thematic inversion of Vulcan's
shield in the *Aeneid*, perversely memorializing Actium from the
perspective of Antony and Cleopatra instead of Augustus. They
proclaim the ascendancy of the *imperium* of sensual pleasure over
that of Rome. The engravings depict Antony in flight from
Octavius—yet not in flight but in pursuit of Cleopatra, and then
awaiting his death in her lap in the secret streams of the Nile
(6–7).

   Rinaldo in his involvement with Armida is another Antony, or
another Aeneas as Mercury finds him in Carthage, or another
Ruggiero as Melissa finds him in the seventh canto of *Orlando
Furioso*. His sword is bedecked with flowers, his locks are per-
fumed; he is Aeneas as Iarbas labels him, a second Paris with his
eunuch train, "a Maeonian band propping his chin and essenced
locks." Rinaldo and Armida are not so much in love with each
other as bound together in mutually gratifying narcissism. She
sees herself reflected in his crystal pendant; he gazes on his own
image in her eyes:

>   Dal fianco de l'amante (estranio arnese)
>   un cristallo pendea lucido e netto.
>   Sorse, e quel fra le mani a lei sospese,
>   a i misteri d'Amor ministro eletto.
>   Con luci ella ridenti, ei con accese,
>   mirano in varii oggetti un solo oggetto:
>   ella del vetro a sé fa specchio, ed egli
>   gli occhi di lei sereni a sé fa spegli.   [20]

Down by the lovers' side there pendant was
   A crystal mirror, bright, pure, smooth, and neat;
He rose and to his mistress held the glass

(A noble page grac'd with that service great);
She with glad looks, he with inflam'd (alas!),
Beauty and love beheld both in one seat;
Yet them in sundry objects each espies,
She in the glass, he saw them in her eyes.

Their love is cupidity by the Augustinian definition, passion moving within the sphere of the self rather than toward God. The narcissism Armida represents is the goal of all unregenerate romance questing.

To retrieve Rinaldo from Armida's enchantment Carlo and Ubaldo have come with another mirror of sorts, a diamond shield. When they hold it up to his eyes, Rinaldo sees himself from another vantage point, that of his epic cause, and is filled with shame (30–31). His recovery is instantaneous and complete (as such moments always are in romance). He comes to his senses like a man waking from sleep (31). The reader cannot help but be struck by the parallelisms between the two states of enchantment and enlightenment. Both the diamond shield of Carlo and Ubaldo and the carved doors of Armida's palace are versions of the same epic symbol, the prophetic shield Vulcan makes for Aeneas in the eighth book of the *Aeneid*. And both the diamond shield and Armida's eyes are mirrors. The instrument of Rinaldo's recovery is functionally identical to that of his entrapment. But in moral terms the diamond shield and Armida's eyes are diametrically opposed. The shield, the symbol of epic endeavor, of the quest for both the Jerusalem of the poem and the New Jerusalem of Revelation, promotes self-knowledge rather than narcissistic indulgence because for Tasso self-knowledge means knowledge of one's place in God's plan.

Still, the superficial parallelisms between enchantment and enlightenment need to be taken into account. Tasso insists on them. They serve as a reminder that his universe, like Augustine's, is not finally a dualistic one. The desire that Armida stirs in Rinaldo is but a perverse manifestation of the love that God requires of all his creatures; the quasi-eternity of her garden is a parody of the eternity to which all Christian pilgrimage aspires. Tasso insists on showing the resemblance of falseness to truth both to establish the parodic nature of the former and to prepare for the resolution of the conflict between love in its two forms, the conversion of the one into the other.

III

Having explored the limitations of the pagan view of things, we are now in a position to see how Christian vision overcomes such limitations. The subject is introduced with the voyage of Carlo and Ubaldo, the first chapter in the story of Rinaldo's spiritual regeneration. Carlo and Ubaldo operate as agents of the hermit sage of Ascalona and his female servant, who correspond to Ariosto's Merlin and Melissa. If Armida's enchanted garden represents nature's attempt at simulating paradisal eternity without the sanction of grace, the magic of the old hermit of Ascalona and his sorceress companion is nature operating within its providential context. The hermit is a pagan convert to Christianity, a reminder, as Tasso's *Allegoria* explains, that "humane wisdome" and "knowledge of the workes of Nature" must proceed finally from "the supernaturall knowledge receiued by Gods grace." (With characteristic symmetry Tasso makes Ismeno, the principal pagan sorcerer, a lapsed Christian.) He has access to all the secrets of nature, but through divine revelation, to which he has been brought by Piero (the church), he has come to understand the greater mystery that all earthly *scientia* is superseded and validated by *sapientia:*

> "Di me medesmo fui pago cotanto,
> ch'io stimai già che 'l mio saper misura
> certa fosse e infallibile di quanto
> può far l'alto Fattor de la natura:
> ma quando il vostro Piero al fiume santo
> m'asperse il crine, e lavò l'alma impura,
> drizzò più su il mio guardo, e 'l fece accorto
> ch'ei per sé stesso è tenebroso e corto."   [14.45]

> ["So learned, cunning, wise, myself I thought,
>   That I suppos'd my wit so high might climb
> To know all things that God had fram'd or wrought,
>   Fire, air, sea, earth, man, beast, sprite, place, and time:
> But when your hermit me to baptism brought,

And from my soul had wash'd the sin and crime,
Then I perceiv'd my sight was blindness still:
My wit was folly, ignorance my skill."]

All power and knowledge, he discovers, derive from God: "He is the architect, the workmen we." Thus the miracles he performs—walking on water (33) and parting the waters of the river to give Carlo and Ubaldo passage (36)—recapitulate instances in Scripture in which nature accedes to divine purpose.[17] The paradox implicit in such maraviglie is that nature remains natural while apparently contradicting its own laws. The hermit's subterranean palace is a wonder constructed without demonic magic (42), and his vault of treasures consists of "riches grown by kind, not fram'd by art" (48). By contrast the enchantments of Armida or Ismeno are art's conspiracy with nature against grace, and thus unnatural.

The hermit of Ascalona equips Carlo and Ubaldo with the implements they will need in rescuing Rinaldo from Armida's island and assigns the sorceress to guide them on their voyage. The voyage (canto 15) makes clear the relation of scientia to sapientia in both spatial and temporal terms. The knights first skirt the impressive Egyptian camp at Gaza, then pass along the northern coast of Africa, studded with the monuments of ancient empires. Among these is Carthage, whose ruins occasion a lament for the mutability of earthly glory:

> Giace l'alta Cartago; a pena i segni
> de l'alte sue ruine il lido serba.
> Muoiono le città, muoiono i regni;
> copre i fasti e le pompe arena ed erba;
> e l'uom d'esser mortal par che si sdegni:
> oh nostra mente cupida e superba!   [20]

[Great Carthage low in ashes cold doth lie,
   Her ruins poor the herbs in height scant pass;
So cities fall, so perish kingdoms high,
   Their pride and pomp lie hid in sand and grass:
Then why should mortal man repine to die,
   Whose life is air, breath wind, and body glass?]

As the travelers move westward toward the pillars of Hercules, they move backward, at first, in time. (But their journey into the past will bring them to a vision of the future; images of decay will be replaced by images of renewal as the journey progresses.) When they reach the ocean beyond the Mediterranean world they come to the geographical and epistemological limits assigned to the classical world, the point at which "Great Hercules" would have "impal'd / The over-daring wit of mankind vain" (25). Beyond are the Elysian Fields and the Fortunate Isles, of which Armida's island is one. Here, then, are the loci of timelessness in classical myth, and here too is the boundary within which human knowledge, pagan and classical knowledge of nature, is confined. To make the point Tasso alludes to Dante's Ulysses (*Inferno* 26), who, driven by a desire "to see and know," ventured beyond the pillars of Hercules only to pass into oblivion(26).

But the present travelers, Carlo and Ubaldo, go beyond the limits fixed by Hercules with a different result since they do so with the advantage of their guide's greater knowledge. They attain something of a critical perspective on classical tradition as they are told that the Fortunate Isles are the stuff of heathen fantasy rather than truth (37). For Carlo and Ubaldo the passage through the pillars now opens a vista into the future as it occasions their guide's prophecy of the voyage of Columbus to the New World (30–32). But Tasso is concerned with more than demythologizing classical legend or asserting the superiority of his age's knowledge of geography. The voyage of Columbus has its place in the tradition of Renaissance millennialism as the fulfillment of eschatological prophecies of the dissemination of God's Word to all nations of the earth in the last age:

> For I wil visit their workes, and their imaginations: for it shal come that I wil gather all nations, and tongues, and thei shal come, and se my glorie. . . . For as the newe heauens, and the newe earth which I wil make, shal remaine before me, saith the Lord, so shal your sede and your name continue.   [Isa. 66.18, 22][18]

The Christian reader sees Isaiah's prophecy of the "newe heauens, and the newe earth" fulfilled in John's vision of "a new heauen, and a new earth" in the form of the New Jerusalem in Revelation (21.1–2). The historical Crusaders saw themselves participating in the gathering of nations at the close of world history of which both Isaiah and John speak.[19] Renaissance Christian millennialists believed that the New World opened by the voyage of Columbus would be the scene of the apocalyptic gathering of nations.[20] In the same vein the guide explains to Carlo and Ubaldo that the divine purpose behind that voyage is to open the remaining regions of the world to receive the Word (29).

Looking back on the journey of Carlo and Ubaldo from Gaza across the Mediterranean to Carthage and to the Fortunate Isles, we now see what had seemed to be regression into the classical past converted to prophecy of the millennium. We are at the point where classical and romance quests are overgone by Christian pilgrimage. A survey of decayed historical empires is replaced with a vision of imperium sine fine in Christian terms, the *imperium* of the universal church. Ulysses' frustrated desire "to see and know" is answered with an allusion to Revelation.

But as always in literary evocations of apocalyptic finality, the distance between then and now is preserved. When Carlo asks for more specific knowledge of the cultures of the Fortunate Isles, his guide defers to the providential decree that fixes the time of full discovery in the future:

> "Ché ancor vòlto non è lo spazio intero
> ch'al grande scoprimento ha fisso Dio;
> né lece a voi da l'oceán profondo
> recar vera notizia al vostro mondo."　　　　　[15.39]

["Nor yet the time hath Titan's gliding fire
　Mete forth, prefix'd for this discoverment,
Nor is it lawful of the ocean main
That you the secrets know, or known explain."]

To know of the promised end and to attain it remain different propositions as long as the quester is bound by the laws of time and nature.

IV

As Tasso tells us in the *Discorsi*, the conversion of romance to epic is a conversion of multiplicity and diversity to coherence and unity. The true Christian epic reveals the order and shape that history assumes when it is understood to be the handiwork of

Providence rather than Fortuna. By this definition the *Liberata* is a Christian epic.

The *Liberata* can be divided into two movements, one initiated by God as he calls on Goffredo to open the siege of Jerusalem in canto 1, the other initiated by Goffredo as he personally engages in the first assault on the city in canto 11, the poem's midpoint. Goffredo's action is in many respects an echo of the event that Christianity places at the midpoint of human history, the intercession of Christ on man's behalf. Goffredo, we note, enters the field of combat as a common soldier and is wounded. As Christ's descent into the world marks a turning point in universal history, Goffredo's gesture serves as the pivotal event in the battle for Jerusalem. The first ten cantos dramatize the steady deterioration of the moral and political fabric of the Christian camp, while the second ten reveal the process of regeneration. During the first movement the pagan forces approach the peak of their strength, while the principal Christian heroes, Rinaldo among them, desert their cause and disperse throughout the landscape. Beginning with canto 11, however, the double pattern of ascending pagan and declining Christian fortunes is reversed.[21]

The God of the poem's first half evokes the deity of the Old Testament—commanding but distant, sublime, and incomprehensible to mortals. We are continually made aware of the gulf between heaven and earth, between the celestial region of harmony and pure act and that of imperfect human endeavor (9.56–57). In the first half of the poem the direction of movement between these two planes is downward (the descents of Gabriele in canto 1 and Michele in canto 9), and it is projected from a height that suggests something of God's detachment from the action he has set in motion. The movement of the second half of the poem is ascent, and, instead of angelic emissaries from God, we hear now an appeal for reciprocity voiced by men. Goffredo emerges from his passivity, and the poem enters a phase in which access to divinity is assured through the mediatory agencies of ceremony, prayer, conversion, baptism, repentance, vision, and contemplation. It is in this phase that the propitiatory effect of Christ's incarnation and crucifixion begins to be felt in the narrative.

At the geometrical center of the poem, as Goffredo ascends Mount Olivet in formal procession before his assault on

Jerusalem, epic action becomes aware of itself as symbolic, as ritualistic recapitulation of an action that has preceded it. Mount Olivet is a setting whose importance in the *Liberata* derives from its importance in the Bible, and in Christian messianic tradition in particular. It is the scene, first, of David's exile from Jerusalem (2 Sam. 15.30) and, later, of Christ's triumphal reentry into Jerusalem (Matt. 21.1) in fulfillment of Old Testament prophecies (Isa. 42.11, Zech. 9.9). The symmetry is, of course, crucial both to the Christian strategy of typological exegesis[22] and to Tasso's poem, which finds here its theme and its structure. David is the type, the *umbra futurorum* of Christ, who in turn transforms the Old Testament ideal of kingship and converts loss to gain. That the Old Testament setting for exile becomes that of Christ's return to Jerusalem signals Christianity's promise of redemption.

Mount Olivet is the scene of two other New Testament events, interrelated by the messianic theme Tasso wishes to invoke. It is the setting for the moment of agony in which Christ reconciles himself to his death in words that inform the concept of chivalric action to which Goffredo's knights are meant to aspire: "Not as I will, but as thou wilt" (Matt. 26.39). And it is the scene of the Ascension (Acts 1.12), where Christ explicitly refers to himself as the fulfillment of Old Testament prophecy. Tasso does not gloss his text with these references but he acknowledges their collective impact in a subtle but direct poetic image. As the Christians climb Olivet and their hymns are returned from the surrounding landscape by Echo, we witness the conversion of classical nature, the spiritualization of a natural world:

> E quasi par che boscareccio coro
> fra quegli antri si celi e in quelle fronde;
> sì chiaramente replicar s'udìa
> or di Cristo il gran nome, or di Maria.   [11.11]

> [It seem'd some choir that sung with art and skill
>   Dwelt in those savage dens and shady ground,
> For oft resounded from the banks they hear
> The name of Christ and of his mother dear.]

If Goffredo divides the twenty cantos of the epic into two distinct halves, Rinaldo further subdivides the poem into quadrants. He is exiled from the Christian camp in canto 5 for killing Gernando and is restored to the cause by Carlo and Ubaldo in canto 16. His presence in the first and last quarters of the poem ensures Christian ascendancy, while his absence in the second and third allows the pagan heroes Argante, Clorinda, and Solimano to dominate. Through Rinaldo's exile and restoration Tasso projects again the universal paradigm of Fall and Redemption.

Taken canto by canto the *Liberata* unfolds in a pattern of bilateral or mirror symmetry. Canto 1 contains parallels in theme and subject to canto 20, canto 2 to canto 19, and so forth. The call to arms comes in the first canto; the battle to liberate the city is finally won in the last. In canto 2 the narrative setting shifts from the Christian camp to Jerusalem for the first time; in canto 19 the Christians enter and sack the city. The Egyptian satrap, Argante, is introduced in canto 2 and slain by Tancredi in canto 19. The city is sighted by the Christian army in canto 3, entered in canto 18. Cantos 4 and 17 contain parallel accounts of Armida appealing for aid, first from the Christian camp, then from the pagans. Canto 4 opens with a council in Hell, in which Pluto offers an infernal account of universal history. It is the first, demonic part of an allusion to Aeneas's visionary descent into Avernus (*Aen.* 6), which is completed in canto 17 when Rinaldo is told of his historical descendants, the princes of the House of Este, Tasso's patrons.

Cantos 5 and 16 are pivotal in their respective halves of the poem since they contain the story of Rinaldo's exile and return. In canto 5 he abandons himself fully to his irascible nature by killing Gernando, and in canto 16 he is released from narcissistic and self-indulgent passion when he sees himself reflected in the diamond shield, the symbol of a higher chivalric purpose. Cantos 6 and 7 withdraw into the uncharted pastoral interior of romance landscape with the adventures of Erminia and Tancredi, while 15 and 14 contain accounts of terrestrial navigation and Goffredo's visionary ascent, both of which provide perspectives for seeing the aimlessness and narrowness of romance. In canto 6 Tancredi is drawn by his misdirected affections away from the field of battle in pursuit of Erminia, whom he supposes to be Clorinda; in canto 15 Carlo and Ubaldo are guided by a prophetess on a mission to release Rinaldo from just such a misdirection of passion, his involvement with Armida, in order to return him to Goffredo. In canto 7 both Erminia and Tancredi are thoroughly immersed (and Tancredi actually imprisoned) in the pastoral world; in canto 14 we see that world from another angle, as Goffredo is transported in a dream to a distance from which terrestrial existence ("this earthly jail") may be regarded with celestial irony:

> "Quanto è vil la cagion ch'a la virtute
> umana è colà giù premio e contrasto!
> in che picciolo cerchio, e fra che nude
> solitudini è stretto il vostro fasto!"   [14.10]

> ["How vile, how small, and of how slender price,
> Is there reward of goodness, virtue's gain;
> A narrow room our glory vain up-ties,
> A little circle doth our pride contain."]

In canto 8 a threat to Goffredo's authority arises with the attempted revolt of Argillano and the Italian troops, which Goffredo suppresses with a majestic assertion of his temporal power. In canto 13 Goffredo averts a similar outbreak of dissension by appealing to heaven in prayer. Canto 9 contains the night raid of Solimano against the Christian camp; canto 12 completes the incorporation of this epic allusion (see *Iliad* 10.299–579, and *Aen.* 9.176–449) by returning again to a night raid, this time that of Clorinda and Argante against Goffredo's battle tower. This refraction of an episode from classical epic is characteristic of Tasso's allusive technique: it permits the reassessment of a heroic action by the standards of a new code. Thus the dying Clorinda's conversion to Christianity and her baptism serve to answer the question of Nisus, her Virgilian predecessor: "Is it God, Euryalus, that puts this fire in our hearts, or does his own wild longing become to each man a God?" Finally, canto 10 contains the council debate of the pagans and represents the beginning of their demise, and canto 11 contains the ceremonial procession of the Christians to Mount Olivet and the first successful assault on Jerusalem.

This survey by no means exhausts the correlations between the matching cantos of the poem but it should demonstrate the centrality of the theme of redemption. The narrative continually and systematically looks back on itself, and on its classical predecessors, from a position of greater moral awareness. Its symmetry is no mere reflex of a Renaissance sense of proportion but an expression in poetic form of the poem's concept of deliverance.

We may examine the symmetrical unfolding of Tasso's theme in more detail by looking at cantos 3, 8, 13, and 18, the midpoints of the four quarters of the poem. I would like to survey these four cantos in terms of the image each gives us of death. For it is ultimately the awareness of human mortality that prompts both the romance and the Christian imagination, and it is in their respective responses to death that their relationship to each other is defined.

V

Death enters the poem for the first time in canto 3 with the first skirmish between Christian and pagan forces. The most notable loss on the Christian side is Dudone, Captain of the Adventurers. Dudone's funeral constitutes an allusion to the funeral games in the fifth book of the *Aeneid*. In contrast to Virgil's ritual, which has sufficient amplitude by itself to mediate between death and sorrow on the one hand and a sense of the continuity of human culture on the other, Dudone's funeral seems at first to elicit only a rather remote consolation:

> "E come a nostro pro veduto abbiamo
> ch'usavi, uom già mortal, l'arme mortali,
> così vederti oprare anco speriamo,
> spirto divin, l'arme del Ciel fatali. . . ."   [3.70]

["And as in our cause we have seen you,
once a mortal man, use mortal arms,
so now we also hope to see you,
a divine spirit, wield the fateful arms of Heaven. . . ."]

[My trans.]

So Goffredo prays, and in canto 18 he is granted a vision of Dudone and the "fleshless spirits" ("ignudi spirti") fighting alongside the living in the decisive battle for Jerusalem. It would be easy to judge Tasso inferior to Virgil here, to see Tasso sadly incapable of bridging in human terms the gulf between present desolation and promised immortality. But in fairness to Tasso it ought to be said that he writes in service to an idealism in which two orders of existence—time and eternity—are separated by a distance not easily traversed.

Immediately after the funeral of Dudone, Goffredo sends his troops to lumber the forest near Jerusalem in order to construct war machines. The image of the forest is introduced without pretensions but its significance greatly expands over the course of the poem. The cutting of trees recalls a motif in the *Aeneid* into which Virgil condenses the most compelling urges of his poem: the desire to preserve pastoral serenity, stability, and timelessness and the antithetical impulse to build, to erect monuments to epic enterprise. Tasso's forest is a terrestrial metaphor (like that in which the Red Cross Knight and Una take refuge in the beginning of *The Faerie Queene*) laden with potential drama and pageantry. But the felling of timber is an act charged with tension:

> L'un l'altro essorta che le piante atterri,
> e faccia al bosco inusitati oltraggi.
> Caggion recise da taglienti ferri
> le sacre palme, e i frassini selvaggi;
> i funebri cipressi, e i pini, e i cerri,
> l'elci frondose, e gli alti abeti, e i faggi,
> gli olmi mariti, a cui talor s'appoggia
> la vite, e con piè torto al ciel sen poggia.   [3.75]

> [One exhorts the other to fell the plants
> and do unwonted outrage to the trees.
> They fall, hewn by the sharp iron,
> the sacred palms and the wild ashes,
> the funereal cypresses, the pines, the turkey oaks,
> the leafy holm-oaks, the lofty firs, the beeches,
> and the husband elms to which sometimes the vine
> clings and climbs toward heaven with its twisted foot.]
>   [My trans.]

The strident rhythms of epic activity overlie an elegiac sense of remorse. Tasso extends to this image the impact of Dudone's death and funeral: it is an image of the world in the shadow of mortality.

The important eighth canto raises again the issue of the death of a Christian hero. The stated subject of the canto is the fall of Sveno the Dane, whose arrival at the Christian camp has been anticipated since canto 1. That Sveno has been awaited so long, that he never actually arrives, and that his death is reported only at second hand, by a witness whose own perceptions are more nearly a matter of faith than of experience (8.27–42), are matters indicative of Tasso's deeper theme. It concerns the nature of testimony itself and the feelings of uncertainty, exclusion, and frustration that attend any human perception of mystery. The witness speaks of having been miraculously healed by holy hermits:

> "Stupido lor riguardo, e non ben crede
> l'anima sbigottita il certo e il vero;
> onde l'un d'essi a me: 'Di poca fede,
> che dubbii? o che vaneggia il tuo pensiero?'"   [8.29]

> ["I gaz'd on them like one whose heart denaith
> To think that done he sees so strangely wrought;
> Till one said thus: 'O thou of little faith,
> What doubts perplex thy unbelieving thought?'"]

Witness, evidence, language, signs, dreams, revelation, and the problem of their authentication are the real subjects of this canto. The reported death of Sveno has a false parallel in the specious report of the death of Rinaldo, which stirs up a crisis in the Christian camp. Argillano, provoked by rumors and false dreams sent by Alecto, accuses Goffredo of Rinaldo's murder and starts a rebellion against the Christian leader. Alecto, the malignant genius of the canto, triumphs, although her success in distorting truth testifies more to the depravity of human perception than to the power of a demonic being.

The account of Rinaldo's "death" is a catalogue of the fallacies to which romance perception is susceptible. The story of Sveno's death portends a tragedy that the discovery of Rinaldo's battered armor beside a headless and mutilated corpse seems to confirm, as a "diverse and uncertain rumor" ("un rumor vario e incerto") begins to spread. Again we find ourselves two or three removes

from the event as the discovery of the body is related by Ali-
prando, who must himself interpolate from the testimony of a
young shepherd:

> "Uscir de la foresta
> scòrse molti guerrieri, onde ei s'ascose;
> e ch'un d'essi tenea recisa testa
> per le sue chiome bionde e sanguinose,
> la qual gli parve, rimirando intento,
> d'uom giovenetto, e senza peli al mento."   [8.54]

> ["He saw repair
> A band of soldiers from that forest's shade,
> Of whom one carried by the golden hair
> A head but late cut off with murd'ring blade;
> The face was fair and young, and on the chin
> No sign of beard to bud did yet begin."]

Romance, which experiences the phenomenal world as an impediment to the search for truths, is made to confront its own
deficiencies: clues are misread, identities mistaken, and unreli-
able witnesses believed. The "evidence" is finally assembled,
with Alecto's help, in Argillano's dream:

> Gli figura un gran busto, ond'è diviso
> il capo, e de la destra il braccio è mozzo;
> e sostien con la manca il teschio inciso,
> di sangue e di pallor livido e sozzo.
> Spira, e parla spirando il morto viso;
> e 'l parlar vien co 'l sangue e co 'l singhiozzo:
> "Fuggi, Argillan; non vedi omai la luce?
> fuggi le tende infami e l'empio duce."   [8.60]

> [She showed him a great torso from which the head
> was sundered, and the right hand lopped off;
> and with the left hand it held the severed skull,
> filthy and livid with blood and pallor.
> It breathed, and breathing the dead visage spoke;
> the words came with blood and sobs:
> "Flee, Argillano. Can you not see the light by now?
> Flee the wicked tents and the impious leader."] [My trans.]

Visual misapprehension leads to moral error, and Argillano sounds an open challenge to Goffredo's authority. In terms conspicuously close to those of the advocates of the Reformation, Argillano inveighs against the faithlessness, arrogance, materialism, and ambition of Goffredo (a distinct misrepresentation of his motives as they are disclosed in 1.8) and claims for himself a personal, unauthorized insight into the truth of things. Tasso subtly satirizes the importunity and frustration produced by Argillano's personal "revelation":

> "Io 'l vidi; e non fu sogno, e, ovunque or miri,
> par che dinanzi a gli occhi miei s'aggiri."   [8.68]

> ["I saw it was no dream before mine eyes,
> Howe'er I look, still, still methinks it flies."]

Tasso's general theme is the abuse of language and vision but the canto contains a more specific injunction against the typical obscurity of romance imagination, here implicitly associated with heresy, the abuse of the Word. In both contexts we are meant to see the poverty of the human intellect when it applies itself to spiritual matters. This is Tasso in his role as spokesman for the Counter-Reformation. At best it might be said that the romance poet experiences many of the same constraints felt by the Christian visionary: a sense of privation and distance, an awareness of being twice removed from an original event, and a need for at least symbolic assurances. But the frustration of the romance poet, Tasso would contend, is far greater and it deepens finally into despair.

In a sense this canto describes an inversion of Tasso's plan to show romance enchantment and magic completed in Christian mystery. Argillano leads us in the opposite direction: miracle is reduced to enigma and error, mystery to romance obfuscation, and Christian revelation to the nightmare of a perturbed and rebellious imagination. To see this in perspective, contrast Argillano's dream with its intended counterpart in canto 18: Argillano's vision of Rinaldo's dismembered corpse is a grotesque, demonic parody of Rinaldo's (and Christ's) transfiguration by grace. A vision of wholeness and holiness is perversely foreshadowed in canto 8 by one of mutilation and death.

Tasso returns to the locale of the woods near Jerusalem in canto 13, this time letting us feel the full impact of its unregenerate nature. The pagan sorcerer Ismeno enchants the forest to prevent the Christians from using it to construct more engines of war. The spell that Ismeno casts is an appropriation by romance convention of a landscape familiar from Dante, an image of the world unredeemed from sin and death. Each Christian hero venturing there encounters a phantom of the anguish or the allure to which he is most susceptible (recall Atlante's enchanted palace in *Orlando Furioso*) and returns to the camp defeated, as it were, by himself. Thus Tancredi strikes a tree with his sword and finds that it embodies the spirit of Clorinda, whom he mistakenly killed in the previous canto; he is made to relive his moment of pathos (13.41–46). Tancredi—"weak in love" ("fievole in amore")—can neither reconcile himself to the death of his lover nor prevail against his own concupiscible passion so long as his love is not directed, as all chivalric energy ought to be, toward God.

It may be inferred from the nature of the enchanted woods that what the chivalric romance heroes lack is the axis on which existential dichotomies ought finally to be aligned: the distinctions between spirit and flesh, illusion and reality, death and life are everywhere collapsed. Clorinda informs Tancredi that she is imprisoned by enchantment in the form of a tree: "I know not whether I should say in the body or in the grave." And Tancredi requires a reminder to the effect that "Those who are living should not make war with the dead." The wood first encountered in canto 3 is now an environment of both ontological and spiritual confusion, a region of death-in-life where trees gush blood and the wind moans in human ululation. Romance imagination has intensified the ambivalence implicit in Tasso's first description of the forest (3.75–76).

Dantesque echoes are audible throughout this canto but they are heard in the narrower, disordered space of romance convention. From these enchanted woods there is as yet no access to Christian cosmology. Mysteries cannot be traced to a divine source but are presented as opaque and awesome *maraviglie*. The romance conventions employed in this canto (enchantment, transformation, illusion) are themselves in need of some kind of verification. It is the need to which Tasso addresses himself in the *Discorsi* when he argues for the theoretical compatibility of maraviglia and *verisimilitudine*.

If romance marvels are made credible on being converted into Christian mysteries, Tasso accomplishes this in canto 18. Rinaldo is sent to break the enchantment of the woods and succeeds, not by virtue of his superior strength or his reason but by an appeal to the greater miracle of grace:

> "Padre e Signor; e in me tua grazia piovi,
>   sì che il mio vecchio Adam purghi e rinovi."   [18.14]

> ["Father and Lord, pour your grace into me
>   so that my old Adam is purged and renewed."]
>   [My trans.]

Once again the setting is Mount Olivet, and again the narrative consciously imitates an event from Christian scripture. Rinaldo, like Christ before him, is transfigured:

> La rugiada del ciel su le sue spoglie
>   cade, che parean cenere al colore;
> e sì l'asperge, che 'l pallor ne toglie
>   e induce in esse un lucido candore;
> tal rabbellisce le smarrite foglie
>   a i matutini geli arido fiore;
> e tal di vaga gioventù ritorna
>   lieto il serpente, e di nov'òr s'adorna.   [18.16]

> [The heav'nly dew was on his garments spread,
>   To which compar'd his clothes pale ashes seen,
> And sprinkled so that all that paleness fled,
>   And thence of purest white bright rays out-stream.
> So cheered are the flow'rs, late withered,
>   With the sweet comfort of the morning beam;
> And so, return'd to youth, a serpent old
>   Adorns herself in new and native gold.]

Tasso's simile extends to nature (to fallen nature, as the Edenic serpent suggests) the transfiguring and renewing power of grace. We recall the perpetual twilight, the "everlasting night" of the enchanted woods (13.2), while from Mount Olivet we are offered a new vision, the sight of darkness dividing from light in a dawn that permits us a glimpse of the cosmic plan:

> Era ne la stagion ch'anco non cede
> libero ogni confin la notte al giorno,
> ma l'oriente rosseggiar si vede,
> ed anco è il ciel d'alcuna stella adorno;
> quando ei drizzò vêr l'Oliveto il piede,
> con gli occhi alzati contemplando intorno
> quinci notturne e quindi matutine
> bellezze incorruttibili e divine.
>
> Fra sé stesso pensava: oh quanto belle
> luci il tempio celeste in sé raguna!
> Ha il suo gran carro il dì; l'aurate stelle
> spiega la notte e l'argentata luna:
> ma non è chi vagheggi o questa o quelle;
> e miriam noi torbida luce e bruna,
> ch'un girar d'occhi, un balenar di riso
> scopre in breve confin di fragil viso.   [18.12–13]

It was the time when 'gainst the breaking day
    Rebellious night yet strove, and still repined;
For in the east appear'd the morning grey,
    And yet some lamps in Jove's high palace shined;
When to mount Olivet he took his way,
    And saw (as round about his eyes he twined)
Night's shadows hence, from thence the morning's shine;
This bright, that dark; that earthly, this divine.

Thus to himself he thought: how many bright
    And splendid lamps shine in heav'n's temple high;
Day hath his golden sun, her moon the night,
    Her fix'd and wand'ring stars the azure sky;
So framed all by their Creator's might,
    That still they live and shine, and ne'er shall die,
Till (in a moment) with the last day's brand
They burn, and with them burns sea, air, and land.

Dawn, spring, dew, and sunlight are all clearly symbolic of Christian spiritual renewal; sunset is a daily reminder of the inevitability of the Apocalypse. But the orderly diurnal and seasonal motions of celestial bodies are palpable, natural events as well. The moment of spiritual renewal has signaled a return to the world of natural processes from that of romance illusion.

From Mount Olivet Rinaldo descends into the enchanted woods, which we now understand as a false parallel to the "marvelous domain of God called the world" ("mirabile magisterio di Dio," *Discourses*, p. 77). Enchanted nature imitates the miracle of regeneration but without attaining to its higher significance:

> E sovra e intorno a lui la selva annosa
> tutte parea ringiovenir le foglie:
> s'ammolliscon le scorze, e si rinverde
> più lietamente in ogni pianta il verde.   [18.23]

> Above and around him, all the ancient wood
> seemed to rejuvenate its leaves:
> the bark softened, and every plant
> more happily took on a new green.   [My trans.]

"Seemed" in this passage is a deliberate qualification, implying moral as well as phenomenological uncertainty. Rinaldo encounters here the phantom of his own previous delinquency, Armida, encased in what appears to be (but is not) a myrtle. This is Ovidian nature, a region of metamorphosis and transformation but not of transfiguration in the sense that Rinaldo has experienced it. Divinity is revealed only in a theatrical and artificial sense: sylvan goddesses appear "as the theater shows them, or as we sometimes see in paintings." Rinaldo remains a silent observer, curious and surprised by what he sees but essentially detached. His spiritual awakening has given him the distance that enables him to cut down the myrtle and end the enchantment of the woods (his false love for Armida, his self-love, the sensuous world).

We may be inclined to object that Tasso sacrifices dramatic realism to moralism at this point, but Rinaldo's act is more than a sudden reflex of moralistic revulsion. This episode is the culmination of a sequence that properly includes Dudone's death and promised resurrection in canto 3, the first foray into the woods, the demonic parody of transfiguration in Argillano's vision of Rinaldo's mutilated corpse in canto 8, and Clorinda's transformation in canto 13. This sequence, taken in its entirety, represents Tasso's attempt to close the distance between the temporal and eternal worlds that opened in our first encounter with death. Rinaldo finally succeeds in placing death (along with the illusions and anxieties associated with it) in perspective. We now see nature restored to its proper status:

> non d'incanti terrible, né lieta;
> piena d'orror, ma de l'orror innato.   [18.38]

> neither with dreadful magic nor with gladness;
> full of horror, but of natural horror.   [My trans.]

The gothic distortions of romance magic are dispelled in the clarifying light of Christian revelation.

We are restored to reality by Christian miracle, Tasso maintains, because this miracle affirms the principle by which the world is ordered and moved. It is this belief on which Tasso bases his claim to be at once a Christian poet and an epic poet. The visionary moment does not so much call the hero out of the world of time as permit him to enter it heroically. He attains the serenity that allows him to confront the world's agonistic dimension. He sees the world's "horror" as natural. Death has its place in the scheme of things. Thus Rinaldo emerges from the false, interior world of the self into the world of human history. He moves toward Jerusalem for the first time.

It is the apparent abruptness of transitions like that of Rinaldo's transfiguration—and later that of Armida's conversion—that bothers most of Tasso's readers.[23] If seeing such changes in terms of the poem's larger pattern partly alters our view of them, it does not make them dramatically convincing. For it is not in the nature of the spiritual transformations with which Tasso presents us to be gradual. They do not permit dramatization. Drama belongs rather to romance, that view of the world as a struggle between diverse and equally powerful forces. Romance is the soul divided against itself, projecting its divisions onto the world. It is Tasso's purpose to expose all such discord as illusory. The transformations undergone by Rinaldo and Armida are necessarily sudden because they are perceptual changes, changes in the perception of change itself. Such changes subsume all psychological issues.

Rinaldo's transfiguration allows us in retrospect to see Argillano's dream vision of Rinaldo's dismembered corpse as parodic. Argillano's vision gives us an anatomy of the romance imagination. Its images are fragmentary, insubstantial, and horrific since they are projected from what is essentially a divisive, anarchistic, and heretical mind. The enchanted woods of canto 13 provide another insight into the nature of romance. In this canto, where Tancredi encounters Clorinda in her state of Ovidian transformation, we see that romance enchantment derives its power from the hero's own inability to accept death's finality. In a sense this longing to circumvent the limits of mortality is analogous to the yearning of the Christian pilgrim for eternity. But it is a false eternity to which the romance imagination finally leads us. Romance gives us an image of humanity undying though dead, whereas Christianity offers a vision of death engaged and transcended and thus breaks the enchanted circle.

Epic action takes place in the world of human history. Tasso's position is that a Christian epic is possible because Christianity provides access to that world. In practice, however, Tasso is less inclined than either Ariosto or Spenser to dwell on the image of an earthly *imperium* even as it might finally, in its restored condition, constitute a reflection of the heavenly city. Tasso concludes his poem with a glimpse of Goffredo, still in his bloody armor, hastening through conquered Jerusalem to the temple, scarcely pausing to contemplate his victory before launching his soul toward the New Jerusalem in prayer (20.144). It is evening but an evening that resonates with apocalyptic overtones. (We recall Rinaldo's meditation on the sun, moon, and stars from the top of Mount Olivet in canto 18: "still they live and shine, and ne'er shall die / Till [in a moment] with the last day's brand / They burn, and with them burns sea, air, and land.") The ending of Tasso's poem is a reminder that all heroic actions, all human efforts to build or to redeem cities, are but interludes in the larger sweep of history beginning with the Fall and ending with the Apocalypse. Ariosto and Spenser too are aware that specific epic actions are circumscribed by universal history, that the dynasties they celebrate are only images of a greater end, but at the same time they give more scope to the present moment than does Tasso. Ariosto celebrates a marriage, Spenser a betrothal (*FQ* 1.12), but Tasso relegates the equivalent event in his poem, the union of Rinaldo and Armida, to an offstage future (thereby maintaining the analogy between such events and those of Revelation). Both Ariosto and Spenser make us feel more keenly than does Tasso the reality of the cities in which dynastic ceremonies take place.

Tasso, moreover, shows little interest in playing the part of the dynastic chronicler. After all, he has chosen as the focus of his epic a city with moral but not, in any limited sense, historical connections to his Ferrara. He seems, in fact, reluctant to immerse himself in the chain of events that links his narrative present and his contemporary world even where literary convention would seem to require that he do so. His imitation of Virgil's description of Vulcan's shield is a case in point. It is one of only two instances in the *Liberata* in which Tasso interrupts his text with dynastic prophecy.[24] Furthermore, Rinaldo's shield (canto 17) depicts only his ancestors, his past. Of the narrative future, the bridge to Tasso's present, the hermit is hesitant to speak:

> "Ma l'arte mia per sé dentro al futuro
> non scorge il ver che troppo occulto giace,
> se non caliginoso e dubbio e scuro,
> quasi lunge, per nebbia, incerta face."   [88]

["But not by art or skill of things future
   Can the plain truth revealed be and told,
   Although some knowledge doubtful, dark, obscure,
   We have of coming haps in clouds up-roll'd."]

From the obscurity that is his future the hermit singles out for specific mention only Alfonso II, the ruler of Tasso's Ferrara. In his encomium Tasso alludes briefly and in a general way to Alfonso's ability to execute justice and to his patronage of the arts (92), but it is clear from the lack of emphasis given to these civic virtues that they are for Tasso secondary considerations. It is as if the preservation and government of historical Ferrara were for Tasso intermediate concerns. He finds his full voice only when he projects an image of Alfonso as a militant champion of what one suspects is a Counter-Reformation orthodoxy:

> "Oh s'avvenisse mai che contra gli empi
> che tutte infesteran le terre e i mari,
> e de la pace in quei miseri tempi
> daran le leggi a i popoli più chiari,
> duce sen gisse a vendicare i tempî
> da lor distrutti, e i vïolati altari:
> qual ei giusta faria grave vendetta
> su 'l gran tiranno e su l'iniqua setta!"   [93]

"But if it hap, against those wicked bands
    That sea and earth infest with blood and war,
And in these wretched times to noble lands
    Give laws of peace false and unjust that are,
That he be sent to drive their guilty hands
    From Christ's pure altars and high temples far;
O what revenge, what vengeance shall he bring
On that false sect and their accursed king!"

Thus does Tasso urge Alfonso to be another Goffredo and so to continue in the spirit of the First Crusade to chasten paganism and heresy. In effect, Tasso urges his readers to accept the invisible reality of the New Jerusalem as more relevant to us as humans than the visible reality of Ferrara. The images of Alfonso and Ferrara quickly fade to reveal those of the Christian warrior and the City of God behind them. Tasso, like his Goffredo, is always impatient to contemplate the *quo tendis*, the anagogical and eschatological implications of things.

CHAPTER FIVE

SPENSER:
The Dynastic Pair, Britomart and Artegall

Book 3 of *The Faerie Queene* is the romance core of the poem, the point at which Spenser seems to have elected to follow Ariosto rather than Virgil in matters of narrative form and content. Book 3 replaces the single hero and the linear, conclusive action of books 1 and 2 with a plot composed of a variety of incidents, a pattern of "Accidents" rather than "intendments," in Spenser's words (Letter to Ralegh), arranged according to the romance principle of entrelacement. The debt to Ariosto is both general and specific, as readers have noted.[1] But book 3 is also the starting point for the poem's dynastic plot, the story of Britomart and Artegall, which although immediately derived from the story of Bradamante and Ruggiero in *Orlando Furioso*, ultimately refers us back to the *Aeneid*. We find ourselves at the familiar point of confluence of romance and epic matter, where the romance poet reveals his epic aspirations.

The apparent confusion of book 3 constitutes a stage of critical reassessment through which classical epic must pass on its way to becoming Christian epic. Spenserian romance consists of a pattern of deliberate reversals of epic norms calculated to elicit awareness of the scope of Christian paradox, to prepare for a revelation of truths held to be beyond the capacity of Virgil to envision. In book 3 Spenser transfers the role of dynastic hero from male Aeneas to female Britomart and substitutes the narrative matter of love for the matter of war not out of sheer perversity but because, like Ariosto and Tasso before him, Spenser seeks to redefine epic imperatives in accordance with the more inclusive idealism of Christianity. Love, we are to discover once again, is not finally an impediment to the establishment of empire; love, at least as it is construed in Augustinian terms,[2] is rather empire's most basic element. Thus in retrospect from book 4 Spenser takes pains to say that he feels no embarrassment for having made love the subject of a heroic narrative:

> The rugged forhead that with graue foresight
>   Welds kingdomes causes, and affaires of state,
>   My looser rimes (I wote) doth sharply wite,
>   For praising loue, as I haue done of late,
>   And magnifying louers deare debate;
>   By which fraile youth is oft to follie led,
>   Through false allurement of that pleasing baite,
>   That better were in vertues discipled,
> Then with vaine poemes weeds to haue their fancies fed.
>
> Such ones ill iudge of loue, that cannot loue,
>   Ne in thier frosen hearts feele kindly flame:
>   For thy they ought not thing vnknowne reproue,
>   Ne naturall affection faultlesse blame,
>   For fault of few that haue abusd the same.
>   For it of honor and all vertue is
>   The roote, and brings forth glorious flowres of fame,
>   That crowne true louers with immortall blis,
> The meed of them that loue, and do not liue amisse. [4.pr.1–2][3]

In attaching to his dynastic hero and heroine the interdependent and mutually perfecting virtues of justice and chastity,[4] Spenser clearly follows Ariosto, whom Spenser understands to have aimed at a reinterpretation of Augustan *imperium* in Christian terms. The institution of justice alone might permit the establishment of an empire such as Anchises envisions in the sixth book of the *Aeneid,* or a "common-weal" corresponding to the Old Testament rule of law, but to represent empire as it can be under the dispensation of New Testament grace, justice must be wedded to the virtues associated with Britomart as she evolves in the course of books 3–5: love, equity, and mercy.[5]

Spenser, I am suggesting, draws on Ariostan romance with a clear understanding of its potential as an instrument for overgoing Virgil. Britomart is a case in point. She is derived from Ariosto but from that part of the *Furioso,* as we have seen, that attempts to assimilate the *Aeneid.* We may trace Britomart's origins to Virgil by a direct route by turning to the *Ciris,* where we find her namesake, Britomartis, a virgin who takes flight into the sea to escape the love of King Minos.[6] Britomartis is the source of Britomart's impulse to identify chastity with virginity and to defend this virtue at all costs. The allusion to the *Ciris* is complicated, however, by the fact that it is not Virgil's Britomartis but his Scylla, the exemplum of unchaste behavior, upon whom Spenser's heroine is in other respects modeled. It is the dialogue between Scylla and her nurse Carme, for instance, that Spenser imitates in 3.2, where Britomart's nurse Glauce endeavors to cure her mistress of a potentially tragic and destructive passion for Artegall. Scylla falls in love with King Minos despite the enmity existing between him and her father, King Nisus, and subsequently betrays her father for her lover's sake. Britomart, as Thomas P. Roche has observed, is a fusion of the two women of the *Ciris,* the chaste Britomartis and the passionate Scylla:

> They represent the two extremes of dedicated virginity and lust, extremes that lead to a god-like transmutation or to a debasement of humanity, bringing with it political as well as personal ruin. Spenser, like Virgil, sees love as a force that can destroy nations as well as individuals, and as a result his Britomart shares qualities with both Britomartis and Scylla. Her chastity is derived from Britomartis, but it is a chastity that springs from a love as passionate as Scylla's.[7]

If this is the problem of Britomart, it is also potentially a solution to a problem, specifically the problem of the *Ciris.* In the Virgilian story a tragic outcome is inevitable, given the antithetical nature of the choices with which characters are presented. In Spenser's revision of the story a resolution of tragic antagonisms is implicit in the fact that a single heroine embodies what were for Virgil conflicting impulses. Spenser has redefined the crisis of the Virgilian epyllion in romance terms as a quest on the part of Britomart for an integrated and a fulfilled selfhood.

If for Virgil the notion of a being in whom chastity and passion are equal forces is an inconceivable paradox, it is not for Spenser. His Britomart is at the outset of book 3 associated with figures of unassailable virginity, Diana and Belphoebe, but as Britomart accedes to her dynastic destiny by pursuing Artegall, "whose image she had seene in *Venus* looking glas" (3.1.8), she effectively relocates chastity in the institution of marriage. Venus will have a place along with Diana in the composition of the expanded ideal that Britomart finally represents. Thus the universe in which Britomart moves is not in the end one of mutually exclusive alternatives. Her passion for Artegall, for instance, is not barred by any enmity between him and her father, as is Scylla's love for King Minos, but by the fact that she has fallen in love with an image in a mirror instead of a real man (3.2.38). To Britomart it seems an even greater dilemma to love "th'only shade and semblant of a knight," and so it may be, but this problem is solved once Artegall's existence is established. In other words, Spenser substitutes a visionary crisis for what in Virgil was an ethical and a political one. Problems of doing become subordinate to the problem of seeing.

The contiguity of romance and epic is apparent in terms of narrative structure as well as character, as an examination of the first three cantos of book 3 reveals. It may at first seem that with book 3 Spenser abandons the formal plan of books 1 and 2 and in doing so discards any epic ambitions he may have entertained. But the cantos that introduce Britomart, however digressive and disordered they may appear, in fact conform within a small compass to epic design as Spenser (following Horace) describes it in his letter to Ralegh:

> A Poet thrusteth into the middest, euen where it most concerneth him, and there recoursing to the thinges forepaste, and diuining of thinges to come, maketh a pleasing Analysis of all.

Thus the *Aeneid*, for instance, begins at a comparatively advanced point in the plot and then brings the reader up to date as Aeneas recounts in books 2 and 3 the story of his previous experiences. Similarly, we encounter Britomart after she has already embarked on her quest for Artegall and then recourse "to thinges forepaste" for two cantos in order to fill in the narrative gap. The correlation between Spenser's and Virgil's narratives is in fact strikingly precise. As Aeneas in book 1 enters Carthage, the counterimage of the city that is his destined goal, so Britomart in canto

1 enters the Castle Joyous, the locus of Chastity's opposite, Malecasta ("badly chaste"). And as Dido is smitten with love for Aeneas, so, in a farcical revision of the *Aeneid*, is Malecasta for Britomart (cf. *Aen.* 4.54–67, and *FQ* 3.1.47).[8] Book 2 of the *Aeneid* retraces the story of Aeneas from the fall of Troy and book 3 tells of the subsequent wanderings of the Trojan remnant from Troy to Carthage, at which point the narrative resumes in the dramatic present. Canto 2 of Spenser's third book likewise involves a fall of sorts as the poet digresses to tell how Britomart first conceived her passion for Artegall. The third canto describes the visit to Merlin's cave, after which we arrive again at the temporal setting of canto 1.

It is the analogy between Britomart's fall into love and the fall of Troy on which Spenser's revision of Virgil turns. With this substitution of an amorous for a heroic-historical theme, the technique of narrative digression acquires a new dimension. To look back into Britomart's past is also to look deeper into her soul. Thus in canto 1 Britomart receives a slight wound from an arrow shot by one of Malecasta's henchmen, Gardante. The next canto, moving not only backward in time but also inward, explores the deeper significance of this incident by recasting it as metaphor. Britomart gazes at the image of Artegall in her father's mirror:

> The Damzell well did vew his personage,
>   And liked well, ne further fastned not,
>   But went her way; ne her vnguilty age
>   Did weene, vnwares, that her vnlucky lot
>   Lay hidden in the bottome of the pot;
>   Of hurt vnwist most daunger doth redound:
>   But the false Archer, which that arrow shot
>   So slyly, that she did not feele the wound,
> Did smyle full smoothly at her weetlesse wofull stound.
>
> [2.26]

The third canto then reverses the process of romance regression as Britomart learns through Merlin's prophecy that her love for Artegall has been sanctioned by Providence. Her passion is not, she discovers, like the fall of Troy an irremediable catastrophe that she must put behind her, but the "hard begin" of her destiny. With this reversal the strategy by which Spenser intends at once to assimilate and to overgo Virgil becomes apparent. The opening movement of the *Aeneid* is preparation for the tragic fourth book, in which Aeneas is compelled to choose between Dido and Rome, love and empire. For Britomart the choice initially seems the same: Her love for Artegall is an apparently destructive affliction that draws her away from her father's kingdom into the recesses of Faeryland. But at the point of farthest withdrawal she discovers that her love will advance rather than thwart the progress of dynastic history. She is not like Aeneas asked to choose between empire and love; she is exhorted to pursue both.

The story of Britomart might be thought of as a revision of the plot of the first four books of the *Aeneid* in terms of the Christian paradox of the *felix culpa*. Like Milton's Adam (*PL* 12.469–78), Britomart will discover that her "fall," as it sets the stage for a revelation of providential benevolence, is in the long run an occasion for joy rather than grief.[9] This is not to say that Britomart as we first encounter her has sinned, but neither has she fully grasped the workings of divine grace. She is virtuous, but her virtue, "stedfast chastity," is designed to operate in a fallen world. It is like temperance a self-dependent and defensive virtue;[10] it manifests itself in the form of resistance to what is perceived as a corrupting environment. Thus Britomart undertakes a quest for love as if love were war. She encloses herself in inpenetrable armor, equips herself with an enchanted spear, and in her first encounter with Artegall engages him in battle. She contains in the lesser world of her self all the conflicts she sees in the larger world in which she moves. She is a woman in a man's costume, a British maiden in Saxon armor, and an aggressor whose actions are motivated by an instinct for self-defense, indeed, by fear.[11]

Britomart's chastity—her capacity to resist the temptation of unchaste behavior, at least—is not really the virtue at risk. Thus her first adventure, the episode in Malecasta's Castle Joyous, is strangely unthreatening. But as Britomart's virtue is as yet unperfected, the episode in canto 1 is not without its relevance to her. Malecasta, or rather her six knights, confront all arrivals at the Castle Joyous with the no-win choice of serving her if they have no lady of their own, converting to Malecasta's service if they have one, or accepting Malecasta as a reward should they triumph in battle over them. As Britomart observes, "the choise is hard" but hers is a special case:

> Therefore a read Sir, if thou haue a loue.
>   Loue haue I sure, (quoth she) but Lady none;
>   Yet will I not fro mine owne loue remoue,
>   Ne to your Lady will I seruice done,
>   But wreake your wrongs wrought to this knight alone,
>   And proue his cause.   [3.1.28]

Britomart is by reason of her sex immune to Malecasta's laws. (That she stands outside the law, but without being unvirtuous, is significant with respect to her relationship with Artegall and her association with the principle of equity in book 5.) Britomart can permit herself to be escorted to the Castle Joyous without thereby committing an unchaste act because she is entitled to a piece of sophistry that allows her to do so without accepting Malecasta's terms.

But in a sense there is for Britomart a greater danger in not having to confront Malecasta directly than there might have been in a less oblique challenge, for Britomart manages to emerge from the Castle Joyous without coming to terms with its implications for her. On the walls of an inner room are tapestries depicting the story of Venus and Adonis, a courtship that is in many respects a parodic version of Britomart's quest for Artegall. Both are narratives viewed from a feminine perspective. Both involve males who are destined to die prematurely. Artegall, like Ariosto's Ruggiero (and like Achilles, whose armor Artegall wears), is to be killed shortly after his marriage to Britomart, "Too rathe cut off by practise criminall / Of secret foes, that him shall make in mischiefe fall" (3.3.28). Likewise Adonis: "For who can shun the chaunce, that dest'ny doth ordaine?" Both are to be awarded a kind of consolation for death, Adonis in his transmutation into "a daintie flowre," Artegall in his posterity.

Venus, to be sure, is like Malecasta the antithesis of chastity. She embodies lust as Shakespeare analyzes it in sonnet 129, an inherently frustrating, inevitably tragic disequilibrium of subject and object. Venus, in whom the distinctions of maternal and connubial, divine and human love are hopelessly blurred, possesses Adonis in his sleep (as Malecasta attempts to do with Britomart) but loses him to the boar when he awakens. And we are meant, finally, to see an important difference between the fates of Adonis and Artegall. Adonis's metamorphosis into a flower is a sterile and an artificial approximation of the consolation offered Britomart for Artegall's death:

> With thee yet shall he leaue for memory
> Of his late puissaunce, his Image dead,
> That liuing him in all actiuity
> To thee shall represent.   [3.29]

As do Ariosto and Tasso before him, Spenser sees that the art generated by desire is a false art. Venus employs a secret art of "sleights and sweet allurements" in her wooing of Adonis (1.35), and this art corresponds to that of the tapestry itself. Both are predominantly visual. The art of cupidinous love, and by extension the art in which that art of love is depicted, are voyeuristic:

> And whilest he bath'd, with her two crafty spyes,
> She secretly would search each daintie lim.   [36][12]

With the death of Adonis the art of Venus and that of the tapestry converge:

> Him to a daintie flowre she did transmew,
> Which in that cloth was wrought, as if it liuely grew.   [38]

The tacit qualification of "liuely" with "as if" establishes the limitations of both the artisan of the tapestry and Venus. Neither can do more than render something lifelike.

Despite the obvious differences between the legend of Venus and Adonis and that of Britomart and Artegall, the parallelism should not lightly be dismissed. As an epic poet, Spenser knew that Venus was not only lust but also the mother of Aeneas and the chief divine advocate of his Roman destiny. And as a Christian poet Spenser knew that love was the basis of the true *imperium*. The disdain Britomart displays for what she sees in the Castle Joyous (40) indicates a lack of self-awareness on her part, a denial of her partial identity with Malecasta. Both Malecasta and Britomart move within the narrow confines of the self, Malescasta with oppressive cupidity, as she imposes her will on all who approach her realm, and Britomart with defensive chastity, as she repels everyone she encounters. Malecasta is in a way the part of Britomart that derives from the Scylla rather than the Britomartis of the *Ciris*. If there is a lesson for Britomart in her experience in the Castle Joyous, it is not so much the need to spurn passion as the need to recognize herself in her opposite. What is required is an understanding of chastity not as restraint but as a force transcending and harmonizing the apparent discord of virginity and lust. The point is pressed home in the closing stanzas of the canto, when Britomart is wounded by an arrow shot by one of Malecasta's knights (Gardante) in the fray following Britomart's rejection of Malecasta's nocturnal advances. The wound suggests at least partial vulnerability to passion on Britomart's part. If she has not reciprocated, Britomart has expressed sympathy for Malecasta's feelings:

> Full easie was for her to haue beliefe,
>> Who by self-feeling of her feeble sexe,
>> And by long triall of the inward griefe,
>> Wherewith imperious loue her hart did vexe,
>> Could iudge what paines do louing harts perplexe.
>> Who meanes no guile, beguiled soonest shall,
>> And to faire semblaunce doth light faith annexe;
>> The bird, that knowes not the false fowlers call,
> Into his hidden net full easily doth fall.   [54]

And so she should, since Britomart shares with Malecasta the fate of having as the object of her desire a figure that has (as yet) no being except as it exists in her own mind.

If Britomart's costume is a clue to understanding her character, she is a creature wholly cut off from the world through her own contrivance. Such insularity has many facets. The armor that protects her innocence also preserves her naiveté, of which there is ample evidence in the encounter with Malecasta:

> For thy she would not in discourteise wise,
> Scorne the faire offer of good will profest;
> For great rebuke it is, loue to despise,

> Or rudely sdeigne a gentle harts request;
> But with faire countenaunce, as beseemed best,
> Her entertaynd; nath'lesse she inly deemd
> Her loue too light, to wooe a wandring guest.   [55]

What is a defense is by the same token a disguise, a "bold deuise" conceived by Glauce, "that therefore nought our passage may empeach" (3.3.53). If she is sometimes gullible, Britomart is elsewhere instinctively disingenuous in her dealings with others, as when she provokes Guyon "with faind gainesay" into extolling Artegall's virtues in canto 2. Both her naiveté and her maidenly guile, however, are in the last analysis simply projections onto the world of her own inner disequilibrium, the product of her infatuation with "th'only shade and semblant of a knight." Britomart is brought to painful awareness of that disequilibrium in canto 2.

The instrument of this awareness is the mirror the great magician Merlin created for Britomart's father King Ryence to reveal to him "what euer foe had wrought, or frend had faynd." The mirror belongs to a general class of romance symbols, among which we may include both Armida's mirror and the diamond shield that Carlo and Ubaldo use to release Rinaldo from Armida's enchantment in the *Liberata*. That is, Merlin's mirror has the capacity, rather ambiguously, to reflect whatever "to the looker appertaynd" (19). As a reflective device it is potentially an instrument of either self-love or historical self-awareness, romance or epic vision, depending on how it is used. King Ryence uses it for the defense of his realm (21). When Britomart uses the mirror, however, the emphasis falls heavily on "selfe":

> Her selfe awhile therein she vewd in vaine;
> Tho her auizing of the vertues rare
> Which thereof spoken were, she gan againe
> Her to bethinke of, that mote to her selfe pertaine.   [22]

The moment is reminiscent of that in which Orlando internalizes the providential storm that saves Paris to create the imagery of romantic passion (*OF* 8.71–86).[13] Britomart's concerns are personal rather than civic, and thus she substitutes a romance obsession for heroic obligation, an image of a lover for one of the city. She adapts the terms of "kingdomes causes, and affaires of state" to the vocabulary of the heart:

> But as it falleth, in the gentlest harts
> Imperious loue hath highest set his throne,
> And tyrannizeth in the bitter smarts
> Of them, that to him buxome are and prone. [23]

She creates an *imperium* for Love and with the disastrous consequences familiar from the Petrarchan sonnet tradition elevates Love to the status of tyrant. The conflation of Mars and Venus, the confusion of the themes of love and war that is everywhere evident in Britomart's dress and behavior, follows in due course.

When she first sees the image of Artegall in Merlin's mirror, Britomart, still innocent of love in "her vnguilty age," continues on her way until the unknown malady begins to disturb her sleep. Glauce attempts to diagnose the disease and vainly sets about applying superficial remedies (34). The wound, however, is discovered to be internal and thus incurable by Glauce's maternal ministrations. As the cause becomes more apparent Glauce suggests that Britomart has fixed her affections on "the semblant pleasing most your mind," a projection of her own imagination, and that this affords the consolation that the image, if unobtainable, cannot be in itself objectionable. It is no consolation, however, for Britomart, who grasps the narcissistic implications:

> But wicked fortune mine, though mind be good,
> Can haue no end, nor hope of my desire,
> But feed on shadowes, whiles I die for food,
> And like a shadow wexe, whiles with entire
> Affection, I doe languish and expire.
> I fonder, then *Cephisus* foolish child,
> Who hauing vewed in a fountaine shere
> His face, was with the loue thereof beguild;
> I fonder loue a shade, the bodie farre exild. [44]

She is, after all, looking in a mirror when she sees Artegall. It remains for Britomart to cross the distance between self and other, and otherness now looms in several senses: Artegall is image rather than substance, Faery rather than British, a figure apparently of the "antique" past rather than the present (25), and male. The threshold at which Britomart now stands may be described as a sexual awakening, a movement from childish, innocent, albeit narcissistic passion to mature adult love.[14] Like Milton's Eve in her first moments of consciousness (*PL* 4.449–91), Britomart must make the transition from self-love to love of another. But the passage is equally, as Spenser's renewed invocation to his muse in the next canto indicates, from amorous to heroic matter:

> Begin then, O dearest sacred Dame,
>> Daughter of *Phoebus* and of *Memorie*,
>> That doest ennoble with immortall name
>> The warlike Worthies, from antiquitie,
>> In thy great volume of Eternitie:
>> Begin, O *Clio*, and recount from hence
>> My glorious Soueraines goodly auncestrie,
>> Till that by dew degrees and long protense,
> Thou haue it lastly brought vnto her Excellence.   [3.4]

Love, the kind of love, that is, through which Britomart will be transformed from a daughter into a mother and in which she is not only a lover but also the object of love, marks the entrance into history. If this is a fall from innocence it is one of those "destined descents" that stirs up "th' Heroes high intents," as the poet puts it in stanza 2, a fall that, taking its meaning from that of Adam and Eve, initiates historical consciousness and may, given the "fatall purpose of diuine foresight," eventually be construed a fortunate one.

Britomart, however, has not yet completed her destined descent. This she will do only when she enters the underworld cavern of Merlin, the creator of the magic mirror, from whom she will hear the dynastic prophecy that finally proves her fall fortunate. She learns that she will marry Artegall and that together they will begin the line that culminates in Elizabeth. But for the moment the way back into the historical world from which she has withdrawn lies in further withdrawal. She must fully grasp the otherness of Artegall, of Faeryland, of the world she sees reflected in the mirror before she can come to perceive the possible oneness of the opposites he and she represent. That she does finally arrive at such a perception, however, is crucial. The movement of the romance quest is circular, from England into Faeryland and back to England. What she discovers of Artegall in Merlin's cave is that he is not a Faery knight (a misapprehension under which he himself labors and from which she must rescue him) but is ""'sprong of seed terrestriall" (3.26). He is "sonne of Gorlois / And brother vnto *Cador*, Cornish king" (27), and thus half brother to Arthur. He is not "antique" but her living contemporary; and if he is male, even that distinction is not irreconcilable, for, as the hermaphroditic image with which Spenser originally concluded book 3 implies, marriage is the blending of the two sexes into a new entity, man and wife made one flesh.

Britomart's journey from the England of King Ryence into Faeryland and back reflects the general strategy of *The Faerie Queene* as it immerses its reader in its fictional and temporally remote environment with the aim of returning his gaze in the end to Elizabethan England. Britomart's initial confusion on seeing in Merlin's mirror the image of Artegall in his armor of "antique mould" thus serves as a warning that Faeryland is a potentially hazardous metaphor. One can easily mistake Spenser's purpose in inviting us to regress into the archaic and fictive setting of his poem. Thus can one forget that romance is for Spenser a liminal experience of disorientation from which one must emerge, finally, into the daylight of the historical world. *The Faerie Queene* continually looks ahead to the time when its allegory can be discarded, when its double images of Belphoebe and Gloriana can resolve into the single figure of Elizabeth.[15] The circular movement of romance wandering must be carried to completion. The danger lies in allowing the imagination to become arrested in the past, in Faeryland, as Britomart does in her initial passionate fixation on Artegall and as the narrator of book 3 does in his meditations on Britomart, the Arthurian era and the classical ages.

Spenser speaks to his reader in book 3 in a voice tremulous with nostalgia for the glories of "antiquity" and with corresponding disdain for the contemporary world:

> Where is the Antique glory now become,
>   That whilome wont in women to appeare?

Where be the braue atchieuements doen by some?
Where be the battels, where the shield and speare,
And all the conquests, which them high did reare,
That matter made for famous Poets verse,
And boastfull men so oft abasht to heare?
Bene they all dead, and laid in dolefull herse?
Or doen they onely sleepe, and shall againe reuerse?

If they be dead, then woe is me therefore:
But if they sleepe, O let them soone awake:
For all too long I burne with enuy sore,
To heare the warlike feates, which *Homere* spake
Of bold *Penthesilee,* which made a lake
Of *Greekish* bloud so oft in *Troian* plaine;
But when I read, how stout *Debora* strake
Proud *Sisera,* and how *Camill'* hath slaine
The huge *Orsilochus,* I swell with great disdaine.

[3.4.1.-2][16]

It is important to realize that Spenser in his capacity as narrator is
not speaking *in propria persona.* That Spenser's narrator burns
with "enuy sore" as he contemplates the supposed superiority of
a former age betrays his limitation. His passion, like that of
Britomart for Artegall, or rather for the antique image of Artegall,
is the result of an incomplete understanding of its object. The
narrator's attitude to history will no less than Britomart's conception of herself need to be revised as the dynastic theme unfolds.
The "Antique glory" for which the Spenserian poet burns is the
Amazonian aggressiveness of Britomart (or that of Radigund in
book 5) before she has been reconciled to Artegall. As a recommendation of a virtue that Elizabeth ought to embody (3.4.3), this
vision of female martial supremacy needs to be reassessed, as it
will be in book 5, in the light of the ideal of justice, which is by its
broadest definition a concept of balance.

The poet's praise of antiquity in the beginnings of each of the
previous three cantos of book 3 reveals similar limitations. Canto
1 applauds the use of arms in "antique times" in these terms:

O goodly vsage of those antique times,
In which the sword was seruant vnto right;

> When not for malice and contentious crimes,
> But all for praise, and proofe of manly might,
> The martiall brood accustomed to fight:
> Then honour was the meed of victorie,
> And yet the vanquished had no despight:
> Let later age that noble vse enuie,
> Vile rancour to auoid, and cruell surquedrie.   [13]

But this hymn to an age "In which the sword was seruant vnto right" ironically follows the scene in which Britomart emerges from nowhere and without cause assaults Guyon, the Knight of Temperance. Canto 2 presents a sophistical interpretation of law as a conspiracy of men, conscious of their inferiority, to preserve their dominance over women:

> But by record of antique times I find,
>   That women wont in warres to beare most sway,
>   And to all great exploits them selues inclind:
>   Of which they still the girlond bore away,
>   Till enuious Men fearing their rules decay,
>   Gan coyne streight lawes to curb their liberty.   [2]

Book 5 will present the history of law from another perspective, as the evolution of justice rather than the erosion of natural female superiority.

The opening stanzas of canto 3 expose the crux of the matter of assessing the poet's praise of antiquity. Antiquity, he tells us, did well to deem love a God:

> That ouer mortall minds hast so great might,
>   To order them, as best to thee doth seeme,
>   And all their actions to direct aright;
>   The fatall purpose of diuine foresight,
>   Thou doest effect in destined descents,
>   Through deepe impression of thy secret might,
>   And stirredst vp th'Heroes high intents,
> Which the late world admyres for wondrous moniments. [2]

At this point it becomes evident that the speaker's notion of "Antiquitie" is tied up with his understanding of "Love." The statement that antiquity named love a god, as Harry Berger suggests, seems to imply an identification of love as eros and may thus recall the argument in the *Symposium* between Socrates and those who would in effect confer on a state of human consciousness the status of an objective deity. "Such a projection," Berger notes, "permits the soul to shift responsibility."[17] One might add that by the Spenserian narrator's definition love resembles the power that tyrannizes the Petrarchan lover—and Britomart in the moment of her first glimpse into Merlin's mirror. But Spenser's description of love is deliberately ambiguous. The reader is left to decide whether the deified love of which the narrator speaks is eros or Christ, who orders mortal minds and directs human actions according to his knowledge of what is best for humanity, not exclusively for himself, and whose "fatall purpose" includes his own destined descent and does not imply the victimization of those who submit to him.

It is the speaker's tone of nostalgia that argues his conception of love as eros, for nostalgia betrays basic feelings of helplessness and hopelessness regarding the present and the future that would be inappropriate in a fully Christian view of history. Deified eros is a whimsical tyrant, a human passion conceived as a force outside and ungovernable by humanity. To make a god of eros is not only to abdicate one's moral responsibility but also to relinquish any genuine claim for personal greatness. Heroic achievements must await the kindling of the "sacred fire" from above. The speaker's disillusionment with the present is thus the consequence of having projected onto it his own moral poverty. Admiration for the past, moreover, is his only recourse, given the inscrutability and unreliability of the god he worships: its only certain actions are those it has already taken. Eros does not, like the God of Scripture, communicate to humanity his plan for history. The narrator's unqualified reverence for the past is not Britomart's intense and complex feeling for Artegall, but both are emotions that arise from a misapprehension of love—and consequently a misconception of the nature of history—that Spenser does not for long leave unchallenged.

In canto 3 Merlin forces Britomart to reassess her conceptions of love and time by embodying the ambiguities with which those issues have been charged. He straddles the two traditions of romance and epic: He is a descendant of both Ariosto's Merlin and Virgil's Anchises. He is the dynastic prophet, the agent of epic historical consciousness, but he is also a romance victim of love, a prisoner held in bondage by his own magic, turned against him by the false Lady of the Lake (3.10–11). His cave is a typically romance locale, "low vnderneath the ground, In a deepe delue, farre from the vew of day," but Spenser locates the place on the map of Wales with the precision characteristic of an epic poet, pausing to point out that it can be visited by the present-day traveler (8). Spenser makes a display of pseudoantiquarian interest in the derivation of the name Cayr-Merdin from Maridunum (7) to invest the moment of Britomart's arrival there with an aura of authenticity.

Merlin is the source of romance maraviglia in book 3:

> For he by words could call out of the sky
>   Both Sunne and Moone, and make them him obay:
>   The land to sea, and sea to maineland dry,
>   And darkesome night he eke could turne to day:
>   Hugh hostes of men he could alone dismay,
>   And hostes of men of meanest things could frame,
>   When so him list his enimies to fray:
>   That to this day for terror of his fame,
> The feends do quake, when any him to them does name. [12]

But this is magic accommodating the requirements of epic verisimilitude in the manner Tasso recommends:

> One same action can then be both marvellous and verisimilar: marvellous when regarded in itself and confined within natural limits, verisimilar when considered apart from these limits in terms of its cause, which is a powerful supernatural force accustomed to performing such marvels.[18]

In this way Merlin's magic finds its ultimate source in Christian miracle. Merlin's powers are distinctly reminiscent of those attributed to Fidelia in 1.10.20:

> And when she list poure out her larger spright,
>   She would commaund the hastie Sunne to stay,

Or backward turne his course from heauens hight;
Sometimes great hostes of men she could dismay;
And eke huge mountaines from their natiue seat
She would commaund, themselues to beare away,
And throw in raging sea with roaring threat.
Almightie God her gaue such powre, and puissance great.

And Fidelia's feats in turn allude to scriptural testimony of the miraculous power of faith. Joshua commands the sun to stand still (Josh. 10.12), Hezekiah turns the sun back (2 Kings 20.10), Gideon dismays the Midianites (Judg. 7), and Christ speaks of a faith capable of moving mountains (Matt. 21.21). Merlin, then, presides over what is by now a familiar transformation: romance becomes epic as epic is redefined in the light of Christian revelation.

For Britomart the encounter with Merlin entails first coming to terms with her basic ambivalences. Until now she has been an innocent tormented with guilt, confronting the world in a posture simultaneously aggressive and defensive, deceptive and naive. Britomart and Glauce approach Merlin cautiously, Britomart in disguise and Glauce with the intention of concealing the true cause of Britomart's complaint by attributing it to demonic possession (18). But Spenser's Merlin, like Ariosto's (and Virgil's Anchises) has long anticipated the hero's arrival, and like Ariosto's Merlin Spenser's will reinterpret what has seemed an instance of romance "misfortune," her love for Artegall (5), as a fortunate fall by virtue of his knowledge of the providential plan:

> It was not, *Britomart*, thy wandring eye,
>   Glauncing vnwares in charmed looking glas,
>   But the streight course of heauenly destiny,
>   Led with eternall prouidence, that has
>   Guided thy glaunce. . . .   [24]

What Britomart will learn from Merlin is that her shame cannot and should not be hidden. Guilt is the first stage of self-knowledge in a fallen world but the second stage involves the perception that salvation ensues from consciousness of sin. What is required is not, as Glauce has thought, a cure but enlightenment, not avoidance of a seemingly tragic fate but acceptance of destiny in a new spirit (25). Thus Merlin penetrates both Glauce's guile and Britomart's disguise:

> The doubtfull Mayd, seeing her selfe descryde,
>   Was all abasht, and her pure yuory
>   Into a cleare Carnation suddeine dyde;
>   As faire *Aurora* rising hastily,
>   Doth by her blushing tell, that she did lye
>   All night in old *Tithonus* frosen bed,
>   Whereof she seemes ashamed inwardly.   [20]

Britomart's blush is a mixture of embarrassment and radiance. The Aurora simile comes from the fourth book of the *Aeneid* (584–85, 6–7, 129), where it occurs in association with Dido's fiery passion for Aeneas in a pattern of imagery that culminates in Dido's funeral pyre. But if Britomart is like Dido in her passion for Artegall, she becomes like Dido with a non-Virgilian result, as Merlin's prophecy makes clear two stanzas later:

> For from thy wombe a famous Progenie
> Shall spring, out of the auncient *Troian* blood,
> Which shall reuiue the sleeping memorie
> Of those same antique Peres, the heauens brood,
> Which *Greeke* and *Asian* riuers stained with their blood. [22]

In its association with Britomart the Aurora simile becomes an assurance that love can be transformed into a positive, generating force like sunlight. The realization of this potential, or the arrival at the moment when Britomart will no longer be constrained by her feelings of shame to lurk behind her "cloudy vele," is the goal of chastity. We shall have arrived there when love can be confessed without shame, when Britomart can reveal herself from behind the defensive armor she wears, and the likeness of the human image to the divine that existed before the Fall is again apparent. [19] In *The Faerie Queene* that moment is adumbrated once again in Britomart's encounter with Artegall in book 4.

> The wicked stroke vpon her helmet chaunst,
>   And with the force, which in it selfe it bore,
>   Her ventayle shard away, and thence forth glaunst

A downe in vaine, ne harm'd her any more.
With that her angels face, vnseene afore,
Like to the ruddie morne appeard in sight,
Deawed with siluer drops, through sweating sore,
But somewhat redder, then bessem'd aright,
Through toylesome heate and labour of her weary
            fight.   [4.6.19]

Merlin's prophecy of Britomart's dynastic future is in a sense a continuation of his lesson in self-awareness. Merlin transposes onto British chronicle matter the romance themes of exile and return and division and reunification. As he forges an analogy between the patterns of romance action and British (and Christian) history, he presents Britomart with an interpretive choice like that which confronts the reader of romance narrative, whether to regard history as an indeterminate cycle of loss and recovery, as romance wandering projected on a national scale, or as a coherent, teleological process, conforming finally to the salvific, providential scheme. Merlin's subject is the exile of the Britons, descendants of Trojan Brutus (see 2.10.9), and the eventual restoration of their line in the person of Henry VII, the first of the Tudor monarchs. The history of the British crown recapitulates romance narrative in tracing a movement from "princely bowre to wastfull wood" (42) and back through an "eternall vnion" of "nations different afore" (49). The Britons are first driven into Wales by the Saxons (33), who are in turn defeated by the Danes (46). The country then falls to William the Conqueror (47), whose line continues until "the terme is full accomplished" and "the Briton bloud their crowne againe reclame" with the advent of Henry Tudor. His marriage to Elizabeth of York, which reconciles the two warring houses of York and Lancaster, marks the end of England's long history of "ciuile armes" (49). Spenser makes of this event an instance of historical recursus, for the Tudor marriage will be a reenactment of the union of Britomart and Artegall, two "warlike minds" which initially confront each other antagonistically. So far so good. British history builds toward the inauguration of an era of "sacred Peace" through marriage, the goal of romance questing as it aligns itself with Christian myth. But the last figure in Merlin's prophecy is not Henry Tudor but

Elizabeth, the "royall virgin," whom we glimpse in a warlike attitude, threatening Spain with her scepter (49). To see what this image means for Britomart and for Merlin's vision of history we shall need to investigate the prophecy more closely.

The first figure in Merlin's prophecy is, of course, Artegall, in whom Spenser continues to interweave romance and historical material. Artegall is related to the Arthur of British chronicle tradition both by analogy and by blood. Artegall is "Arthur's equal" (Art / egal), a status Spenser implies by assigning Artegall the place in history reserved for Arthur in the chronicles. Artegall, moreover, shares Arthur's eventual fate: Artegall will be "Too rathe cut off by practise criminall / Of secret foes" (28), as Arthur will be betrayed by his nephew Mordred. Both destinies recapitulate that of Ariosto's Ruggiero, who will be killed by the treacherous Gano (OF 3.24). But Artegall's existence may also be accounted for historically; he may be Arthur's half brother, son of Igerne (Arthur's mother) and Gorlois.[20] Merlin seems to draw equally from British chronicle material and from Ariosto (cf., for instance, st. 23 and OF 3.17–18). But Merlin also draws on Scripture, if only to keep his audience conscious of the ultimate authority for all prophetic utterance.

With Merlin's reference to Conan, the unidentified son of Britomart and Artegall, the scriptural matrix begins to emerge. Artegall's son is depicted in symbolic language that echoes Old Testament prophecy: "Like as a Lyon, that in drowsie caue / Hath long time slept, himselfe so shall he shake"(30). The allusion is to Jacob's prophecy concerning his twelve sons in Genesis 49.9: "Iudah, as a lions whelpe shalt thou come vp from the spoile, my sonne. He shal lie downe & couche as a lion, & as a lionesse. Who shal ster him vp?"[21] The Geneva Bible glosses Judah as a type of Christ, which may help explain Merlin's curious tentativeness in speaking of the final outcome of Conan's career: "And if he then with victorie can lin [cease], / He shall his dayes with peace bring to his earthly In." Conan's victory is indefinite, not because Merlin's foreknowledge of British history is suddenly imperfect but because the "faire accordaunce," the simultaneous "victorie" and "peace" toward which the prophecy moves, is as much a scriptural and a spiritual as a historical event.

At this early stage in Merlin's prophecy the relevance of scriptural allusion to British history remains unclear. As elsewhere in

Britomart's experience, enlightenment comes retrospectively. For the moment, in fact, the prophecy of British history is susceptible to a different reading altogether. If Merlin's prophecy is read, as in one sense it asks to be, from the perspective of a narrowly conceived British bias, the pattern of exile and return evident throughout confirms history as a static and moribund process. Vortipore succeeds Artegall's son "In kingdome, but not in felicity;" but his son Malgo "shall full mightily / Auenge his fathers losse, with speare and shield" (31).[22] British ascendancy is only temporary, however, because Malgo's son Careticus is subsequently overwhelmed by the Saxons and Gormond (34). The to and fro rhythm of history continues as Saxon Etheldred, acting in the interests of the papal emissary Augustine, massacres the British monks at Bangor. They are then in turn avenged by Cadwan (35), whom, according to Geoffrey of Monmouth, the Briton princes subsequently elect their king.[23] The tragic cycle then extends into the next generation as Cadwan's son Cadwallin (Cadwallo) wreaks a mighty vengeance (36) on Edwin, son of the Saxon Etheldred. Merlin's bias is transparent in his rhetorical coloring. Augustine is "ambitious"; Pellite, the false prophet who predicts disaster to the British cause (Geoffrey 12.4), is a "wicked" sorcerer; the Saxon Penda is "fearefull" whereas Cadwallin is moved by an immitigable, righteous, heroic wrath. Merlin's partisan passion is of sufficient intensity to carry him through the account of Cadwallin's killing of the Saxon martyr, the "good" and "godly" King Oswald, without evident remorse (38–39).

The cycle of exile and return, defeat and retribution, might have continued indefinitely, one imagines, were it not that the hand of Providence begins to reveal itself in British affairs. Cadwallader, ravaged by divine "plagues and murrins pestilent," is forced into an exile from which his return is barred by heavenly decree:

> For th'heauens haue decreed, to displace
> The *Britons,* for their sinnes dew punishment,
> And to the *Saxons* ouer-giue their gouernment.   [41]

Thus the age of British kings passes and is lamented by Merlin in terms that evoke simultaneously the fall of Troy and the Fall, humanity's expulsion from the Edenic "bowre" to the "wastfull wood":

> Then woe, and woe, and euerlasting woe,
>> Be to the Briton babe, that shalbe borne,
>> To liue in thraldome of his fathers foe;
>> Late King, now captiue, late Lord, now forlorne,
>> The worlds reproch, the cruell victours scorne,
>> Banisht from Princely bowre to wastfull wood:
>> O who shall helpe me to lament, and mourne
>> The royall seed, the antique *Troian* blood,
> Whose Empire lenger here then euer any stood. [42]

Merlin's lament is in effect a challenge to Britomart to reveal what she has learned from the spectacle of historical flux. To her credit she does not yearn for one more turn of the wheel; she grasps the problem of British history as Merlin has so far unfolded it:

> Ah but will heauens fury neuer slake,
>> Nor vengeaunce huge relent it selfe at last?
> Will not long misery late mercy make. . . ? [43]

"Mercy," that is, must replace "vengeaunce huge" if the tragic pattern of British history is to be changed.

Stanzas 41–43 mark the emergence of a moral perspective on historical events. One feels it is as much Britomart's response to what she has thus far witnessed as it is fate that determines the next event, the ascension of Henry VII to the British throne after an 800-year hiatus in the Briton–Trojan line of kings. Henry is the agent of a spiritual as well as a political renovatio:

> Tho when the terme is full accomplishid,
>> There shall a sparke of fire, which hath long-while
>> Bene in his ashes raked vp, and hid,
>> Be freshly kindled in the fruitfull Ile
>> Of *Mona*, where it lurked in exile;
>> Which shall breake forth into bright burning flame,
>> And reach into the house, that beares the stile
>> Of royall maiesty and soueraigne name;
> So shall the Briton bloud their crowne againe reclame. [48]

The advent of the Tudor dynasty brings with it an assurance that "sacred Peace" will finally establish itself in England and the nation will lay aside "ciuile armes" (49). British history thus far is in a sense Britomart's internal struggle transferred to a larger canvas. Britomart's experience of alienation, the confrontation with otherness precipitated by her discovery of Merlin's mirror, has its historical counterpart in the sequence of foreign invasions of the British realm. Britomart in turn recapitulates the central historical catastrophe when on leaving Merlin's cave she dons Saxon rather than British armor to serve as her disguise (58). But as she does so she also begins the process of assimilating contraries that eventually leads to "eternall vnion" of "nations different afore" in the realm of history and to her marriage to Artegall in the realm of her own experience. Merlin's prophecy exhorts Britomart to embrace a more inclusive ideal than virginity, to emerge from the "Princely bowre" of the self.

But the last event in British history mentioned by Merlin seems strangely out of line with the prophecy of an era of "sacred Peace" under Henry VII. In stanza 49 we catch a glimpse of Elizabeth dealing a blow to "the great Castle" (Castile) with her "white rod" (a reference to the defeat of the Spanish Armada in 1588). At this point the reader is reminded that Elizabeth is as much as Britomart the intended audience of Merlin's prophecy. If Britomart's vision of British history is in effect an extended look at herself in Merlin's mirror, let us recall that *The Faerie Queene* is also a mirror in which Elizabeth is invited to see herself (2.pr.4, 3.pr.5). Like Britomart, in whom Elizabeth may see herself represented as martial virginity, Elizabeth is urged to embody a more fully evolved virtue.[24] In the proem to the next book the poet states openly what Merlin now says indirectly by begging Elizabeth to modify the "vse of awfull Maiestie" with "melting loue":

> To her I sing of loue, that loueth best,
> And best is lou'd of all aliue I weene:
> To her this song most fitly is addresst,
> The Queene of loue, and Prince of peace from heauen blest.

> Which that she may the better deigne to heare,
> Do thou dred infant, *Venus* dearling doue,
> From her high spirit chase imperious feare,
> And vse of awfull Maiestie remoue:
> In sted thereof with drops of melting loue,
> Deawd with ambrosiall kisses, by thee gotten
> From thy sweete smyling mother from aboue,

thinking of himself as a Faery knight to seeing himself as an English knight and as a Christian saint (10.60–61). In him the realms of Faery, history, and the spirit are ordered hierarchically, each clarifying as it transcends the last. He is to become an *English* saint but his becoming one is contingent on his awareness of his spiritual destiny, his discovery of his future identity as an English *saint*. The act of killing the dragon that earns Red Cross his place in English history becomes fully meaningful only as its eschatological significance emerges. Spenser's legend of the Faery knight converges with history as history in turn converges with Christian myth.

In the proem to book 2 Spenser announces a departure from the poetics of the first book involving the excision of eschatological concerns. The poet asserts that his narrative is "antique history," "matter of iust memory" rather than "painted forgery," and to prove his case he argues an analogy between his discovery of Faeryland and the recent discoveries of the Americas. "Who euer heard of th'Indian *Peru?*" Yet it surely existed before it came to be known by Europe: "Why then should witlesse man so much misweene / That nothing is, but that which he hath seene?" There is perhaps in this a muted echo of the Pauline injunction to acknowledge the truth of what "eye hath not seen, nor ear heard," but the explicit issue is no longer spiritual revelation. The level of veracity to which the poet seems to aspire is that attainable by the geographer or the historian. The figure of the prophet has disappeared; the governing narrative metaphor is not now strictly that of a pilgrimage but that of the voyage for discovery.

In canto 9 time is represented as perceived in the "brain" of Alma's Castle. The future is a chamber buzzing with "Deuices, dreames, opinions vnsound, / Shewes, visions, sooth-sayes, and prophesies" (9.51); the present is a gallery of "lawes, of iudgements, and of decretals; / All artes, all science, all Philosophy" (53); the past is the written record of "things foregone through many ages." The difference between this and Contemplation's revelation of universal and spiritual history is that now we are exploring the mind of man rather than that of God. Alma's Castle reveals the limitations of the human perception of time: it is at best, as Augustine describes it, a present of things present, a present of things past, and a present of things future.[27] As a written record of history, the documents in Eumnestes' library, "Some made in books, some in long parchment scrolles, / That were all worme-eaten, and full of canker holes" (57), are to be distinguished from Fidelia's "sacred Booke, with bloud ywritt," which "none could read, except she did them teach" (1.10.19). Eumnestes can convey an impression of time as duration but he cannot, like Contemplation, glimpse eternity. He is not like Contemplation a blind visionary but merely "an old oldman, halfe blind," who possesses "liuely vigour . . . in his mind" (55; cf. 1.10.47). And as his knowledge does not extend from first things to last, what he does know is necessarily disordered (58).

Arthur and Guyon each read a chronicle from Eumnestes' library: Arthur, *Briton Moniments*, which traces the history of the British crown from Trojan Brutus to Uther Pendragon, Arthur's father, in much the same manner as any contemporary Tudor chronicle, and Guyon, *Antiquitee of Faery Lond*, which is pure fabrication, a history of "Elfin kynd" from Quick to Gloriana. The two chronicles are fact and fiction juxtaposed, the dualism established as the epistemological framework of book 2 in the proem. The chronicles, as Berger and Roche have shown, complement each other strategically.[28] They are mutually delimiting. The faery chronicle is formally more complete, beginning with a myth of genesis and ending with an encomium to Elizabeth or her allegorical counterpart Gloriana. The progress of the Elfin race contains no reversals of fortune; the line of succession is unbroken. Arthur's chronicle, by contrast, records the disruptions and reversals of actual history. The British hero has to adjust to genuine adversity, human frailty and depravity, losses and deaths. Its image of nobility, however, is thus fully exercised and breathed, to paraphrase Milton, in the dust and heat of human experience. If this chronicle is formally less complete, the virtues, the moral and legal institutions whose evolution it traces, are greater than those of the Elfin chronicle. In the light of *Briton Moniments* the history of the Elfin race appears suspiciously felicitous: There is nothing in it to prevent the Elfin reader from coming away from it with an illusion of unqualified self-sufficiency.

The point of the juxtaposition of the two chronicles seems to be that the question posed in the proem (Is the narrative of book 2

> For till the world from his perfection fell
> Into all filth and foule iniquitie,
> *Astraea* here mongst earthly men did dwell,
> And in the rules of iustice them instructed well. [5.1.5]

The aspect of justice Artegall is most successful in administering involves discriminating between truth and falsehood where they first seem indistinguishable, as when in canto 1 of book 5 he correctly decides between the claims of Sir Sanglier and an anonymous squire for possession of the same lady. Justice uncovers duplicity and discredits fraud. Or, to translate into the vocabulary of romance narrative, justice penetrates disguises. Artegall is thus capable in precisely the area in which the romance heroine is deficient (recall Britomart's naiveté in the Castle Joyous). Justice corrects the errors to which romance vision is liable to the extent that it overvalues resemblances. The point is made by contrasting Satyrane's tournament in honor of the false Florimell in 4.4 (the canto in which Artegall first meets and is overthrown by Britomart) and Marinell's tournament on the occasion of his wedding to the true Florimell in 5.3. The former, in which Britomart is champion of the third day of battle, culminates in the erroneous presentation of the girdle of chastity to the false Florimell, the simulacrum, the soulless phantom of beauty. The latter, in which Artegall is champion of the third day, ends in the exposure of the false Florimell and her equally false escort Braggadocchio by Artegall and the presentation of the girdle of chastity to the true Florimell, now bride of Marinell. Chastity now finds its proper context in marriage, and the chivalrous tournament reaches its proper conclusion as a public celebration of concord. When Artegall is triumphant, illusions are dispelled.

As justice defines the limits of chastity, so chastity does for justice. As James E. Phillips has analyzed what Spenser calls his "treatise" on justice (5.3.3), the subject falls into three subtopics, Justice, Equity, and Mercy or Clemency:

> where Justice is the absolute, measure-for-measure equation of exact reward and punishment according to the letter of the law, where Equity is the taking into account of the individual circumstances in each case, and where Mercy or Clemency is the human and divine impulse to forgive.[32]

The Artegall of the first four cantos operates with perfect effi-
ciency according to the principles of Justice Absolute with the
help of the iron man Talus, whose name suggests *lex Talionis*, the
Old Law administered according to the letter, untempered by
mercy. When he encounters the Amazonian Radigund, however,
we discover that Justice Absolute has its limitations, because of
which Artegall is dependent upon Britomart. Artegall is overcome by Radigund not through her superior force but by virtue of
an inherent deficiency in the concept of justice he figures—a deficiency that renders Talus useless to him (5.19). He accepts the
terms of combat that Radigund proposes and is subsequently
bound by them (as Britomart is not when she similarly accepts the
terms of Malecasta's six knights):

> But these conditions doe to him propound,
>   That if I vanquishe him, he shall obay
> My law, and euer to my lore be bound,
> And so will I, if me he vanquish may;
> What euer he shall like to doe or say:
> Goe streight, and take with thee, to witnesse it,
> Sixe of thy fellowes of the best array,
> And beare with you both wine and iuncates fit,
> And bid him eate, henceforth he oft shall hungry sit.
>
> [4.49]

He finds himself on the horns of a dilemma, however, when in a
scene reminiscent of his battle with Britomart (4.6) he unmasks
Radigund and discovers "A miracle of natures goodly grace / In
her faire visage voide of ornament" (5.5.12). "Ruth of beautie"
prevents him from continuing the fight but the initial conditions
of battle bind him to Radigund's service:

> So was he ouercome, not ouercome,
>   But to her yeelded of his owne accord;
> Yet was he iustly damned by the doome
> Of his owne mouth, that spake so warelesse word,
> To be her thrall, and seruice her afford.
> For though that he first victorie obtayned,
> Yet after by abandoning his sword,
> He wilfull lost, that he before attayned.
> No fayrer conquest, then that with goodwill is gayned.
>
> [5.5.17]

> But vertuous women wisely vnderstand,
> That they were borne to base humilitie,
> Vnlesse the heauens them lift to lawfull soueraintie.
>
> [5.5.25]

The injunction against female rule is for Spenser a law of nature but may also be traced back to the Pauline text in which the Renaissance found confirmation of its notions of hierarchy and order:

> For the housband is the wiues head, euen as Christ is the head of the Church, & the same is the sauiour of his bodie. Therefore as the Church is in subiection to Christ, euen so let the wiues be to their housbands in euerie thing.   [Eph. 5.23–24]

Since equity is that part of justice that accommodates exceptions, the cases of Britomart and Elizabeth are properly introduced at this point.[37] Yet they constitute exceptions of such magnitude that they cannot simply be relegated to an appendix to the body of codified law. Spenser's intention is not simply to apologize for Elizabeth but to present her accession to the throne as an exception that advances and expands the concept of imperial justice. Spenser's previous attempts to prepare for the advent of Elizabeth's rule have been based on the relatively weaker argument of historical precedent (2.10.54, 3.3.54). Spenser's justification of female sovereignty in 5, however, is fully integral to the evolution of the book's titular virtue.

As a negative exemplum of female sovereignty and as a dramatization of the shortcomings of Justice Absolute, the Radigund episode sets the stage for Britomart's climactic vision of Equity in Isis Church in canto 7. Here again Spenser's focal theme is "true iustice" (1), but Britomart's vision is climactic to more than one theme. Here too Spenser comes as close as ever in his poem to fulfilling the expectations of the dynastic theme in a marriage between two principal figures. If Britomart's experience in Isis Church is something short of a marriage, it nonetheless establishes the terms on which such a marriage could be based. Spenser's subject is no less marriage than equity, no less sexuality than "Common-weale," for in Spenser's thought these issues are fundamentally interinvolved. We are at the center of book 5 but now we see through the eyes of the heroine of book 3; in other words, the concept of justice will be illuminated by chastity and chastity will be enlarged by justice. The issues of love and empire now fully intersect, as they have promised to do from the outset of the dynastic narrative.

As critical commentary on canto 7 has shown, Britomart's vision can be interpreted as an allegory of Elizabethan jurisprudence[38] and as a marriage debate,[39] or as "an initiation into womanhood."[40] The Temple of Isis has been identified as Parliament[41] but it is also explicitly a "church" in which the priests of Isis celebrate a mass (17). It clearly has aspects of both to the extent that it serves as the *templum* of both "magnificke chastity" and "true iustice."[42]

Spenser's principal sources for his conception of Isis Church are Plutarch (*Of Isis and Osiris*) and Diodorus Siculus (*Bibliotheca* 1.11–22), in which Osiris is a euhemerized Egyptian god of justice and Isis is associated with equity. Spenser follows Plutarch in identifying Osiris, like his Artegall, with the sun and Isis, like Britomart, with the moon: "For that they both like race in equall iustice runne" (7.4).[43] The temple of Isis is attended by priests whose rites and customs (among which is observance of "stedfast chastity" [7.9]) are with some exceptions and variations drawn from the sources. The following are the details of Britomart's experience in Isis Church. She is escorted into the temple, where she sees the idol of Isis:

> One foote was set vppon the Crocodile,
>> And on the ground the other fast did stand,
>> So meaning to suppresse both forged guile,
>> And open force: and in her other hand
>> She stretched forth a long white sclender wand.
>> Such was the Goddesse; whom when *Britomart*
>> Had long beheld, her selfe vppon the land
>> She did prostrate, and with right humble hart,
> Vnto her selfe her silent prayers did impart. [5.7.7]

Britomart spends the night under the wings of Isis.[44] In her sleep she has a dream "which did close implie / The course of all her

search that Isis made for the mangled body of Osiris, went up and down gathering up limb by limb still as they could find them. We have not yet found them all, Lords and Commons, nor ever shall do, till her Master's second coming.

The myth of Isis and Osiris here finds its meaning in the context of Christian myth. The unending search Isis makes for the mangled pieces of the body of Osiris is a reminder that we exist in a fallen world in which knowledge of Truth will always be imperfect. As inhabitants of this fallen world (and as readers of Spenser's allegory), we must resign ourselves to our limitations: We may grope toward a vision of divine truth but we shall not arrive at the goal "till her Master's second coming."

Most of the complexity of Britomart's dream resides, appropriately, in the figure of the serpentine crocodile, which the priestly interpreter identifies as both Artegall and Osiris. Here Spenser seems to have taken liberty with his sources in order to emphasize the doubleness of Britomart's perception of Artegall since Plutarch, for one, associates the crocodile with the treacherous brother of Osiris–Artegall, Typhon, who continually frustrates the attempts of Isis to gather together the pieces of the body of Osiris. Moreover, Spenser's crocodile is ambivalent in its own right, representing "both forged guile / And open force." This ambivalence has suggested to some readers the double-edged sword of Machiavellian statecraft,[51] to others the conflicting imperatives of common law and Roman law[52] or the uncontrollable vacillation between cruelty and false pity (*crudelis misericordia*) of law conceived without equity.[53] As it pertains to the legend of Chastity the crocodile may also suggest the twin cupidinous passions of ire and lust. And from associations elsewhere in the poem the serpentine crocodile–dragon figure has acquired meanings ranging from sin and error to truth and faith. Book 1 traces its transformation from the dragon of Error (1.1.13–26) to that at the feet of the proud, imperial Lucifera (4.10), to the serpent upon which Orgoglio sets Duessa in "royall maiestye" (7.16–18), to the dragon on the crest of Arthur's helmet (7.31), to the snake in the cup of Fidelia (10.13), to the dragon Red Cross finally slays. The serpent arises from the poem's Protean principle, from the notion of mutability over which the poet perceptually seeks a victory.

Britomart's dragon is at first a savior as it devours the threatening fire and storm, then an apparent antagonist, at one point reduced to "humblesse meeke," then raised to the status of partner in procreation. To the extent that the dragon is associated with Artegall it is more than reasonable to assume that its ambivalence is descriptive of justice in its presently incomplete state of evolution. To the extent that the perspective of the dream is Britomart's, it is equally reasonable to assign the ambivalence to Britomart herself, who still alternates between maidenly naiveté and masculine martial aggression, whose love is blind in the double sense of not fully knowing its object and not being able to see anything else. What is horrific in the aspect of the crocodile is at least partly a projection as well as a cause of her "fearfull fright" (16).

Whatever the crocodile may be taken to represent, the point seems to be that what is called for is a change in the way of seeing things. Britomart is carried from an initial state of "felicity" (whether this is an Edenic innocence or the first relatively peaceful years of Elizabeth's reign) through "fright" to a promise of "ioyance" restored (23) as the temple priest explains to her the historical significance of her dream. Whatever narrower configuration of history the changes in Britomart suggest, they also suggest the providential movement of history from Fall to Redemption. The moment in 5.7 parallels that in 1.10 in which Contemplation purges Red Cross of despair by informing him of his historical identity and his heroic, spiritual destiny. For Britomart too this is a moment of revelation and historical self-awareness. The priest sees through her disguise, recognizing her to be the destined progenitress of the Tudor line (21). The lesson is essentially the same as in book 1, in which the figure of the serpent undergoes so many transformations. An understanding of the providential plan is in itself sufficient to dispel nightmarish unrealities and to resolve ambivalences and discord. When we know that the snake takes its real meaning from its place in Fidelia's cup (1.10.13), we know by the same token that to see it as the Dragon of Error is to be in some sense complicit in that error. Conversely, the view of things that is least horrific, the experience of forces as creative rather than destructive, the vision of something whole and harmonious rather than discordant, is the

is merely a symbolic appropriation of the meaning of that event to the poem. The dynastic marriage stands in the same relation to the scriptural event as Tasso's historical Jerusalem does to the New Jerusalem of Revelation. But Spenser's imagination is more profoundly influenced by his consciousness of the lag between becoming and being.[57] He differs from Ariosto and Tasso in the degree to which he invests even his symbolism with a sense of indeterminacy.

We cannot know what Spenser might have done with the marriage theme had he finished writing *The Faerie Queene*, but what we have of the poem is enough to establish Spenser's reluctance to put an end to vicissitude, to banish mutability utterly from his thought. Consider, for instance, what seems at first to be the exception to Spenser's rule of prohibiting narrative closure in a celebration of marriage, the marriage of Thames and Medway in the eleventh canto of book 4. Marriage is celebrated but only because the problem of time has been evaded by virtue of the special status of the principals. The marriage of Thames and Medway, the convergence of two rivers in a common "bed," can be presented with a kind of narrative immediacy because the same quality of immediacy pertains to it throughout time. It is both a single, finite occurrence and an ongoing natural phenomenon; it stands simultaneously within time and outside time. The poet here conspires with nature to reconcile sequential, historical time with timelessness. In such moments the poet allows himself a glimpse of cosmic harmony and order realized in fact. Elsewhere, however, his fiction cannot evade the laws of temporality, which preclude the perfect coincidence of the actual and the ideal.

The last five cantos of book 5 bring narrative fiction and Elizabethan history to their closest proximity in *The Faerie Queene*. At times the narrative is scarcely more than sustained allusion to specific contemporary events. The vision that thrusts Britomart into English national history by revealing her role as cofounder of the Tudor dynasty propels the poem in that direction as well. As the distance between the poem's narrative and actual historical events closes, readers have sensed a critical change in the nature of Spenser's allegory and a diminution of the scope of his prophetic vision.[58] The problem has recently been stated by Michael O'Connell.[59] On the one hand the narrative's fidelity to historical incident seems to come at the expense of allegorical coherence and on the other hand the urge to preserve the logical integrity of allegory leads to blatant distortions of historical fact. Thus in canto 11, for instance, Artegall chastises Bourbon for having "forborne" the "good shield" given him by Red Cross (Henri IV's decision to abandon his Protestantism in order to better his chances of coronation) but assists him in the rescue of Flourdelis (France) from a "rude rout" of peasants nonetheless. The narrative follows history accurately (Elizabeth continued her alliance with France despite her disappointment with Henri's conversion to Roman Catholicism) but the narrative seems therefore to fail by the standards of moral allegory. Bourbon is never forced to realize that by discarding the shield of Protestant faith "fro dangers dread his doubtfull life to saue" he has ironically abandoned that which "most safety to him gaue / And much did magnifie his noble name" (5.11.46). Indeed his experience arguably proves the contrary.[60] If this is allegory betraying itself in order to follow history, the Belge episode in canto 10 would seem to illustrate the reverse. There Arthur liberates Belge (the Low Countries) from the tyranny of Gerioneo (Philip II of Spain) and restores her to her throne "And from her balefull minde all care be banished" (10.39). The episode affirms the moral supremacy of English Protestantism in its contest with Spanish Catholicism but the narrative flies in the face of historical fact. A triumph so decisive and final as that implied by Arthur's defeat of Gerioneo was never actually achieved. We seem to be witnessing the collapse of a moral vision of history as it tests itself against the experience of history, or the betrayal of the promise of a Tudor "apocalypse" as the poem emerges from the remote Arthurian past into the Elizabethan present. The vision of what ought to be comes up short as it is measured against what is.[61]

We attribute disillusionment to the poet of book 5 if we see the crisis of that book to be a perilous collision of what ought to be and what is, but this is to misconstrue Spenserian prophecy as more fragile than it is. Prophecy is not for Spenser a form of wish fulfillment; it is not a bubble of optimism that is susceptible to deflation when what is hoped for fails to materialize. Instead it is

is unswervingly bound. Elizabeth is justice enhanced by the principle of equity and tempered by mercy or clemency.

To see the scope of Spenser's idealism one needs to appreciate the boldness with which he has dealt with current Elizabethan history in his legend of Justice. The Radigund and Isis Church episodes confront what might be considered one of the two greatest legal dilemmas of Elizabethan government, the question of rule by a woman. Mercilla's trial of Duessa raises the other, the question of a monarch's immunity from the law. The trial of Mary, Elizabeth understood, threatened to establish a precedent that could return to undermine her own claim to supralegal authority. In each instance Spenser takes an issue that constituted an assault on the ideological foundations of Tudor *imperium* and makes of it an occasion to reaffirm and expand the ideal. The fact of female rule conflicts with the enshrined principle of male social and legal supremacy but leads to the concept of equity, of valid exception to the law, which ultimately saves justice from its own undoing. The subjection of Mary/Duessa to the authority of the law challenges the theory of the monarch's divine right but leads to the institution of what is for a Christian society the highest principle of justice, mercy. We recognize the characteristic logic of all romance action: What is apparently disruptive can be seen from another angle as an integral part of a system that finally admits no discord.

Mercilla, as T. K. Dunseath notes,[66] symbolizes the cosmic harmony that existed when Astraea walked the earth (pr. 5):

> All ouer her a cloth of state was spred,
>> Not of rich tissew, nor of cloth of gold,
>> Nor of ought else, that may be richest red,
>> But like a cloud, as likest may be told,
>> That her brode spreading wings did wyde vnfold;
>> Whose skirts were bordred with bright sunny beams,
>> Glistring like gold, amongst the plights enrold,
>> And here and there shooting forth siluer streames,
> Mongst which crept little Angels through the glittering
>> gleames.   [5.9.28]

As mercy, the third and greatest component of justice, Mercilla resolves the ambiguities of previous phases of the dynastic narrative. Like the Elizabeth of Merlin's prophecy in book 3, Mercilla raises her scepter in defense of her realm, but this scepter is explicitly what the "white rod" of book 3 was not, a "sacred pledge of peace and clemencie" (30). The crocodile coiled at Isis's feet that is in Britomart's dream first "swolne with pride of his owne peerelesse powre" and then reduced to "humblesse meeke" has its counterpart in the "huge great Lyon" at Mercilla's feet. But this symbol of power is firmly controlled "With a strong yron chaine and coller . . . / That once he could not moue, nor quich at all" (33). The priestly interpreter of canto 7 soothes Britomart by promising that what seemed horrific in her dream signified her marriage to Artegall. Britomart, however, must live with the promise of that marriage; Mercilla is the promise fulfilled—literally, as she is Elizabeth, the royal descendant of Britomart and Artegall, and allegorically, as she is the concept of justice resulting from the union of law and equity.

Therefore, from Mercilla's vantage point, law and equity are understood not to be at odds with each other, as they sometimes appear to be in earlier stages of the allegory. Equity is not merely the body of necessary exceptions to law and so a principle potentially at variance with Justice Absolute; equity is rather justice brought nearer to perfection. And mercy is not simply a third element of justice but the sum of all its parts. To make the point Spenser provides an analogy in the celestial imagery of cantos 7 and 9. Britomart experiences her vision in Isis Church nocturnally, in the absence, that is, of the sun/Artegall/Osiris. As she sees marriage—the implicit subject of the dream—from her perspective alone, it appears nightmarish and violent. Artegall is present, however, at Mercilla's court, and the imagery surrounding her indicates that the sun has been returned to its proper place in the heavens. The towers of her palace "outshine the dimmed skye / And with their brightnesse daz'd the straunge beholders eye" (21); her skirts are "bordred with bright sunny beams" (28) and the natural sun is there to mark the time of day (35). The restoration of the sun signifies that the imbalance of Britomart's vision has been corrected. Justice fully evolved comprehends both Britomart and Artegall, Isis and Osiris, the moon and the sun, "For that they both like race in equall iustice runne."

The issue at Duessa's trial is the familiar romance one of dis-

contemplates mutability with humility and patience. He requires his heroes to endure with equanimity the sentence that stays their course, as does Red Cross when he is told he must play out his earthly drama before he can ascend to the New Jerusalem (1.10.63) or Artegall when is is called away from Irena before he has completed the task of reforming her realm (5.12.27). The Spenserian hero must continue the romance quest, knowing that Envy, Detraction, and the Blatant Beast lie in wait to hound him but knowing also that all movement, however errant or aimless it may seem to be, is governed by "Eternall Providence."

But the differences among Spenser and Ariosto and Tasso are temperamental rather than philosophical ones. In the end all three poets were engaged in a common pursuit: All three sought to reflect in their poetry the change in the nature of things Christ had effected. All fixed their gazes on the image of an *imperium* in which Justice was wedded to Grace and saw there what entitled them—indeed obliged them—to overgo Virgil. If Spenser sensed more acutely than Ariosto or Tasso the difficulty of bringing his poem to completion, at least it was not with Virgil's uncertainty and melancholy that Spenser faced what lay ahead.

Epilogue

The last great Christian epic is not strictly speaking a dynastic poem. In his middle years Milton abandoned his plans for an Arthuriad, a work that might have resembled more closely those of Ariosto, Tasso, and Spenser than does *Paradise Lost*. Milton came to speak with disdain of the "long and tedious havoc" of heroic romances, with their "tilting Furniture, emblazon'd Shields, / Impreses quaint, Caparisons and Steeds" (*PL* 9.34–35). He professed an impatience with chivalric conventions as his own poem turned to "the better fortitude / Of Patience and Heroic Martyrdom / Unsung." Milton could not write a dynastic poem because as the Restoration approached he could see no contemporary institution in which he might place his hopes for millennial reform, no manifestation of dynasty that did not in fact obstruct the goal of salvation. His old distaste for monarchy remained strong: God had not made Man lord over other men (*PL* 12.69–70). His protestantism gave him a focus at once too narrow and too wide for the dynastic theme. His subject was the redemption of the individual soul or that of humanity in general but not that of a chosen nation.

In a sense the idea of a Christian dynastic epic is inherently problematic. Boethius identifies the difficulty:

> "The whole race of men on this earth springs from one stock. There is one Father of all things; One alone provides for all. . . .
>
> "Thus, all men come from noble origin. Why then boast of your ancestors? If you consider your beginning, and God your

of historical accidents we are apt to read his prophecy of the Elizabethan era as a flight of fantasy or as deliberately ironical, and thus as evidence of underlying skepticism or despair.

Perhaps an even greater barrier between the modern reader and the Renaissance poet appears when the issue of Renaissance imitation of Virgil is raised. We are inclined to assert the greater accuracy of our image of Virgil and to mistrust that which seems to have been filtered through a Christian ideology. The interpretive imitations of the *Aeneid* in the Renaissance, one might feel, tell us more about the interpreter than the text. Here again our distance from the Renaissance conception of history is a factor, for the Renaissance Christian poet's view of the *Aeneid* is inextricably bound up with his view of time. He could not contemplate Virgil's poem apart from his understanding that history is a teleological process, the progressive disclosure of God's plan for human salvation. The Renaissance poet's purpose is not so much to produce a faithful reconstruction of the *Aeneid* as to determine its place and its meaning in the universal scheme of things that he believed had been revealed with the advent of the New Covenant. Interpretation is not for him simply an antiquarian exercise, an effort to catalogue, clarify, and analyze the elements of the original text as if the significance of that text were wholly contained within itself. These, the preoccupations of an empiricist epistemology, had only begun to come into play by the seventeenth century. This is not to say that the Renaissance poet condescended to Virgil. In my examination of Renaissance reactions to the *Aeneid* I have emphasized the Christian thinker's awareness of the consequences of Virgil's coming before the New Dispensation, but I hope I have left room in the course of the argument to show the extent of their respect for him. They sought, in the end, to affirm Virgil's place in their culture, not to banish him from it.

Notes

INTRODUCTION

1 I adapt the term from Peter V. Marinelli, "The Dynastic Romance: A Study in the Evolution of the Romantic Epics of Boiardo, Ariosto and Spenser" (Ph.D. diss., Princeton University, 1964).

2 *The Works of Edmund Spenser: A Variorum Edition*, ed. Edwin Greenlaw, Charles G. Osgood, Frederick M. Padelford, et al., 11 vols. (Baltimore: Johns Hopkins University Press, 1932–57), I.168–69. All quotations from *The Faerie Queene* (hereafter cited as *FQ*) are taken from this edition.

3 *The Art of Poetry*, trans. Edward Henry Blakeney, *Literary Criticism: Plato to Dryden*, ed. Allan H. Gilbert (1940; rpt. Detroit: Wayne State University Press, 1962), p. 133.

4 *W. H. Auden: Collected Poems*, ed. Edward Mendelson (New York: Random House, 1976), p. 455.

5 Northrop Frye, *The Return of Eden: Five Essays on Milton's Epics* (Toronto: Toronto University Press, 1965), p. 14; *Anatomy of Criticism: Four Essays* (Princeton: Princeton University Press, 1957), pp. 318–20.

6 Tasso, *Discourses on the Heroic Poem*, trans. Mariella Cavalchini and Irene Samuel (Oxford: Clarendon Press, 1973), p. 40.

7 For an instance of the use of the term *overgo* in this sense, see Gabriel Harvey, "A Gallant Familiar Letter," in *Elizabethan Critical Essays*, ed. G. Gregory Smith (Oxford: Oxford University Press, 1904), 1.115–16. Harvey refers to Spenser's own use of the term.

8 Torquato Tasso, *La Gerusalemme Liberata*, from *Opere di Torquato Tasso*, ed. Bartolo Sozzi, 3d ed. (Turin: Unione Tipografico-Editrice Torinese [UTET], 1974).

9 Tasso, *Jerusalem Delivered*, trans. Edward Fairfax, ed. John Charles Nelson (New York: Capricorn Books, [1963]).

10 Gerhart B. Ladner, *The Idea of Reform: Its Impact on Christian Thought and Action in the Age of the Fathers*, rev. ed. (1959; rpt. New York: Harper & Row, 1967), pp. 1–5.

11 Augustine, writing to refute those who would attribute the decline of his

contemporary Rome to Christianity, argues that God gives earthly kingdoms to the good and the bad alike, not fortuitously, but according to a plan concealed from mortals. But felicity, as opposed to prosperity, God gives only to the good (*City of God* 4.33).

12   *The City of God*, trans. Marcus Dods (New York: Random House, 1950), 14.28.

13   On the distinction between *caritas* and *cupiditas*, see, for instance, Augustine, *On Christian Doctrine* 3.10.16.

14   See, for instance, *City of God* 12.2.

15   Maphaeus Vegius, "The Thirteenth Book of the *Aeneid*," trans. Thomas Twyne (1584), in *Maphaeus Vegius and his Thirteenth Book of the Aeneid: A Chapter on Virgil in the Renaissance*, ed. Anna Cox Brinton (Stanford: Stanford University Press, 1930), p. 79. Latin lines 437–39; English lines are unnumbered.

16   Cited in Brinton, pp. 27–28.

17   For example, Juan Luigi de la Cerda (ca. 1560–1645), Ruaeus (1643–1725), and Tarquinius Gallutius (1514–49), who describes the "Thirteenth Book" as a fifth wheel. See Brinton, pp. 31–32.

18   An anonymous *Ovide Moralisé* of the beginning of the fourteenth century, ll. 4671–742, ed. C. de Boer, in *Verhandelingen der Koninklijke Nederlandsche Akademie van Wetenschappen, Afd. Letterkunde*, 43 (Amsterdam: NorthHolland, 1938), pp. 128–30; and a fifteenth-century "Ovide Moralisé en Prose," 14.17, ed. C. de Boer, *Verhandelingen*, 61.2 (1954), 364–65.

19   See, for instance, M. Y. Hughes on Spenser's imitations of book 6 of the *Aeneid* in "Virgil and Spenser," *University of California Publications in English*, 2, no. 3 (1929), 371–77.

20   Domenico Comparetti, *Vergil in the Middle Ages*, trans. E. F. M. Benecke, 2d ed. (New York: Macmillan Co., 1908); H. Theodore Silverstein, "Dante and Vergil the Mystic," *Harvard Studies and Notes in Philology and Literature*, 14 (1932), 51–82; D. C. Allen, *Mysteriously Meant: The Rediscovery of Pagan Symbolism and Allegorical Interpretation in the Renaissance* (Baltimore: Johns Hopkins University Press, 1970); David Thompson, *Dante's Epic Journeys* (Baltimore: Johns Hopkins University Press, 1974); Michael Murrin, *The Allegorical Epic: Essays in Its Rise and Decline* (Chicago: University of Chicago Press, 1980). For further bibliography, see Leslie George Whitbread, trans., *Fulgentius the Mythographer* (Columbus: Ohio State University Press, 1971), p. 115.

21   As opposed to scholiastic. See Earl G. Schreiber and Thomas E. Maresca, introduction to Bernardus Silvestris, *Commentary on the First Six Books of Virgil's Aeneid* (Lincoln: University of Nebraska Press, 1979), p. xi.

22   The notion that the life of man (and the history of the world) divides into six ages can be found in Augustine. See *De Genesi contra Manichaeos* 1.23–24; and *City of God* 10.14, 16.12, and 16.43.

23   "The Exposition of the Content of Virgil," trans. Whitbread, par. 12. Hereafter I shall refer to this work by paragraph numbers given parenthetically in the text.

24   Schreiber and Maresca, p. xi. The trend toward Platonic interpretations culminates in Landino (*Camaldulensian Dialogues*), who sees the dialectic be-

tween active and contemplative virtues as central to the *Aeneid*. Dido thus represents not so much the danger of concupiscence as the temptation to pursue the active life. For a discussion of Landino, see Murrin, *Allegorical Epic*, pp. 27-50.

25 On the subject of Anchises' doctrine of metempsychosis and Augustine's objections to it, more will be said later (see below, pp. 62-64). Fulgentius's comment refers to *Aeneid* 6.724-51.

26 Bernardus Silvestris, *Commentary*, preface (Schreiber and Maresca, p. 5).

27 Murrin, pp. 48-49.

28 Ibid., p. 49.

29 Ibid. Murrin observes:

> God, the One above or identical with supreme being, cannot accept predication, since to say he is this or that would limit his essence.... Ordinary knowledge seems to be precisely predicative knowledge, but how can anything the essence of which is to have no predicates (any predicate being the expression of determinateness) be known? The Neoplatonist decided that "it can be 'known' only in a negative way, i.e., by first positing and then negating all possible predicates. *Agnoscendo cognoscitur.*"

30 Bernardus Silvestris, *Commentary* 6.108 (Schreiber and Maresca, p. 52). See 1 Cor. 13.12, "For now we see through a glass darkly; but then face to face," and the discussion of this allusion in Bernardus by Thompson, *Dante's Epic Journeys*, pp. 27-28, 82-83.

31 *Purgatorio* 22.67-69, trans. John D. Sinclair (New York: Oxford University Press, 1939). As Charles S. Singleton notes in his *Commentary* to the *Purgatorio* (Princeton: Princeton University Press, 1973), Statius's words echo Augustine, *De symbolo: sermo ad catechumenos* 4.4 (col. 664): "O Iudaei, ad hoc ferentes in manibus lucernam Legis, ut aliis viam demonstretis, et vobis tenebras ingeratis" ("O Jews, you carry in your hands the torch of the law, and while you light the way for others, you are yourselves enshrouded in darkness"). See also *Purgatorio* 27, where Dante leaves Virgil behind, and the analysis of this moment by Singleton in *Dante Studies 2: Journey to Beatrice* (1958; rpt. Baltimore: Johns Hopkins University Press, 1977), esp. pp. 257-67. In terms of the concept of justice, which will be of concern in this study, Singleton describes the relation between Virgil and Dante as follows:

> Virgil as guide, and as a kind of light, is not merely the natural light of reason as this is given to every man, but he is also that light as it was given to those philosophers and wise men who, like himself, came before Christ and were pagans. In allegory, he is the light which was given to them in that period of history, before the light of grace was come, which is Christ. Therefore, when Virgil declares that he "discerns no further" than that justice to which he brings his charge, we are not to overlook the extension of meaning evident in this historical sense. If Virgil discerns no further than this, it must be that "the philosophers," the *savi* who dwell as he

does in Limbo, discerned no further, that this, and no more than this, was their conception of justice. Virgil represents them and their limits of vision. [p. 57)

32 On the preservation of the earthly, literal, and historical sense of things within the context of allegorical interpretation in general, see Erich Auerbach, "Figura," *Scenes from the Drama of European Literature* (1959; rpt. Gloucester, Mass.: Peter Smith, 1973), esp. p. 73.

CHAPTER ONE

1 Augustine quotes from Anchises' prophecy more than a dozen times in *The City of God*, and from his discourse on reincarnation eight times, usually to illustrate what Augustine takes to be the fallacy of the Platonic conception of the dualism of body and soul and the shortcomings of the conception of history that proceeds from that error. Augustine's appraisal of Virgilian and Platonic views of history are examined more fully in the next chapter.

2 The Renaissance view of the *Aeneid* is developed in later chapters; the purpose of the present chapter is to show in general terms how the *Aeneid* invites the Renaissance perception of the poem as the product of a limited (pagan) and in fundamental ways tragic vision.

3 Text and translation of the *Aeneid* are from the Loeb edition, *Virgil*, trans. and rev. H. Rushton Fairclough (1935; rpt. Cambridge: Harvard University Press, 1967).

4 Charles Paul Segal, "*Aeternum per saecula nomen*, The Golden Bough and the Tragedy of History: Part II," *Arion*, 5, no. 1 (1966), p. 45. I am indebted to both this and part 1 of the same article, *Arion*, 4, no. 4 (1965), 617–57. Segal's reading of book 6 is consistent with a trend in modern interpretation to see in the *Aeneid* "a pessimism about the cost of history, an acute sensitivity to the suffering of the individuals who participate in it" (pt. 1, p. 618).

5 *City of God* 14.5, for instance. See also Fulgentius, "The Exposition of the Content of Virgil," par. 23 (Whitbread, pp. 132–33). Fulgentius, in a dialogue with the ghost of Virgil, uses Aeneas's question to establish the shortcomings of the classical poet:

> "Are you not the one who pleaded on mystic lines in the *Eclogues:*
> And now the virgin returns, Saturn's kingdomes return;
> Now a new race is sent forth from high heaven;
> and yet now is not your mind dozing off when you snore out something smacking of the Academy and say 'O Father, am I now to believe that exalted souls go hence to heaven and once more return to their sluggish bodies'? Why, among such sweet apples, must you include sour blackberries and put out the torch of your luminous wisdom?"
> He smiled as he replied:"I would not be a pagan if I did not leaven so many Stoic truths with a pinch of Epicurean foolishness. No one is permitted to know all the truth except you Christians, on whom shines the sun of truth."

See also Mario A. Di Cesare, *The Altar and the City: A Reading of Vergil's Aeneid* (New York: Columbia University Press, 1974), pp. 114-15.

6   *Giordano Bruno's The Heroic Frenzies,* "Argument of the Nolan," trans. Paul Eugene Memmo, Jr., *University of North Carolina Studies in the Romance Languages and Literature,* 50 (1964, 1965), 74.

7   Brooks Otis, *Virgil: A Study in Civilized Poetry,* 2d ed. (1964; rpt. Oxford: Clarendon Press, 1966), pp. 300-01.

8   For a fuller discussion of the anticipations in book 6 of Anchises' promise of *aeternum nomen,* see Segal, pt. 1, pp. 634-54.

9   Michael Putnam elaborates on the significance of the death of Palinurus in a discussion of book 5 in *The Poetry of the Aeneid: Four Studies in Imaginative Unity and Design* (Cambridge: Harvard University Press, 1966), pp. 64-104. Putnam notes some of the ways in which Palinurus seems a part of Aeneas, "that part of Aeneas which pertains to voyaging, to wandering, and to a meaningless search for a goal which has, almost until this very moment, remained unstipulated" (p. 98). The death of Palinurus figures "the death of a total concept," a way of life in which the hero struggles "for what in his own terms he thought was right." At this point the hero "must yield to a higher fate and a different world."

10   Segal, pt. 1, p. 653.

11   Adam Parry, "The Two Voices of Virgil's *Aeneid,*" *Arion,* 2, no. 4 (1963), 79.

12   Otis, pp. 268-69.

13   Ibid., pp. 300-01.

14   Translation by Marcus Dods.

15   Lines 806-07, 832-35, 847-53. The historical prophecy can be divided in different ways. See Otis (pp. 301-03), who suggests two major divisions before the Marcellus passage (854-86), and Gilbert Highet, *The Speeches in Vergil's Aeneid* (Princeton: Princeton University Press, 1972), p. 101, who follows Norden by suggesting division into seven parts.

16   See Di Cesare, pp. 117-18.

17   See also 5.18.

18   Parry, p. 78.

19   See Kenneth Quinn, *Virgil's Aeneid: A Critical Description,* 2d ed. (Ann Arbor: University of Michigan Press, 1969), pp. 172-74.

20   Ibid., pp. 26-58.

21   On the difference between Virgil's concept of fate and the Christian notion of Providence, see W. A. Camps, *An Introduction to Virgil's Aeneid* (London: Oxford University Press, 1969), pp. 41-50. T. S. Eliot suggests in "Virgil and the Christian World," *On Poetry and Poets* (New York: Farrar, Straus and Cudahy, 1957), that the virtues and concepts stressed in the *Aeneid (labor, pietas, fatum)* anticipate Christian emphases, making Aeneas "the prototype of a Christian hero" (pp. 147-48). But Eliot is careful to note what finally divides the Virgilian and Christian worlds: "The term which one can justifiably regret the lack of in Virgil is *amor....* There is tenderness and pathos enough in the *Aeneid.* But Love is never given, to my mind, the same significance [as in Dante] as a principle of order in the human soul, in society and in

the universe that pietas is given; and it is not Love that causes *fatum*, or moves the sun and the stars." Eliot's reading of the *Aeneid* is indebted to that of Theodore Haecker, *Virgil, Father of the West*, trans. A. W. Wheen (London: Sheed and Ward, 1943).

22   On the general subject of the "epistemological skepticism" of the *Aeneid*, particularly as evident in Anchises' disquisition, see Michael Murrin, *The Allegorical Epic*, pp. 27-50. Murrin suggests that the *Aeneid* shows the effect of the thinking of the New Academy (the Platonists Arcesilas, Carneades, Clitomachus, Philo), with its contention that "all sense evidence is merely probable, can never be trusted completely" (p. 38). The issue of Virgil's skepticism inevitably takes one to the famous crux with which Virgil closes book 6: Why does Aeneas exit the underworld through the gate of false dreams? On this, and its implications for Virgil's "perception of Roman history as a long Pyrrhic victory of the human spirit," see Wendell Clausen, "An Interpretation of the *Aeneid*," *Harvard Studies in Classical Philology*, 68 (1964), 145-47.

CHAPTER TWO

1   On the general subject of Augustine's interest in Virgil, see John J. O'Meara, "Augustine the Artist and the *Aeneid*," *Mélanges offerts à Mademoiselle Christine Mohrmann* (Utrecht: Anvers, 1963), 252-61, and "Virgil and Saint Augustine: the Roman Background to Christian Sexuality," *Augustinus*, 13 (1968), 307-26. On the subject of allusions to the *Aeneid* in the *Confessions*, see Eugene Vance, "Augustine's *Confessions* and the Grammar of Selfhood," *Genre* 6, no. 1 (1973), 1-28. Vance suggests that Aeneas's long "auto-scopic" narrative, his account of the fall of Troy in the court of Dido, serves as a poetic model for the *Confessions* (pp. 14-15).

2   Saint Augustine, *Confessions*, trans. R. S. Pine-Coffin (1961; rpt. London: Penguin Books, 1975).

3   The case against classical poetry is extended in *The City of God*, where Augustine condemns the poets for their role in promoting the pagan gods and commends Plato for expelling poets from the ideal state (2.14). See also Nancy Lenkeith, *Dante and the Legend of Rome* (London: The Warburg Institute, 1952), pp. 33-35. To emphasize only Augustine's negative comments on classical poetry, however, would be misleading. See also *On Christian Doctrine* 2.18.28 and 2.40.60.

4   *On Christian Doctrine*, trans. D. W. Robertson, Jr. (New York: Bobbs-Merrill, 1958).

5   See O'Meara, "Augustine the Artist and the *Aeneid*," p. 258.

6   O'Meara, *The Young Augustine: The Growth of St. Augustine's Mind up to his Conversion* (New York: Longmans, Green and Co., 1954), pp. 5-11.

7   For a brief discussion of discrepancies in dating in Augustine's various accounts of events in his life, see C. C. Martindale, "A Sketch of the Life and Character of St. Augustine," *St. Augustine* (1930; rpt. New York: Meridian Books, 1957), pp. 82-101.

8 Courcelle, in fact, maintains that the autobiographical section of the *Confessions* is for Augustine secondary in importance to the exposition of Scripture with which tbe *Confessions* conclude (Pierre Paul Courcelle, *Recherches sur les Confessions de Saint Augustin* [Paris: De Boccard, 1950], p. 23).

9 O'Meara, *Young Augustine*, pp. 11–13.

10 For evidence of Augustine's notion that universal history is recapitulated in an individual's life in the *Confessions*, see 11.28.

11 O'Meara (*Young Augustine*, p. 174) provides the following gloss: "The group of ascetics at Trier may well have some connection, as has been suggested, with the visit to that place about 336 of the author of the famous life of St. Antony referred to—St. Athanasius. The further suggestion of Courcelle that one of the two men so converted to a life of asceticism was St. Jerome, has, not without some reason, been put aside by Theiler."

12 The bibliography of critical commentary on this scene is long but for a convenient summary of some of the interpretive positions taken, see O'Meara, *Young Augustine*, pp. 182–85. O'Meara takes issue with Courcelle's contention that the scene is literary and fictitious.

13 Translation by William Watts (1631), Loeb edition, *St. Augustine's Confessions* (1912; rpt. Cambridge: Harvard University Press, 1977).

14 The fact that there are two conversions here suggests a parallelism with Ponticianus's story. See Courcelle, *Recherches*, pp. 197–202. Two later allusions to the *tolle lege* passage are worth pursuing: (1) Dante's Paolo (another Paul, but one who has undergone a conversion of a disastrous kind) echoes Augustine as he and Francesca recall reading Lancelot, "how love constrained him"; "quel giorno più no vi leggemmo avante" see *Inferno* 5.121–38). (2) Petrarch reenacts the *sortes* in "The Ascent of Mont Ventoux," where he opens his copy of the *Confessions* to the passage that reads, "And men go to admire the high mountains, the vast floods of the sea, the huge streams of the rivers, the circumference of the ocean, and the revolutions of the stars—and desert themselves" (*Conf.* 10.8). His thoughts then move backward from Augustine to St. Anthony and finally to Virgil:

> Happy the man who succeeded in baring the causes of things
> And who trod underfoot all fear, inexorable Fate and
> Greedy Acheron's uproar   (*Georgics* 2.490–92),

from which he draws this moral:

> How intensely ought we to exert our strength to get under foot not a higher spot of earth but the passions which are puffed up by earthly instincts.

(trans. Hans Nachod, *The Renaissance Philosophy of Man*, ed. Ernst Cassirer, Paul Oskar Kristeller, and John Herman Randall, Jr. [1948; rpt. Chicago: University of Chicago Press, 1971], pp. 36–46).

15 Adam Parry, "The Two Voices of Virgil's *Aeneid*," p. 80.

16 On the subject of Platonism in Augustine's thought, see Charles Boyer, *Christianisme et Néo-Platonisme dans la Formation de Saint Augustin*, rev. ed. (1920; rpt.

Rome: Catholic Book Agency, 1953); Raymond Klibansky, *The Continuity of the Platonic Tradition during the Middle Ages* (London: Warburg Institute, 1939); O'Meara, *Young Augustine*, pp. 131–55.

17 Translation by Marcus Dods.

18 See, for instance, Karl Löwith, *Meaning in History* (Chicago: University of Chicago Press, 1949), pp. 166–90.

19 See Theodor E. Mommsen, "St. Augustine and the Christian Idea of Progress," *Medieval and Renaissance Studies*, ed. Eugene F. Rice, Jr. (Ithaca: Cornell University Press, 1959), pp. 265–98.

20 See *City of God* 1.1, and Sermon 105.9, 10.

21 As Augustine puts it elsewhere, the orders of nature and grace are not ultimately opposed; the order of grace, rather, is that through which nature is "liberated and controlled" (*Retractations* 2.68).

CHAPTER THREE

1 For background on the sixteenth-century debate on narrative theory see Bernard Weinberg, *A History of Literary Criticism in the Italian Renaissance* (Chicago: University of Chicago Press, 1961), II, 954–1073, and Baxter Hathaway, *The Age of Criticism: The Late Renaissance in Italy* (Ithaca: Cornell University Press, 1962).

2 The Ruggiero–Bradamante story is also derived from Boiardo, but Boiardo as he recapitulates the Virgilian dynastic theme. For further discussion of the terms *epic* and *romance* and the relationship between these two narrative categories, see below, pp. 113–15, 123–26.

3 Italian text: *Orlando Furioso*, ed. Lanfranco Caretti, 2d ed. (Torino: Einaudi, 1971). The English translation is by Allan Gilbert (2 vols., New York: S. F. Vanni, 1954).

4 *City of God* 14.28.

5 In so doing I follow the example of Peter V. Marinelli, *The Dynastic Romance*. See also C. P. Brand, *Ludovico Ariosto: A Preface to the "Orlando Furioso"* (Edinburgh: Edinburgh University Press, 1974), pp. 107–25, for a discussion of the dynastic theme.

6 Benedetto Croce, *Ariosto, Shakespeare and Corneille*, trans. D. Ainslie (New York: H. Holt and Co., 1920), pp. 64–65. See also Giuseppe Toffanin, *Il Cinquecento, Storia Letteraria d'Italia* (Milan: F. Vallardi, 1929), p. 186, and for a reading stressing Ariosto's pessimism, Raffaello Ramat, *Per la storia dello stile rinascimentale* (Messina: G. d'Anna, 1953), pp. 45–73. The Crocean attitude reemerges more recently in C. P. Brand: "Ariosto does not polemicise: he has no sense of mission, no real political or social message for his trouble-laden times. . . . His reaction is one of lament and protest, mingled with nostalgia for a past age which he knows is really in his imagination" (p. 125). Robert M. Durling, by contrast, emphasizes the seriousness of Ariosto's political and social commitment in *The Figure of the Poet in Renaissance Epic* (Cambridge: Harvard University Press, 1965), pp. 112–81.

7 A. Bartlett Giamatti, *The Earthly Paradise and the Renaissance Epic* (Princeton:

Princeton University Press, 1966), p. 139. See also Durling, who warns against attending only to the urbane tone of Ariosto's narrating persona and not to Ariosto himself, who is fundamentally moral, if not overtly and sententiously so (pp. 132–36).

8   The double allusion to the *Aeneid* is noted by D. S. Carne-Ross, "The One and the Many: A Reading of *Orlando Furioso*, Cantos 1 and 8," *Arion*, 5, no. 2 (1966), 224.

9   As L. Caretti notes in his edition of the *Furioso*.

10 The final reversal in this pattern of associations comes in canto 19, where Angelica is seen playing Dido to Medoro's Aeneas (st. 33–35).

11 See Giamatti, "Headlong Horses, Headless Horsemen: An Essay on the Chivalric Epics of Pulci, Boiardo, and Ariosto," *Italian Literature: Roots and Branches*, Essays in Honor of Thomas Goddard Bergin, ed. Giose Rimanelli and Kenneth John Atchity (New Haven: Yale University Press, 1976), pp. 265–307. Giamatti observes that "Orlando is not simply a victim" but does so within the context of a reading of canto 23 that tends to make the moral issue disappear. Orlando's madness is described as a failure to retain self-possession and equanimity when confronted with the discovery that experience does not conform to the rules of the Petrarchan code of love. Thus for Giamatti, Orlando's madness serves as Ariosto's "warning against putting one's faith and hope in any system, verbal or cultural" (p. 301). Such is the attitude of the narrator but not, I think, the attitude Ariosto intends the reader to take.

12 Augustine's conversion is precipitated by his reading of Rom. 13.13–14: "Not in glotonie, and dronkenes, nether in chambering and wantonnes, nor in strife and enuying: But put ye on the Lord Jesus Christ, and take no thoght for the flesh, to fulfil the lustes of it" (Geneva Bible).

13 E. M. W. Tillyard describes this as one of the requirements of epic, *The English Epic and Its Background* (1954; rpt. New York: Oxford University Press, 1966), pp. 12–13.

14 Eugenio Donato offers an interesting analysis of "the conjunction of literature and madness" or desire in the *Furioso* in "'Per Selve e Boscherecci Labirinti': Desire and Narrative Structure in Ariosto's *Orlando Furioso*," *Barroco*, 4 (1972), pp. 17–34. "Ariosto's narrative," Donato argues, "does not fit into the canonic forms of a literature that claims the possibility of disclosing the truth of desire." It is less "a discourse about desire and about the truth of desire" than "a discourse of desire" (p. 31). But Donato errs, it seems to me, in suggesting that the *Furioso* therefore lacks a critical perspective on madness and cupidity. The problem arises when one mistakes the narrating persona for Ariosto himself or when one ignores the existence of the poem's second narrator, the one presenting the Ruggiero–Bradamante plot.

15 See Franco Pool, *Interpretazione dell'Orlando Furioso* (Florence: La Nuova Italia, 1968) on the narrator's assertion of absolute and arbitrary authority over the vicissitudes of his plot (p. 17).

16 William J. Kennedy, *Rhetorical Norms in Renaissance Literature* (New Haven, Yale University Press, 1978), pp. 148–49. See also Eduardo Saccone,

"Cloridano e Medoro," *Il soggetto del 'Furioso' e altri saggi* (Naples: Liguori, 1974).

17 David Quint, "Astolfo's Voyage to the Moon," *Yale Italian Studies*, 1 (1977), 398-408. For a contrasting view, see Durling, p. 149.

18 Durling, pp. 117-32. See also Kennedy, pp. 135-51. Kennedy suggests that it is Ariosto's intention to reconcile two diverse conceptions of the epic narrator, a Virgilian and an Ovidian one. The distinction Kennedy draws between the two is useful in the present context. The Virgilian narrator "maintains rhetorical distance" and "confronts a homogeneous Augustan audience with a programmatic and propagandistic aim" whereas the Ovidian narrator, the master of small forms like the tale and the isolated dramatic incident, exhibits a "penchant for detail and descriptive embroidery [and a] mercurial alternation of tone and mood, which most often depend upon the speaker's own characterization" (pp. 136-37).

19 See Jean Bodel, *Les Saisnes* 1.6.

20 Edmund G. Gardner, *The King of Court Poets* (New York: Dutton, 1906), p. 49.

21 Bradamante bears some resemblance to the *Venus armata* of Renaissance Neoplatonism (Edgar Wind, *Pagan Mysteries in the Renaissance*, rev. ed. [1958; rpt. New York: Norton, 1968], pp. 75-80, 89-96). She has her epic prototype in the Venus who appears to Aeneas in the guise of Diana in the first book of the *Aeneid* (314-20). In such a figure Renaissance mythographers saw many allegorical implications. Neoplatonists saw the embodiment of the *discordia concors* of amorous desire and militant chastity (Wind, p. 77) and thus a configuration of virtue reconciled to pleasure. In variant traditions the armor Venus wears may be that of Diana (Chastity), Minerva (Wisdom), or Mars (War). In the latter case the figure may evoke the warfare of love, or love's cruelty, but also love victorious over hate (Wind, p. 92). Ariosto's martial heroine has been compared to the allegory of *fortezza-carità* (O. Fischel, *Raphael* [London: Kegan Paul, 1948], I. 91, cited in Wind, p. 92n), a translation of Venus-Diana or Venus-Mars into the union of the virtues of fortitude and Christian charity. In all cases the figure embodies a discord but one capable of being resolved finally into concord in Neoplatonistic paradox. Bradamante, however, has yet to resolve the discord evident in her transsexuality, her conflicted dedication to chastity and to love; and for her no such resolution can be achieved independently of Ruggiero.

22 See the "Brief and Summarie Allegorie" Harington appends to his translation of the *Furioso* (1591): *Orlando Furioso*, trans. Sir John Harington, ed. Robert McNulty (Oxford: Clarendon, 1972), p. 567.

23 On Bradamante as a figure for Chastity, see Fornari's allegorical commentary on the *Furioso*, *La Spositione... sopra l'Orlando Furioso*, 2 vols. (Florence, 1549-50), I.184. Fornari's is probably the best of several sixteenth-century allegorical commentaries on the *Furioso*, a list of which would include those by Lodovico Dolce, 1542, Clemente Valvassori, 1553, Ieronimo Ruscelli, 1558, Giuseppe Horologgio, 1563, Tommaso Porcacchi, 1568, and Orazio Toscanella, 1574. On the tradition of such commentary, see Marinelli, *Dynastic Romance*, pp. 241-303; Paul J. Alpers, *The Poetry of the Faerie Queene* (Princeton: Prince-

ton University Press, 1967), pp. 137–99; and D. C. Allen, *Mysteriously Meant,* pp. 283–88. Most of the commentaries (Fornari's is an exception) are rather ad hoc undertakings and thus do not assist the reader in seeing the larger structures involved in Ariosto's narrative. To the extent that they reduce Ariosto's poem to a series of discrete platitudinous truisms, the commentaries are perhaps of limited use, but they document the existence of a Renaissance readership to which Ariosto's famous sense of irony was not an impediment to an appreciation of the essentially moral nature of his fiction.

24 Harington equates the hippogriff with passion, here as yet ungoverned by reason ("Allegorie," p. 559). Here, as he frequently does, Harington may be following Fornari, for whom the hippogriff figures the appetite or will (*Spositione* 2.17). The episode of Ruggiero's flight to Alcina's island is one of the few that Fornari singles out for complete allegorization. Alcina's island represents the world and the attendant attractions of cupidity, which include the lust for earthly power and fame. Logistilla's realm, by contrast, is the seat of learning and virtue. Fornari's Platonism is evident in his interpretation, which emphasizes the need to subordinate the sensible appetite to reason.

25 See Giamatti, *Earthly Paradise.*

26 For Fornari (1.181), Atlante represents a militant cupidity, here manifesting itself in the form of a love that contemplates its object to the exclusion of any higher awareness of God. It is against the overprotective love of Atlante that Bradamante, as Chastity, must work in order to restore Ruggiero to his divine mission. Chastity, in other words, becomes a force for active, heroic participation in history, as will be the case in Spenser.

27 Ariosto echoes Virgil precisely (cf. *OF* 7.60, and *Aen.* 4.271–76).

28 Thomas M. Greene, *The Descent from Heaven: A Study in Epic Continuity* (New Haven: Yale University Press, 1963), p. 125.

29 The Italian text and English translation are from Robert M. Durling, *Petrarch's Lyric Poems* (Cambridge: Harvard University Press, 1976).

30 Ariosto's recommendation of this virtue serves to counterbalance St. John's ironic assertion that all epic poetry gives a false and flattering picture of its patrons (35.24–25).

31 Harington's remarks on the kinship of Alcina and Logistilla are helpful, particularly as they express the notion that in an ideal (prelapsarian, postredemptive) state the passions and reason are not antagonistic forces but component parts of an integral whole:

> Perhaps it will seeme straunge to some, as it did to my selfe at the first reading, how it comes to passe that *Logestilla* and *Alcyna* are sisters. . . . The exposition is this:
>   The nature of man (by which is understood our appetite or affection) which ought to be subject to reason and to be governed thereby, this nature (I say) was at the first a lawfull child of God and was by the spirite of God framed to his own likeness . . . ; but when this first perfection was lost and that same great rebellion was made to the overthrow of that quiet and settled state, the heart became so weake as it was not able to endure the

continuall assaults of the passions. . . . And now every part of the body engenders such seeds of concupiscence that nature is become a bastard sister to reason and usurpes that governement that is due onely to her and leaveth her onely one castell which was so strongly scituated that it was impregnable, so that now reason is retirde as it were to her principall fortresse, to the head, the rest of this kingdome being possessed (by *Alcyna*) by pleasure and fond delights ("Allegorie," pp. 562–63).

32   Ruggiero, to be sure, is guilty of some backsliding in subsequent adventures, as when he attempts to rape Angelica (10.114) and when he enters Atlante's enchanted palace. But this only serves to dramatize the need to carry the process of regeneration to its final stage, conversion and baptism: reason by itself, unsustained by grace, is insufficient to guarantee a perfect and lasting reformation.

33   For example, Fulgentius, *Exposition of the Content of Virgil*, 12, and Silvestris, *Commentary*, trans. Schreiber and Maresca, p. 7.

34   At midday, ô King, I sawe in the way a light
           from heauen, passing the brightnes of the sunne,
           shine rounde about me, and them which went with me.
              So when we were all fallen to the earth, I heard
           a voice speaking vnto me, and saying in the
           Hebrewe tongue, Saul, Saul, why persecutest thou
           me? It is hard for thee to kicke against prickes.
                                             [Geneva Bible, Acts 26.13–14]

35   For example, Greene, pp. 138–43.

36   Brand, for one, finds the arbitrariness of this and other religious miracles in the poem to be an obstacle to crediting Ariosto with "any deep religious conviction" (p. 123).

37   Augustine, *De bono coniugali* 3.

38   As Giamatti observes, "Angelica, 'di sé tolto' by love in canto 1, is matched by Ruggiero, 'in sé raccolto' for love in canto 46" ("Headlong Horses, Headless Horsemen," p. 304).

39   Marinelli (pp. 236–38) notes the symbolism and the deliberate contrast with the *Aeneid,* where Turnus receives his fatal wound in the breast.

40   This is an allusion to the alternate Helen myth, usually derived from Euripides and Plato (*Republic* 9.586), in which Helen is said never to have gone to Troy but to Egypt, where she remained under the protection of King Proteus until Menelaus recovered her after the war. For sources and implications, see Frank J. Groten, Jr., "The Tradition of the Helen Legend in Greek Literature" (Ph.D. diss., Princeton University, 1955), and Thomas P. Roche, Jr., *The Kindly Flame: A Study of the Third and Fourth Books of Spenser's Faerie Queene* (Princeton: Princeton University Press, 1964), pp. 152–54. Among the implications is the notion that the Trojan war was futile, Helen being absent from Troy. This has its relevance for Ariosto, for whom true empire is based finally on love rather than warfare.

41   This is a reference to the Donation of Constantine, a forgery (as Lorenzo Valla had proved) claiming to document the first Christian emperor's gift of west-

ern imperial territories to the church. For Ariosto, the gift is legally dubious (34.80) and injurious to the integrity of both church and empire (17.78).

42   As Gardner notes (p. 48), Ariosto seems to have praised Ippolito with a conspicuously ironic intent elsewhere, as in *Carmina* 2.2.

43   Gardner offers this description of the real Ippolito: "Licentious and worldly, haughty and overbearing, Ippolito was utterly devoid of reverence for God or man; some ability as a diplomatist, according to the cynical, materialistic standpoint of the age, coupled to physical courage and a certain amount of skill in military matters, was the nearest approach to virtue he possessed" (pp. 47–48).

44   In a letter to Mario Equicola (18), Ariosto vents his spleen: "It is true that I am making some little addition to my *Orlando Furioso*...; but latterly on one side the Duke, on the other the Cardinal (the one having taken from me a possession that for more than thirty years belonged to our House, the other another possession worth nearly ten thousand ducats, *de facto* and without even summoning me to show my reasons), have given me other things to think of than fables" (Gardner, pp. 145–46).

45   Fornari gives this event a prominent place in his Neoplatonic interpretation of the poem. The triumphal entry of the paladins into Paris signifies the arrival of the soul at its spiritual haven after its journey through the world (2.290). This interpretation reveals one of the difficulties involved in imposing Neoplatonic allegorical schemes on the *Furioso* because the event as Ariosto presents it does not imply a withdrawal from the historical world but an emergence into it.

46   I have already noted a similarity between the marriage of Bradamante and Ruggiero and the betrothal of Una and Red Cross in the fact that each ceremony contains what may be considered a ritualistic challenge to the bonding of the lovers. Note further that in both cases the challenger argues that an earlier obligation prohibits the present contract: Rodomonte cites Ruggiero's former allegiance to Agramante (46.105), and Archimago presents a letter from Duessa claiming that Red Cross has already plighted himself to her (1.12.26). In each case the solution to the problem involves abrogating a literal promise, or affirming the priority of the spirit over the letter. One should also observe that Rodomonte, armed in the scaly hide of a dragon (18.12), anticipates Spenser's dragon or rather that both of these recall the serpent of the first Eden.

CHAPTER FOUR

1   Tasso's lord and patron was Alfonso II (1533–97), fifth Duke of Ferrara, grandson of Alfonso I, and son of Ercole II. For background on Tasso's life, see C. P. Brand, *Torquato Tasso* (Cambridge: Cambridge University Press, 1965), and A. Solerti, *Vita di Torquato Tasso* (Turin, Rome: E. Loescher, 1895).

2   Tasso, *Discorsi del Poema Eroico*, III (to be discussed below).

3   Ibid. The text to which I shall refer throughout this chapter is *Discourses on the Heroic Poem*, trans. Mariella Cavalchini and Irene Samuel (Oxford: Clarendon

Press, 1973). Hereafter page numbers from this translation will be given in the text of the chapter. On unity of epic action, see pp. 65-68.

4 Tasso's *Allegoria della G. L.* appeared in the first Bonná edition (1581). The English translation appears in the first edition of Fairfax's translation of the poem (1600).

5 See A. Bartlett Giamatti, "Spenser: From Magic to Miracle," *Four Essays on Romance*, ed. Herschel Baker (Cambridge: Harvard University Press, 1971), pp. 15-31. Giamatti argues that romance has a visionary dimension, "an impulse to reveal divinity" (p. 17), and that this impulse is completed in Christian revelation.

6 On the impact of the Pazzi translation of the *Poetics* (1536) on Italian literary criticism, see Bernard Weinberg, *A History of Literary Criticism in the Italian Renaissance*, I.371-73. On the general importance of the rediscovery of the *Poetics*, see pp. 349-423. For a discussion of the Christianization of classical poetic theory among Tasso's predecessors and contemporaries, see "Platonism: Triumph of Christianity," ibid., pp. 297-348. On Tasso's synthesis of Aristotelian and Neoplatonic thought in the *Discorsi*, see Annabel M. Patterson, "Tasso's Epic Neoplatonism: The Growth of his Epic Theory," *Studies in the Renaissance*, 18 (1971), 105-33.

7 For general commentary on Tasso's epic theory see Ettorre Mazzali, *Cultura e poesia nell'opera di Torquato Tasso* (Bologna: Cappelli, 1957); B. T. Sozzi, "La Poetica di Tasso," *Studi Tassiani*, 5 (1955), 3-58; Weinberg, *History*; and Baxter Hathaway, *The Age of Criticism*.

8 Tasso's *Discorsi del Poema Eroico* evolve from the earlier *Discorsi dell'Arte Poetica* (as early as 1561-62, as late as 1567-70), which were written after *Rinaldo* and during the period Tasso was at work on the *Liberata*. Tasso's revision of the *Discorsi* did not get under way until after the completion of the *Liberata* (1575), probably in 1587, when he saw the published text of the *Discorsi*, although he had contemplated revisions as early as 1574. The *Discorsi del Poema Eroico* may thus be considered prefatory to *Gerusalemme Conquistata*, the revised version of the *Liberata*. But they can also justifiably be studied as a postscript to the poem he had just completed, first simply because they are his fullest mature statement on epic theory, and second because they are theoretically harmonious with the *Liberata*. They continue to argue for the inclusion of romance elements within a Christian epic (a point on which Tasso's revisions in the *Conquistata* show him becoming nervous). Indeed, the *Discorsi* are written in defense of the *Liberata* against Gonzaga, Speroni, and others who criticized its moral and stylistic impurity. The *Discorsi* were published along with a collection of letters (*Lettere Poetiche*) written in the same spirit (see Mariella Cavalchini, intro., *Discourses*, pp. xi-xx).

9 Tasso's use of the Platonic hierarchy of faculties as a structuring principle in the *Liberata* is explained in the *Allegoria*:

> *Godfrey* which holdeth the principall place in this storie, is no other in the Allegorie but the *Vnderstanding....Rinaldo*, which in action is in the second degree of honour, ought also to be placed in the Allegorie in the answerable degree: but what this power of the mind, holding the second

degree of dignitie is, shall be nowe manifested. The *Irefull* vertue is that, which amongst all the powers of the minde, is lesse estranged from the nobility of the soule, insomuch that *Plato* (doubting) seeketh whether it differeth from reason or no. . . . But when it doth not obey Reason, but suffers it selfe to be carried of her own violence, it falleth out, that it fighteth not against concupiscence, but by concupiscence, like a dogge that biteth not the theeues, but the cattle committed to his keeping.

On the arrangement of the principal heroes of the Christian army in the *Liberta* according to a Neoplatonic hierarchy of virtues, see Greene, *Descent from Heaven*, p. 211.

10   On Tasso's response to Mazzoni's Platonism, see Hathaway, *Age of Criticism*, pp. 390–96.

11   Boethius, *The Consolation of Philosophy* book 3, prose 11; Augustine, *Soliloquies* 1.1–4. In each case the Christian thinker assimilates Platonic or Plotinian notions of unity, truth, and goodness.

12   *Consolation* 3.11.

13   For a contrasting view of romance, see that of Giraldi, summarized in Weinberg, p. 438. Giraldi argues that romance may be considered a separate genre from epic and is thus not subject to the same requirements.

14   This basic attitude of inclusiveness is evident in the *Allegoria:*

The reasonable part ought not (for heerein the Stoiks were very much deceiued) to exclude the *Irefull* from actions, nor *vsurpe* the offices thereof, for this vsurpation shoulde bee against nature and iustice, but it ought to make her her companion and handmaid: So ought not *Godfrey* to attempt the aduenture of the wood himselfe, thereby arrogating to himselfe the other offices belonging to *Reinaldo.*

15   All citations from the *Liberata* are from *Opere di Torquato Tasso,* ed. Bortolo T. Sozzi, 3d ed. (Torino: UTET, 1974), vol I. The English translation is mine. Unless otherwise noted, the translation used hereafter is that of Edward Fairfax, *Jerusalem Delivered,* ed. John Charles Nelson.

16   See A. Bartlett Giamatti, *The Earthly Paradise and the Renaissance Epic,* pp. 199–210.

17   Matt. 14.26; Exod. 14.21.

18   In addition to Isa. 66.18 and 22, see Isa. 11.12, Mic. 4, and Rev. 7.9.

19   For a further discussion, see Norman Cohn, *The Pursuit of the Millennium* (1957; rpt. New York: Harper Torchbooks, 1961), pp. 44–45.

20   John Leddy Phelan, *The Millennial Kingdom of the Franciscans in the New World,* 2d ed., rev. (Berkeley: University of California Press, 1970), pp. 17–28, 72–73.

21   On Tasso's recommendation of double peripeteia for epic plots, see *Discourses,* pp. 79–80.

22   For a further discussion of typology and its applications to the *Liberata,* see Thomas P. Roche, Jr., "Tasso's Enchanted Woods," *Literary Uses of Typology,* ed. Earl Miner (Princeton: Princeton University Press, 1977), pp. 49–78.

23   See, for example, Greene, p. 213, and Giamatti, who winces when Armida suddenly and completely submits to Rinaldo's demand that she forsake

paganism (p. 209). "Indeed, there is something desperate here in Tasso's effort to bring Armida into line with Christianity. The shift implied by these words is too great, and we are finally unconvinced of Armida's redemption. The inner conflicts which were dramatized so beautifully in the garden remain to haunt the poem" (pp. 209–10). Giamatti rightly rejects the readings of those who would suggest that Tasso is "more of Armida's party than God's" but then offers that Tasso's problem "was simply that he could see no way of radically reconciling the two" (p. 209). The point, however, is that for Tasso no such reconciliation is required (see Roche, pp. 69–72). Conversion as Tasso conceives it does not take place on a middle ground. Here dramatic imperatives must give way to moral ones. Once again, as in the case of Ruggiero's baptism and conversion in *Orlando Furioso*, it is appropriate, I think, to invoke Augustinian doctrine: To admit the necessity of accommodating Armida's former self in the moment of her conversion is implicitly to admit something like the fallacy of Manichaean dualism, the assumption that the universe contains two antagonistic realities or substances, both of which have parts to play in shaping human nature. But for Augustine, Ariosto, Tasso, and Spenser there is but one order of reality. The sudden discontinuities we observe in the characters of Renaissance epic must be understood, as Michael Murrin notes in a discussion of Spenser, in the context of Pauline spiritual rebirth (*Allegorical Epic*, p. 149).

24   The other comes at the end of canto 10, where Piero speaks in general terms of a future era of cooperation between the descendants of Rinaldo and the church.

CHAPTER FIVE

1   See R. E. N. Dodge, "Spenser's Imitations from Ariosto," *PMLA*, 12 (1897), 151–204; S. J. McMurphy, *Spenser's Use of Ariosto for Allegory*, University of Washington Publications, 2, 1924; *The Works of Edmund Spenser: A Variorum Edition*, III.367–76; Josephine Waters Bennet, *The Evolution of 'The Faerie Queene'* (1942; rpt. New York: Burt Franklin, 1960), pp. 138–53; Alpers, *The Poetry of The Faerie Queene*, pp. 160–99.

2   Augustine, *City of God* 14.28.

3   All quotations from *The Faerie Queene* are from the *Variorum Edition*. On the question of the suitability of love as a subject for a heroic poem, see above, pp. 117–19.

4   John E. Hankins argues the interdependence of chastity and justice in *Source and Meaning in Spenser's Allegory: A Study of the Faerie Queene* (Oxford: Clarendon Press, 1971) and points to this as evidence of the influence of Francesco Piccolomini's *Vniuersa Philosophia de Moribus* (1583) on Spenser's poem (pp. 151; 2–16). For Francesco, as for Spenser, chastity and justice may initially seem to clash with each other but only as imperfectly understood. Justice, for instance, might express itself as an insistence that chastity abandon its self-interest in refusing to love in return when love is bestowed. In the long run, however, the two virtues are harmonious: chastity and justice are mutually

fulfilled as chastity comes to acknowledge its obligation to a lover and husband. On Ariosto's association of Bradamante with chastity and Ruggiero with justice, see above, chap. 3.

5 As Angus Fletcher notes in *The Prophetic Moment: An Essay on Spenser* (Chicago: University of Chicago Press, 1971), Spenser's concept of justice, fully evolved, implies the transformation of Old Law by New Law: "Equity, with the spirit of the Redeemer, looks for the New within the Old Law, a prophetic search" (p. 286).

6 The derivation of Britomart from the *Ciris*, which Spenser would have attributed to Virgil, is noted by Merritt Y. Hughes, "Virgil and Spenser," *University of California Publications in English*, 2, no. 3 (1929), 348-54, and discussed by Thomas P. Roche, Jr., *The Kindly Flame: A Study of the Third and Fourth Books of Spenser's Faerie Queene* (Princeton: Princeton University Press, 1964), pp. 53-55, and James Nohrnberg, *The Analogy of The Faerie Queene* (Princeton: Princeton University Press, 1976), pp. 446-47.

7 Roche, p. 54.

8 Note also, as Dodge points out (pp. 183, 191), that Britomart's encounter with Malecasta is an ironic reversal of Ruggiero's with Alcina (*OF* 7.21).

9 The history of the notion of the Fortunate Fall is traced by A. O. Lovejoy, "Milton and the Paradox of the Fortunate Fall," *English Literary History*, 4, no. 3 (1937), 161-79. See also Nohrnberg, p. 443.

10 Milton describes chastity in similar terms in the *Apology for Smectymnuus* (*Complete Prose Works*, Yale, 1953, I. 891-93) and in *Comus*, where, as A. S. P. Woodhouse has pointed out ("The Argument of Milton's *Comus*," *University of Toronto Quarterly*, 11 [1941-42], 46-71), chastity is a self-dependent, Platonic virtue, verging on but falling somewhat short of the higher and more dynamic virtue of virginity. Chastity can repel vice but cannot elevate itself to the order of grace.

11 Britomart's fear is evident not in her own behavior but as it is projected in the figure of Florimell, who in st. 15 of the first canto suddenly dashes across the landscape like a comet portending "death and dolefull drerihed," pursued by a "griesly Foster." The incident recalls the opening of *Orlando Furioso*, where Angelica makes a similar entrance, but Florimell's relevance to Britomart can be established, once again, by referring to the *Ciris*, where Florimell's flight to the sea is anticipated in the story of Britomart's namesake, Britomartis. That Florimell is an aspect of Britomart is suggested again in her first encounter with Artegall, whom she perceives as the wrathful knight of *salvagesse sans finesse* (4.4.39).

12 See C. S. Lewis's comments on the tapestries of Venus and Adonis (*The Allegory of Love: A Study in Medieval Tradition* [Oxford: Oxford University Press, 1936], p. 332): "The bad Venus is a picture not of 'lust in action' but of lust suspended—lust turning into what would now be called *skeptophilia*."

13 See above, pp. 74-78.

14 For a discussion of the opening cantos of book 3 in terms of the theme of a sexual awakening, see Nohrnberg, pp. 429-52.

15 Within the world of the poem, as Spenser tells us in the letter to Ralegh, the

image of Elizabeth has been divided into her two persons, "the one of a most royall Queene or Empresse" (Gloriana), "the other of a most vertuous and beautifull Lady" (Belphoebe).

16 For a discussion of the meaning of *antiquity* in a "psycho-cultural" sense in book 3, see Harry Berger, Jr., "The Faerie Queene, Book III: A General Description," *Criticism*, 11 (1969), 234–61, reprinted in *Essential Articles for the Study of Edmund Spenser*, ed. A. C. Hamilton (Hamden: Archon, 1972), pp. 395–424. Berger notes, "Antiquity is not merely 'a long time ago' . . . but also a particular primitive phase of psycho-cultural experience . . . when eros was manifested primarily as hostility" (p. 399). The narrator's nostalgia for this kind of past implies a mind as immature as that which conceives of chastity only as self-defense.

17 Ibid., pp. 407–08.

18 Tasso, *Discourses on the Heroic Poem*, trans. Cavalchini and Samuel, p. 38. See above, pp. 125–26.

19 Roche, pp. 56–60.

20 On the historical identity of Artegall, see Carrie A. Harper, *The Sources of the British Chronicle History in Spenser's Faerie Queene*, Bryn Mawr College Monographs, 7 (1910), 144. Both Arthur and Artegall are sons of Igerne, but Arthur's father was Uther Pendragon, Artegall's Gorlois. Bennett (pp. 81–89) notes that Artegall appears in the chronicles, notably that of Geoffrey of Monmouth (9.12), as one of the knights of the Round Table and one of the most famous of the legendary earls of Warwick, the house to which Spenser's patron, the Earl of Leicester, belongs. The genealogy of Artegall and Britomart, then, may be intended as a compliment to Leicester and the Dudleys, establishing their royal blood. But Artegall and Britomart are also clearly the ancestors of Elizabeth (3.3.49), which is an invitation to see Artegall as a substitute for Arthur. Spenser has made it as easy as possible for the reader to equate Arthur and Artegall by leaving Artegall's son unnamed (st. 29). After this genealogical parenthesis, the lines of Arthur and Artegall converge in the next generation with Vortipore. Observe also that the prophecy of Artegall's and Britomart's lineage is a continuation of that of Arthur in 2.10.1–68. Seen from one angle, the substitution of Artegall for Arthur may be taken as an evasion of the problem of asserting Arthurian ancestry for the Tudors, as Tudor monarchs themselves had done. From another angle, however, the strategy appears to be a way of permitting Spenser to preserve such a connection. Elizabeth already exists in the poem as Gloriana (and Belphoebe), Arthur's contemporary; to portray her as Arthur's descendant Spenser must introduce either Elizabeth or Arthur in another personage. See Roche, pp. 47–50.

21 *Variorum* III. 229–30.

22 Harper notes (ibid., p. 230): "In making Vortipore less successful than Conan and in the end unfortunate Spenser differs entirely from any known authority . . . out of consideration for the listening Britomart, who was naturally more concerned in her son than in her grandson," but also to prepare for

Malgo's revenge in the next generation (which also seems to be Spenser's invention). Spenser seems to be concerned with establishing the cycle of loss and revenge from the outset of the prophecy.

23 Geoffrey of Monmouth, *History of the Kings of Britain* 12.1.

24 The point is made by Berger, "*The Faerie Queen*, Book III: A General Description," p. 402.

25 On this there is general agreement among Spenser critics of the last thirty years. See W. B. C. Watkins, *Shakespeare and Spenser* (Princeton: Princeton University Press, 1950), p. 125; Harry Berger, Jr., *The Allegorical Temper: Vision and Reality in Book II of Spenser's Faerie Queene* (1957; rpt. New Haven: Archon, 1967), pp. 161–207; M. Pauline Parker, *The Allegory of The Faerie Queene* (Oxford: Clarendon Press, 1960), pp. 34–36; and Greene, *Descent from Heaven*, pp. 330–33. It is important, however, not to mistake the fluidity of meaning in Spenser's allegory for rootless relativism. My own understanding of Spenser's allegory is closest to that of Roche, who notes that although the "web of interrelationships" implied by allegory is often unseen in the poem, as in the temporal world, it is assumed that those relationships are "contained within the mind of God" (p. 8).

26 See Berger, *Allegorical Temper*, pp. 78–80. Berger contrasts the concept of memory implied in the portrait of Eumnestes with memory in Platonic doctrine: "In Plato, memory's function is to recollect the eternal, bring forth the ideas graven in the soul before its descent to earth." In a sense, Memory in Alma's Castle represents a move toward Christian thought, in which "the object of memory is no longer a fixed number of Forms in heaven but an endless unfolding of events in time" (79). It seems to me, however, that Spenser stops just short of articulating the Christian conception of history in 2.9 and 10. Note, for instance, the obliquity of the reference to the Incarnation in 10.50.

27 *Conf.* 11.20.

28 On the chronicle matter in 2.10, see Berger, *Allegorical Temper*, pp. 89–114, and Roche, pp. 34–50.

29 Roche, pp. 195–211, esp. p. 200.

30 Ibid., p. 200.

31 Ibid., p. 89.

32 James E. Phillips, "Renaissance Concepts of Justice and the Structure of The Faerie Queene, Book V," *Huntington Library Quarterly*, 33 (1970), 103–20, reprinted in *Essential Articles*, ed. A. C. Hamilton, p. 473.

33 See Kathleen Williams, *Spenser's Faerie Queene: The World of Glass* (London: Routledge and Kegan Paul, 1966), p. 170.

34 On Elizabeth's iconographical association with the moon, see Frances A. Yates, *Astraea: The Imperial Theme in the Sixteenth Century* (London: Routledge and Kegan Paul, 1975), pp. 76–78, 216.

35 The reader should keep in mind, however, that Artegall's effeminization by Radigund is not in the long run destructive; instead it is a necessary stage of humiliation leading to self-awareness, and it prepares for the relationship

between Artegall and Britomart depicted in Isis Church. See T. K. Dunseath, *Spenser's Allegory of Justice in Book Five of The Faerie Queene* (Princeton: Princeton University Press, 1968), p. 136.

36 Phillips, pp. 479–80.

37 See William Nelson, *The Poetry of Edmund Spenser* (New York: Columbia University Press, 1963), pp. 268–69. Nelson cites Jean Bodin, *The Six Bookes of a Commonweale*, trans. Richard Knolles, 1606, ed. K. D. McRae (Cambridge: Harvard University Press, 1962), p. 764:

> For that to say truely, the law without equitie, is as a bodie without a soule, for that it concerning but things in generall, leaveth the particular circumstances, which are infinit, to be by equalitie sought out according to the exigence of the places, times, and persons: whereunto it behoveth the magistrat or judge so to apply the laws, whether it be in tearmes of justice, or in matter of estate, as that thereof ensue neither any inconvenience nor absurditie whatsoever.

38 Frank Kermode, "*The Faerie Queene*, I and V," *Bulletin of The John Rylands Library*, 47 (1965), 123–50, reprinted in *Essential Articles*, ed. A. C. Hamilton, pp. 280–88; René Graziani, "Elizabeth at Isis Church," *PMLA*, 79 (1964), 376–89.

39 Jane Aptekar, *Icons of Justice: Iconography and Thematic Imagery in Book V of The Faerie Queene* (New York: Columbia University Press, 1969), pp. 97–107.

40 Fletcher, *Prophetic Moment*, p. 268.

41 Graziani, p. 377.

42 Fletcher, p. 259.

43 For an analysis of the cosmic symbolism, see Alastair Fowler, *Spenser and the Numbers of Time* (London: Routledge and Kegan Paul, 1964), pp. 208–15.

44 As the editors of the *Variorum* suggest (V.216), the nocturnal vision is based on that of Lucius the Ass in Apuleius, *Metamorphoses* 11.4–8. See also Geoffrey 1.11, in which Brutus receives in his sleep in the Temple of Diana a prophecy of the new Troy his sons will establish in Britain.

45 Roche (p. 81) observes that the imagery recalls Britomart's triumph over Busyrane (3.12), itself a narrative of sacrificial destruction preliminary to Britomart's encounter with Artegall.

46 Fletcher, p. 271.

47 Graziani, p. 384; see also the discussion of the topos of "The World Upsidedown" and Virgilian *adynata* in E. R. Curtius, *European Literature and the Latin Middle Ages*, trans. Willard R. Trask (Princeton: Princeton University Press, 1953), pp. 94–98, and Fletcher, pp. 106–21.

48 For example, the uprising of the Northern Earls, 1569, and the Ridolfi plot, 1571 (Graziani, p. 381).

49 Ibid., pp. 382–87.

50 Kermode, p. 284.

51 Aptekar, pp. 119–24.

52 Kermode, pp. 281–88.

53 Graziani, p. 382.

54 As Roche suggests (note to 1.10.13 in *Edmund Spenser: The Faerie Queene*, ed. Thomas P. Roche, Jr. [New York: Penguin Books, 1978]): "The serpent may be related to the brazen serpent of Moses (Num. 21.8–9) which is a type of Christ crucified."

55 *Allegory of Love*, p. 315.

56 Yates, *Astraea*, pp. 68–74.

57 One of the most eloquent descriptions of this aspect of Spenser's poetry is found in Greene, *The Descent from Heaven*, pp. 330–35.

58 For example, A. C. Hamilton, *The Structure of Allegory in The Faerie Queene* (Oxford: Clarendon Press, 1961), p. 170.

59 Michael O'Connell, *Mirror and Veil: The Historical Dimension of Spenser's Faerie Queene* (Chapel Hill: University of North Carolina Press, 1977), pp. 147–60.

60 Ibid., pp. 154–55.

61 O'Connell summarizes the argument as follows:

> The Legend of Justice fails finally to be prophetic poetry. Spenser appears to lack the conviction of the prophet who knows what is just and fashions the vehicle of his prophecy to express his conviction. When the poem falters, it is not because of the poet's inclination to consider political and historical issues, for prophetic poetry must move in just such a direction. Nor must we suppose that his support of established power and a successful monarch necessarily leads him astray; Spenser is ever his queen's champion, but his poetic interpretation of her career had previously achieved a delicate and complex, if partisan, intelligence. Rather he fails when he makes history as it is, not a vision of history as it should be, the vehicle of his prophetic morality. In doing so he paradoxically betrays a want of faith in history. [p. 156]

62 As Isabel G. MacCaffrey has shown, Spenser's allegory, like Tasso's, is rooted in the belief that "the invisible world that attracts our dreams and our yearning for realization could be more 'real' than the visible." Thus it becomes one of the tasks of allegory "to reproduce what Whitehead, describing the genesis of mental life from the flux of 'illimitable' ordinary experience, calls 'complete occasions': comprehended experiences, rescued from submergence in the confusion of the quotidian," *Spenser's Allegory: The Anatomy of Imagination* (Princeton: Princeton University Press, 1976), pp. 3, 8. Such, I believe, is Spenser's objective in book 5.

63 Here I must disagree with Hamilton, who remarks that the "last three cantos are distanced from fact by the increasing element of fairy tale—the final episode is pure fairy tale—and the obvious emphasis upon the ideal" (p. 190).

64 Fletcher, p. 5.

65 As O'Connell suggests (pp. 156–60).

66 *Spenser's Allegory of Justice*, pp. 208–12.

67 The double meaning of "let" is pointed out in Roche's edition of *The Faerie Queene* (p. 1205).

68 Phillips, "Renaissance Concepts of Justice," p. 481; Hamilton, p. 178; Nelson, pp. 266–69.

69 On Elizabeth's vacillations, or rather the efforts of Protestant propagandists to portray her as reluctant and sorrowful at the necessity of imposing the sentence of execution urged by her council and Parliament, see James E. Phillips, *Images of a Queen: Mary Stuart in Sixteenth-Century Literature* (Berkeley: University of California Press, 1964), pp. 124-25, and 202. In fairness to Spenser, it ought to be noted that the problem he faces here is similar to Milton's in the third book of *Paradise Lost:* Justice conceived as righteousness and mercy paradoxically united is difficult to represent dramatically. But st. 50 shows human pity unable to avert the course of justice; Mercilla's tears do not imply that mercy has been suppressed.

EPILOGUE

1 *The Consolation of Philosophy,* trans. Richard Green (New York: Bobbs-Merrill, 1962), III, poem 6.

Index